How to Read a Chinese Poem

如何阅读唐诗

How to Read a Chinese Poem

A Bilingual Anthology of Tang Poetry

如何阅读唐诗

张畅繁译注

Translated and Annotated by

Edward C. Chang

Library of Congress Cataloging-in-Publication Data

How to read a Chinese Poem: A Bilingual Anthology of Tang Poetry / translated and annotated by Edward C. Chang, English and Chinese.

Library of Congress Control Number: 2007904271

Publisher: BookSurge Publishing
North Charleston, South Carolina

ISBN: 1-4196-7013-1
1. Chinese poetry. 2. Tang poems. 3. Translations into English. 4. Bilingual anthology. 5. Classical Chinese poetry. 6. Regulated verse. 6. *Jintishi.* 7. Chang, Edward.

Cover design by Mimi Chang and Emily Wang

Visit www.booksurge.com to order additional copies.

For

Kiersten,
Evelyn,
Kendal,
and Andersen

Contents

PART 3
Seven-Character Regulated Verses

PART 4
Five-Character Truncated Verses

PART 5
Seven-Character Truncated Verses

Part 6
About the Poets

Preface

A few years ago, a friend sent me a copy of Eliot Weinberger's *Nineteen Ways of Looking at Wang Wei: How a Chinese Poem Is Translated* (Asphodel Press). I was intrigued by this little book because it shows how a four-line poem could be translated in so many different ways and with so many different interpretations.

Weinberger's book influenced my decision to undertake this book project. With so many versions of translation of Chinese classical poetry available in the market, I didn't think much more can be gained by adding another one to the list. I did feel, however, there is a need for a book to show how each regulated verse in the *Three Hundred Poems of the Tang Dynasty* can be analyzed and appreciated from a bilingual perspective. I believe that such a book will be helpful to those who want to gain a better and deeper understanding of the Chinese regulated poetry.

A Chinese regulated verse, which can take either the form of *jueju* (four-line truncated verse) or *lushi* (eight-line regulated verse), must follow a prescribed tonal pattern called *ping-ze*. In the case of *lushi*, it must also demonstrate some sort of parallelism. This poetic form certainly has a lot to do with why the Tang period is considered the golden age of poetry in China.

This book differs from other books of poetry translation in that each poem is given a bilingual annotation with respect to the literal meanings of each key word. In addition, the tone and pinyin transliteration of each Chinese character is provided for reference. Here, even a reader who does not know the Chinese language can learn to recite the original poem and get a feel on how the original poem should sound like. Also, by providing both a word-for-word and literary translation, the reader can better understand what the poet was thinking.

This book is particularly designed for the following readers:

1. Those who cannot read Chinese but want to know more about how regulated poems are written and how they sound in Chinese.
2. Bilingual students who are looking for a useful tool to help them understand Chinese poetry in depth.
3. Overseas Chinese who are interested in reading and writing Chinese regulated verses.

I wish to thank Dr. Alan Zhang for reviewing my manuscript and giving me his valuable comments. I also want to thank Lun Cheung Ku for his frequent encouragement and advice. The completion of this book would be impossible without the continuous support and encouragement from many individuals, particularly Mimi, Emily, Stephanie, Anthony, and Norman.

PART 1

**Introduction to Chinese
Regulated Poetry**

1. What is Jintishi?

All of the Tang poems included in this book were originally written in the form of *jintishi* during the Tang Dynasty (618—907 A.D.). Known as the golden age of poetry in China, Tang Dynasty had produced many great poets such as Du Fu (Tu Fu), Li Bai (Li Po), Wang Wei, Meng Haoran, and Li Shangyin.

So, what is *jintishi*?

Jintishi (近體詩) literally means "modern-style poetry" in Chinese. Actually, *jintishi* is nothing modern at all. In fact, its origin could be traced as far back as the Six Dynasties (222—589 A.D.) when Shen Yue (沈約) and Zhou Yong (周顒) first outlined the rules governing the tone and rhythm of Chinese characters. However, it was not until the Tang Dynasty that *jintishi* was fully developed and adopted as a popular poetic form in Chinese classical poetry.

The term *jintishi* was originally used to distinguish this type of poetic form from *gutishi* (古體詩), the ancient-style poetry. In contrast to *gutishi*, which is under no constraints in terms of *ping ze* (alternating the level and deflected tones), *jintishi* must adhere to a certain tonal pattern, rhyme scheme, and parallelism. The two basic forms of *jintishi* are *lüshi* (律詩) and *jueju* (絕句). In this book, both *lüshi* and *jueju* are considered to be regulated verse.

Lüshi takes the following two forms:

Wulü (五律): an eight-line regulated verse with five characters to a line.
Qilü (七律): an eight-line regulated verse with seven characters to a line.

Jueju takes the following two forms:

Wujue (五絕): a four-line truncated verse with five characters to a line.
Qijue (七絕): a four-line truncated verse with seven characters to a line.

2. How was poetry defined in Ancient China?

Ask any poet today to define poetry. You are likely to get as many definitions as there are poets.

But in ancient China, the definition of poetry was quite direct and simple. Poetry was generally considered to be a form of verbal expression that conveyed how one felt in the heart.

We can develop some insight into the nature of Chinese poetry by examining the Chinese character that means poetry 詩 (shi).

As shown, 詩 is composed of two parts: 言 (yan) and 寺 (si). The phonetic element 寺 was originally written as 志 (zhi), meaning "feelings in the heart." The radical 言 has something to do with "words or speech." Thus, the character 詩 suggests that poetry is the speech of the heart.

The early definition of poetry can be found In the Book of Songs (詩經):

"When it is in the heart, it is *zhi* (志); when *zhi* is expressed in words, it is poetry."

Thus, the function of poetry was to convey in words how one felt. Few people wrote poems just for the sake of self enjoyment; they wrote poems because they wanted to share with others their feelings and to evoke similar emotional experiences in their readers or listeners.

3. Why did poetry become the most popular art form in ancient China?

Among all Chinese arts, poetry was considered to be the most popular art form in ancient China. Poetry provided a convenient medium for people to convey their aspirations or sentiments. Since the reason for writing poetry was to express one's own feelings and to inspire these feelings in others, it makes sense for poems to be written so that people could understand. A poem that was too difficult to be understood by even the educated elites would most likely generate very little resonant effect on its readers.

For this reason, Chinese poems tend to be relatively short in length and less abstruse in surface meaning. This does not mean that people of this generation will not have any problem reading classical poems. Actually, classical poetry could be quite difficult to read as they were written in the literary language—a language that is vastly different from the kind of vernacular Chinese language that we use today. But for the poets' contemporaries, reading classical poetry was probably just as easy as reading vernacular verses by the modern Chinese.

The introduction of *jintishi* during the Tang Dynasty had added a new dimension to the poetic forms already in use. Although *gushi* or *gutishi*, the ancient-style poetry, used rhymes and was less restrictive in form and style, it did not have the kind of musicality that *jintishi* offered. With its emphasis on tonal variations, rhythm, and rhyme scheme, *jintishi* was far more effective in creating a resonant effect on the mind and ears of the reader or listener. Because it brought music to the ears, more and more poets from all walks of life had joined the *jintishi* bandwagon. From the rulers to common people, from intellectual elites to the less educated, just about everyone participated in reciting or chanting, if not writing, poetry. Poetry also became an important part in human social interactions. No social gathering and ceremonial service would be complete without including a few lines or couplets as part of the activities. In fact, poetry was so popular during the Tang and Song dynasties that it was often used as a tool to communicate personal feelings in lieu of direct messages.

4. Can Chinese regulated verse be translated?

In a strict sense, a regulated verse cannot be translated without losing some poetic elements. For one thing, there is no way to translate the sounds and musicality that have become an integral part in Chinese regulated poetry. It is true that such things as ideas, imageries, and feelings can usually be translated from one language to another; it is, however, impossible to translate the sounds and tones that help to heighten the effect of one's emotion and imagination.

Some Chinese words, through cultural conditioning, have acquired the ability to elicit certain emotional responses beyond their surface meanings. Unfortunately, when a regulated verse is translated into a different language, the emotional response aroused by cultural connotations of the original words could be lost along with their sound and musical effects.

The following poem 楓橋夜泊 (Mooring by Maple Bridge at Night) by Zhang Ji illustrates the difficulty of translating any poem from one language to another. Because of the differences in their cultural and language backgrounds, a Chinese native who reads the original poem and an American who reads the English version would most certainly react differently to the imageries and implied meanings in terms of emotional arousal and association.

月落烏啼霜滿天
江楓漁火對愁眠
姑蘇城外寒山寺
夜半鐘聲到客船

8

While classical Chinese poetry was considered to be the speech of the heart, regulated poetry provided the sound, rhythm, and musical element that made such "speech" more effective. For this reason, a regulated verse was not just written for reading, it was written for chanting as well. Thus, when we read a translated regulated verse, we should remember that a regulated verse was essentially written more for the ears than for the eyes.

5. How was the tone classified in Classical Chinese?

In the Chinese language, characters having the same sound may have different tones. There are four tones in classical Chinese phonetics: *ping* (平), *shang* (上), *qu* (去), and *ru* (入).

> *ping* (平) is the level tone (the first and second tone in modern standard Chinese pronunciation).
>
> Examples: 東 (dōng), 家 (jiā), 身 (shēn), 春 (chūn), 陽 (yáng), 田 (tián), 青 (qīng), 川 (chuān).
>
> *shang* (上) is the falling-rising tone (the third tone in modern standard Chinese pronunciation).
>
> Examples: 水 (shuǐ), 古 (gǔ), 馬 (mǎ), 口 (kǒu), 我 (wǒ).
>
> *qu* (去) is the falling tone (the fourth tone in modern standard Chinese pronunciation).
>
> Examples: 地 (dì), 未 (wèi), 路 (lù), 外 (wài), 大 (dà), 下 (xià), 又 (yòu).
>
> *ru* (入) is the "entering" tone. The entering tone is pronounced in a short and abrupt manner.

Examples: 目 (mù), 月(yuè), 物 (wù), 力 (lì),
八 (bā), 國 (guó), 十 (shí), 學 (xué), 雪 (xuě),
北 (běi), 給 (gěi), 七 (qī), 哭 (kū) .

The level tone in modern standard pronunciation includes
both the high and level tone (陽平) as well as the rising tone
(陰平). In mandarin Chinese, there is no entering tone.
Those characters classified as entering tone in classical
Chinese now can fall under any one of the four tones in
mandarin pronunciation.

6. What is parallelism?

In both *wulu* (an eight-line regulated verse with five characters to a line) and *qilu* (an eight-line regulated verse with seven characters to a line), some form of parallelism must be present in addition to tonal variations. Parallelism means that the verbal units at the same position within a couplet must be balanced in terms of word order and parts of speech. Parallelism can take many forms, including contrast, analogy, and similarity. In an eight-line verse, only the two middle couplets require parallelism.

To illustrate how parallelism is used, let's take a look at the following poem by Wang Wei: 山居秋暝 "Autumn Evening in a Mountain Retreat."

空山新雨後
天氣晚來秋
明月松間照
清泉石上流
竹喧歸浣女
蓮動下漁舟
隨意春芳歇
王孫自可留

Since each five-character line normally consists of an initial disyllabic unit and a final trisyllabic unit, we can separate them to see how parallelism is performed.

明○月△   松○間○照△
míng yuè   sōng jiān zhào
bright moon   shines through the pines

清○泉○　　　　　石△上△流●
qīng quán　　　　shí shàng liú
clear spring　　　　flows over the rocks

In the above couplet, the words to be matched are 明月 and 清泉. As can be seen, 月(moon) and 泉(spring) are both nouns while 明 (bright) and 清(clear) are adjectives. In the trisyllabic unit that follows, 松間照 (to shine through the pines) and 石上流 (to flow over the rocks), are also appropriately matched.

竹△喧○　　　　　歸○浣△女△
zhú xuān　　　　guī huàn nǚ
bamboos rustling　　clothes-washing girls are returning

蓮○動△　　　　　下△漁○舟●
lián dòng　　　　xià yú zhōu
water lilies moving　　fishing boat is coming down

In the above couplet, the first characters 竹 (bamboos) and 蓮(water lilies) are both nouns while喧 (to rustle) and 動 (to move) are verbs. In the second unit, 歸浣女 (clothes-washing girls are returning) and 下漁舟 (the fishing boat is coming down) are matched in grammatical relationship.

13

7. What are the tonal patterns of Chinese regulated poetry?

Before getting into the tonal patterns of *jintishi* or regulated verse, it is helpful to know the symbols used in this book to represent the tones of *ping* and *ze*. Characters that are pronounced in the level tone are referred to as the *ping* tone; characters that are pronounced in a deflected manner belong to the *ze* tone. A *ze* tone comprises the tones of *shang*, *qu*, and *ru*.

○ = *ping* (level) tone
△ = *ze* (deflected) tone
● = rhyme (*ping* tone)
▲ = rhyme (*ze* tone)
◯̲ = can be replaced by a *ze* tone
△̲ = can be replaced by a *ping* tone

The five-character regulated verse:

The five-character regulated verse can be either "*ze* start" or "*ping* start." In a *ze* start, the second character of the first line must be in a *ze* (deflected) tone. By the same token, the second character in a *ping* start must be in a *ping* (level) level tone.

A. *Ze* Start

14

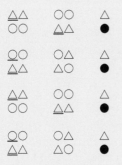

Note: The first line can be substituted with the following tones: ▵▵   ▵○   ●

B. *Ping* Start

Note: The first line can be substituted with the following tones: ○○   ▵▵   ●

Some rules to be observed:

In general, the first and third character in each line may be in either *ping* or *ze* tone as long as the condition known as *"lone ping"* (孤平) will not occur. That is to say, a level tone in any line should not be surrounded by two deflected tones as shown below:

△○   △△   ●

The above condition can be "*rescued*" by placing a level-tone character at the third position as illustrated below:

△○   ○△   ●

Also, within each couplet, the second and fourth characters of the first line must be different in tone from those of the second line. For example, if the second character of the first line is a deflected (*ze*) tone, then the second character of the second line must be a level (*ping*) tone, and vice versa. On the other hand, the second and fourth characters must be of the same tones for the beginning and ending lines of the two adjacent couplets. For example, if the fourth character of line 4 is in level tone, then the fourth character of line 5 must also be in level tone.

The seven-character regulated verse

The following are the two basic tonal patterns of the seven-character regulated verse:

A. *Ze* Start

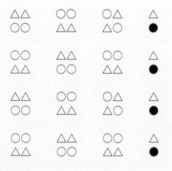

Note: The first line can be substituted with the
following tones: △△ ○○ △△ ●

B. *Ping* Start

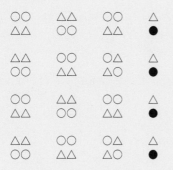

Note: The first line can be substituted with the
following tones: ○○ △△ △○ ●

The rules governing the five-character regulated verse
also apply to the seven-character regulated verse. In general,
characters placed at the first, third, and the fifth positions are
more flexible in the sense that they may be changed to a
different tone.

However, any changes in tonal placement must not
result in having one single-level (*ping*) tone surrounded by
two deflected (*ze*) tones, as shown in the following case:

<u>○</u>○ △△ △○ △

This means that the level tone normally placed at the
fifth position should not be changed to a deflected tone as it
will cause the sixth character to be a *"lone ping"* (孤平).

In addition, the last three characters in a line should not
be all in level tones, as shown in the following case:

◯◯   △△   ◯◯   ●

The five-character truncated verse

Jueju is a curtailed version of *jintishi* that has only four lines. *Jueju* can take the form of five or seven characters to a line. Parallelism is not required in *jueju*.

The following are the tonal patterns of the five-character truncated verse:

A. *Ze* Start (level-tone rhyme)

Note: The first line can be substituted with the following tones: △△   △◯   ●

B. *Ping* Start (level-tone rhyme)

Note: The first line can be substituted with the following tones: ◯◯   △△   ●

C. *Ze* Start (deflected-tone rhyme)

D. *Ping* Start (deflected-tone rhyme)

The seven-character truncated verse

The following are the two basic tonal patterns of the seven-character truncated verse:

A. Ze Start (level-tone rhyme)

Note: The first line can be substituted with the following tones: △△ ○○ △△ ●

B. *Ping* Start (level-tone rhyme)

```
○○   △△   ○○   △
△△   ○○   △△   ●
△△   ○○   ○△   △
○○   △△   △○   ●
```

Note: The first line can be substituted with the following tones: ○○   △△   △○   ●

C. *Ze* Start (deflected-tone rhyme)

```
△△   ○○   ○△   ▲
○○   △△   ○○   ▲
○○   △△   △○   ○
△△   ○○   ○△   ▲
```

D. *Ping* Start (deflected-tone rhyme)

```
○○   △△   ○○   ▲
△△   ○○   ○△   ▲
△△   ○○   △△   ○
○○   △△   ○○   ▲
```

Deflected tone is infrequently used as a rhyme in both *wujue* (five-character truncated verse) and *qijue* (seven-character truncated verse). The rules governing five-character regulated verse also apply to seven-character regulated verse.

PART 2

Five-Character Regulated Verses

五言律诗

Bai Juyi 白居易

草

离离原上草	離離原上草
一岁一枯荣	一歲一枯榮
野火烧不尽	野火燒不盡
春风吹又生	春風吹又生
远芳侵古道	遠芳侵古道
晴翠接荒城	晴翠接荒城
又送王孙去	又送王孫去
萋萋满别情	萋萋滿別情

Grass*

How lushly
the grasses grow on the plain!
Year after year,
they wither before flourishing.
No wildfire can
burn them all.
When spring winds blow,
they sprout once more.
Far away, their fragrance
pervades the ancient road;
on a clear day, their green
extends to the ruined wall.
Now it is you whom I must
see off, my dear friend.
How can the luxuriant grass
not feel my parting pain!

白居易　草

離○離○ lí lí lushly	原○上△ 草△ yuán shàng cǎo grass on the plain
一△歲△ yī suì one year	一△枯○榮● yī kū róng one cycle of flourishing and withering
野△火△ yě huǒ wildfire	燒○不△盡△ shào bù jìn can't burn them all
春○風○ chūn fēng spring winds	吹○又△生● chuī yòu shēng blow and grow again
遠△芳○ yuǎn fāng distant fragrance	侵○古△道△ qīn gǔ dào invades ancient road
晴○翠△ qíng cuì clear green	接△荒○城● jiē huāng chéng touches the ruined wall
又△送△ yòu sòng again to see	王○孫○去△[1] wáng sūn qù my friend leaving here
萋○萋○ qī qī luxuriantly	滿△別△情● mán bié qíng full of parting feelings

* Bai Juyi wrote this poem when he was only sixteen. It was said that he went to Chang'an, the capital city, to call on Gu Kuang, a well-known poet at the time. When Gu saw Bai Juyi's given name 居易, which literally means easy to live, he joked that it was very expensive to live in Chang'an. After Gu read this poem, he said with a sigh, "A person with such a talent shouldn't find it too hard to live here!"

[1] Literally, a descendant of nobility, it refers to an old friend here.

○ = ping (level) tone
△ = ze (deflected) tone
● = rhyme (ping tone)

Cui Tu 崔涂

除夜有怀

迢递三巴路
羁危万里身
乱山残雪夜
孤烛异乡人
渐与骨肉远
转于僮仆亲
那堪正漂泊
明日岁华新

迢遞三巴路
羈危萬里身
亂山殘雪夜
孤燭異鄉人
漸與骨肉遠
轉於僮僕親
那堪正漂泊
明日歲華新

Reflections on New Year's Eve

The roads to the Three Ba's
lie far away from home.
This much-traveled body
has taken its toll.
The mountain in the evening
is partially covered with old snow.
A traveler from another part of the land
holds a candle in his hand.
Gradually I am farther away
from my kinsfolk.
Increasingly I become
close to the servants.
How can I stand
such a drifting life?
Tomorrow will be
the first day of a new year!

崔涂　除夜有懷

迢○遞△ tiáo dì faraway	三○巴○路△[1] sān bā lù Three-Ba Road
羈○危○ jī wēi tough to travel	萬△里△身● wàn lǐ shēn much-traveled body
亂△山○ luàn shān rough mountain	殘○雪△夜△ cán xuě yè night of accumulated snow
孤○燭△ gū zhú single candle	異△鄉○人● yì xiāng rén a person from another land
漸△與△ jiàn yǔ each passing day	骨△肉△遠△ gǔ ròu yuǎn farther from relatives
轉△於○ zhuǎng yú gradually become	僮○僕△親● tóng pú qīn intimated with servants
那△堪○ nǎ kān can't bear	正△漂○泊△ zhèng piāo bó this kind of drifting life
明○日△ míng rì tomorrow	歲△華○新● suì huá xīn a new year will begin

[1] The Three Ba's, which include Bajun, Badong, and Baxi, are near the Yangtse Gorges in Sichuan Province.

Cui Tu

崔涂

孤雁

几行归塞尽	幾行歸塞盡
念尔独何之	念爾獨何之
暮雨相呼失	暮雨相呼失
寒塘欲下迟	寒塘欲下遲
渚云低暗渡	渚雲低暗渡
关月冷遥随	關月冷遙隨
未必逢矰缴	未必逢矰繳
孤飞自可疑	孤飛自可疑

A Lonely Wild Goose

Lines of wild geese returned
to the frontier and vanished.
Alone by yourself,
for where are you bound?
Crying for your missing mates
in evening rain,
you hesitantly
drop down to the cold pond.
With clouds over the islet,
you fly low in dim light.
No one follows you
but the cold frontier moon at a distance.
You may not necessarily
be shot by a stringed arrow,
but be on guard,
when flying alone!

崔涂　孤雁

幾△行○ jǐ háng several lines	歸○塞△盡△ guī sài jìn returned to frontier and disappeared
念△爾△ niàn ěr thinking of you	獨△何○之● dú hé zhī alone where to go
暮△雨△ mù yǔ evening rain	相○呼○失△ xiāng hū shī crying for lost mates
寒○塘○ hán táng cold pond	欲△下△遲● yù xià chí descending hesitantly
渚△雲○ shǔ yún clouds over islet	低○暗△渡△ dī àn dù fly low to cross over
關○月△ guān yuè frontier moon	冷△遙○隨● lěng yáo suí follows quietly from distance
未△必△ wèi bì not necessarily	逢○矰○繳△[1] féng zēng zhuó will be shot by an arrow
孤○飛○ gū fēi flying alone	自△可△疑● zì kè yí be on guard yourself

[1] A bird-shooting arrow with a silk cord attached to it.

Dai Shulun 戴叔伦

江乡故人偶集客舍

天秋月又满
城阙夜千重
还作江南会
翻疑梦里逢
风枝惊暗鹊
露草覆寒蛩
羁旅长堪醉
相留畏晓钟

天秋月又滿
城闕夜千重
還作江南會
翻疑夢裡逢
風枝驚暗鵲
露草覆寒蛩
羈旅長堪醉
相留畏曉鐘

Meeting an Old Friend from Jiangnan at an Inn

Once again in autumn
the moon is full.
So deep is the night
in the capital.
What a pleasant surprise
to see you from Jiangnan!
But I can't be sure
that we are not in a dream.
A wind in the branches
startles the hidden magpie.
Beneath the dewy grass
the crickets feel the chill.
A traveler away from home
ought to drink to the fullest.
So reluctant to part,
we are afraid of the morning bell.

戴叔倫　江鄉故人偶集客舍

天○秋○
tiān qiū
time now is in autumn

月△又△滿△
yuè yòu mǎn
full moon again

城○闕△¹
chéng què
capital city

夜△千○重●
yè qián chóng
the night is very deep

還○作△
hái zuò
could still

江○南○會△
jiāng nán huì
meet as in Jiangnan

翻○疑○
fān yí
even suspect

夢△裡△逢●
mèng lǐ féng
seeing you in a dream

風○枝○
fēng zhī
wind in branches

驚○暗△鵲△
jīng àn què
startles the hidden magpie

露△草△
lù cǎo
dewy grass

覆△寒○蛩●
fù hán qióng
covers shivering crickets

羈○旅△
jī lǚ
a traveler

長○堪○醉△
cháng kān zuì
often feels good to get drunk

相○留○
xiāng liú
wanting to stay

畏△曉△鐘●
wèi xiǎo zhōng
afraid of morning bell

¹ The capital city Chang'an was where the poet met his old friend from Jiangnan, a region south of the Yangtze River.

Du Fu

杜甫

月夜

今夜鄜州月	今夜鄜州月
闺中只独看	閨中只獨看
遥怜小儿女	遙憐小兒女
未解忆长安	未解憶長安
香雾云鬟湿	香霧雲鬟濕
清辉玉臂寒	清輝玉臂寒
何时倚虚幌	何時倚虛幌
双照泪痕干	雙照淚痕乾

On a Moonlit Night

At this very moment
tonight in Fu Zhou,
you are watching the moon
alone in your boudoir.
Far away, I feel for my
young children
who do not understand
why Chang'an is on your mind.
The fog moistens
the locks of your hair;
the clear moonlight
chills your arms.
When can we lean
by the thin curtain
and let the moonlight
shine on the traces of our tears?

杜甫　月夜

今○夜△　　　　　　鄜○州○月△ [1]
jīn yè　　　　　　　fū zhōu yuè
tonight　　　　　　　Fu Zhou's moon

閨○中○　　　　　　只△獨△看 ●
guī zhōng　　　　　zhǐ dú kān
in the boudoir　　　you alone watching

遙○憐○　　　　　　小△兒○女△
yáo lián　　　　　　xiǎo ér nǚ
afar, pitying for　　my little children

未△解△　　　　　　憶△長○安 ● [2]
wèi jiě　　　　　　　yì cháng ān
don't understand　why thinking of Chang'an

香○霧△　　　　　　雲○鬟○濕△
xiāng wù　　　　　yún huán shī
fragrant fog　　　　moistens the hair bun

清○輝○　　　　　　玉△臂△寒 ●
qīng huī　　　　　　yù bì hán
clear moolight　　chills the fair arms

何○時○　　　　　　倚△虛○幌△
hé shí　　　　　　　yǐ xū huǎng
when　　　　　　　to lean on see-through curtain

雙○照△　　　　　　淚△痕○乾 ●
shuāng zhào　　　lèi hén gān
shining on our　　dried traces of tears

[1] Fu Zhou was in present-day Fu County, Shanxi Province.
[2] On his way to Lingwu, Du Fu was captured by An Lushan's rebellious army and taken to the Chang'an City.

Du Fu　　　　　　杜甫

春 望

国破山河在	國破山河在
城春草木深	城春草木深
感时花溅泪	感時花濺淚
恨别鸟惊心	恨別鳥驚心
烽火连三月	烽火連三月
家书抵万金	家書抵萬金
白头搔更短	白頭搔更短
浑欲不胜簪	渾欲不勝簪

Spring View

The country is ruined;
the mountains and rivers remain.
Springtime in the city,
grass and trees are densely green.
Facing hard times,
flowers trigger my tears;
fearing separation,
birds startle my heart.
Beacon fires
last for three consecutive months.
A letter from home
is worth ten thousand gold coins.
Ah, my gray hair
gets too thin to scratch.
It simply
can no longer hold a hairpin!

杜甫　春望

國△破△
guó pò
country ruined

山○河○在△
shān hé zài
mountains and rivers remain

城○春○
chēng chūn
city in springtime

草△木△深 ●
cǎo mù shēn
grass and trees grow deep

感△時○
gǎn shí
facing hard times

花○濺△淚△
huā jiàn lèi
flowers trigger tears

恨△別△
hèn bié
hating separation

鳥△驚○心 ●
niǎo jīng xīn
birds startle my heart

烽○火△
fēng huǒ
beacon fires

連○三○月△
lián sān yuè
last for three months

家○書○
jiā shū
a letter from home

抵△萬△金 ●
dǐ wàn jīn
worth ten thousand gold coins

白△頭○
bái tóu
white hair

搔○更△短△
sāo gèng duǎn
shorter the more I scratch

渾○欲 △
hún yù
it simply

不△勝○簪 ●[1]
bù shèng zān
can't bear a hairpin

[1] A hairpin was used to hold the hair together by both men and women in ancient times.

Du Fu 杜甫

春宿左省

花隐掖垣暮　　　　花隱掖垣暮
啾啾栖鸟过　　　　啾啾棲鳥過
星临万户动　　　　星臨萬戶動
月傍九霄多　　　　月傍九霄多
不寝听金钥　　　　不寢聽金鑰
因风想玉珂　　　　因風想玉珂
明朝有封事　　　　明朝有封事
数问夜如何　　　　數問夜如何

Lodging at the Left Imperial Court* on a Spring Night

Flowers at sunset look darkish
by the wall of the court.
Jiu, jiu, the birds chirp,
looking for a place to perch.
Stars hanging low,
thousands of houses appear shaking;
the moon shines brilliantly
onto the farthest limits of the sky.
Unable to sleep, I keep
hearing the turn of the golden key.
Wind blowing,
I think of the jade horse-bells.
Early morning tomorrow,
I must report to the throne.
Repeatedly I ask,
what time is it now?

杜甫　春宿左省

花○隱△
huā yǐn
flowers hiding

啾○啾○
jiū jiū
'jiu, jiu'

星○臨○
xīng lín
stars hanging low

月△傍△
yuè bàng
moon is close to

不△寢△
bù qǐn
unable to sleep

因○風○
yīn fēng
because of wind

明○朝○
míng zhāo
next morning

數△問△
shuò wèn
ask several times

掖△垣○暮△
yè yuán mù
by palace walls at sunset

棲○鳥△過●
qī niǎo guō
birds ready to perch

萬△戶△動△
wàn hù dòng
thousands of houses shake

九△霄○多●
jiǔ xiāo duō
the sky with abundant light

聽○金○鑰△[1]
tīng jīn yuè
listen to golden key

想△玉△珂●[2]
xiǎng yù kē
think of jade bridle

有△封○事△
yǒu fēng shì
must report to the throne

夜△如○何●
yè rú hé
how is the night

* The left wing of the imperial palace in which Du Fu served as an imperial advisor.
[1] The golden key to the door of the palace.
[2] A bridle that was decorated with jade-like shells.

Du Fu　　　　　　　　　杜甫

金光门

此道昔归顺	此道昔歸順
西郊胡正繁	西郊胡正繁
至今残破胆	至今殘破膽
应有未招魂	應有未招魂
近侍归京邑	近侍歸京邑
移官岂至尊	移官豈至尊
无才日衰老	無才日衰老
驻马望千门	駐馬望千門

Gate of Golden Light*

This was the road through which
I joined the then new court.
The rebels were in full control
at the western outskirts.
The thought of it strikes
intense fear even now.
There may still be souls
out there to be called back.
I returned to the capital
as the Emperor's close courtier.
Could it be his idea
to banish me away?
Without talent,
I gradually become weak and old.
Let me halt my horse
and take a look at the thousand gates.

杜甫　金光門

此△道△
cǐ dào
this road

昔△歸○順△
xī guī shùn
through which I once escaped

西○郊○
xī jiāo
west outskirts

胡○正△繁●
hú zhèng fán
the rebels were numerous

至△今○
zhì jīn
until now

殘○破△膽△
cán pò dǎn
may cause intense fear

應○有△
yīng yǒu
should have

未△招○魂●
wèi zhāo hún
souls not yet called back

近△侍△
jìn shì
as a courtier

歸○京○邑△
guī jīng yì
I returned to the capital city

移○官○
yí guān
assigned to a new post

豈△至△尊●
qǐ zhì zūn
could it be the emperor's idea

無○才○
wú cái
without talent

日△衰○老△
rì shuāi lǎo
getting weak and old

駐△馬△
zhù mǎ
halting the horse

望△千○門● [1]
wàng qiān mén
looking at a thousand doors

---

[*] In the second year of Zhide (757), Du Fu escaped from Chang'an to join the court of the new Empeor Suzong at Fengxiang. On the way to Fengxiang, he passed through the Gate of Golden Light. The following year, he was demoted and banished to Hua Zhou as a result of his loyalty to the disgraced minister Fang Quan. For the second time, he passed the same gate.

[1] Refers to the palace.

Du Fu

杜甫

月夜忆舍弟

戍鼓断人行
秋边一雁声
露从今夜白
月是故乡明
有弟皆分散
无家问死生
寄书长不达
况乃未休兵

戍鼓斷人行
秋邊一雁聲
露從今夜白
月是故鄉明
有弟皆分散
無家問死生
寄書長不達
況乃未休兵

Thinking of My Younger Brothers on a Moonlit Night

Nobody is out on the road
to hear the drums
of the garrison troops.
Only a solitary wild goose
honks at the autumnal frontier.
White Dew begins tonight.
The moon looks brighter
over my hometown.
My younger brothers
are all in different places.
Dead or alive,
no home to find.
The letters I mailed
can no longer be delivered.
What can I expect
with fighting still going on?

杜甫　月夜憶舍弟

戍△鼓△　　　　　　　　斷△人○行●
shù gǔ　　　　　　　　duàn rén xíng
drums of the garrison troops　no one on the road

秋○邊○　　　　　　　　一△雁△聲●
qiū biān　　　　　　　　yī yàn shēng
autumn at frontier　　　sound of a lone goose

露△從○[1]　　　　　　今○夜△白△
lù cóng　　　　　　　　jīn yè bái
dew beginning to　　　turn white tonight

月△是△　　　　　　　　故△鄉○明●
yuè shì　　　　　　　　gù xiāng míng
moon is　　　　　　　　brighter at hometown

有△弟△　　　　　　　　皆○分○散△
yǒu dì　　　　　　　　jiē fēn sàn
younger brothers　　　all in different places

無○家○　　　　　　　　問△死△生●
wú jiā　　　　　　　　wèn sǐ shēng
no home　　　　　　　　to find out alive or dead

寄△書○　　　　　　　　長○不△達△
jì shū　　　　　　　　cháng bù dá
mailing a letter　　　always undeliverable

況△乃△　　　　　　　　未△休○兵●
kuàng nǎi　　　　　　　wèi xiū bīng
not to mention　　　　fighting still goes on

[1] Beginning around September 8 or 9, White Dew is one of the twenty-four climatic periods of the lunar year.

Du Fu 杜甫

天末怀李白

凉风起天末	涼風起天末
君子意如何	君子意如何
鸿雁几时到	鴻雁幾時到
江湖秋水多	江湖秋水多
文章憎命达	文章憎命達
魑魅喜人过	魑魅喜人過
应共冤魂语	應共冤魂語
投书赠汨罗	投書贈汨羅

Thinking of Li Bai at a Remote Corner

Cool wind arises
from the edge of the sky.
My friend, how do you feel?
When will the wild geese
bring me your messages?
Autumn waters swell
the rivers and lakes.
Writings
often bring us bad fate.
Demons enjoy
swallowing those who pass by.
Why not share your grievances
with the ghost of Qu Yuan?
Drop in the Miluo River
a poem to show your pain!

杜甫　天末懷李白

涼○風○ liáng fēng cool wind	起△天○末△ qǐ tiān mò rises from sky's edge
君○子△ jūn zǐ gentleman	意△如○何● yì rú hé how do you feel
鴻○雁△[1] hóng yàn swan geese	幾△時○到△ jǐ shí dào when to arrive
江○湖○ jiāng hú rivers and lakes	秋○水△多● qiū shuǐ duō autumn waters swell
文○章○ wén zhāng writings	憎○命△達△ zēng mìng dá detest good fate
魑○魅△ chī mèi demons	喜△人○過● xǐ rén guō enjoy people passing by
應○共△ yīng gòng should share	冤○魂○語△[2] yuān hún yǔ words with the grievous soul
投○書○ tóu shū drop a letter	贈△汨△羅● zèng mì luó to the Miluo River

[1] Wild swans and geese are often messengers in Chinese poetry.

[2] Refers to the ghost of Qu Yuan (343—290 B.C.), a poet and statesman of the state of Chu. Qu Yuan drowned himself in the Miluo River because his concerns for his country were completely ignored.

Du Fu 杜甫

奉济驿重送严公四韵*

远送从此别	遠送從此別
青山空复情	青山空復情
几时杯重把	幾時盃重把
昨夜月同行	昨夜月同行
列郡讴歌惜	列郡謳歌惜
三朝出入荣	三朝出入榮
江村独归处	江村獨歸處
寂寞养残生	寂寞養殘生

Seeing Yan Wu Off Again at Fengji Courier Station

We have come a long way;
here we must part.
The blue mountain is left behind
with an empty feeling.
When shall we
raise wine cups again
as we did last night,
strolling together in moonlight?
People in all nearby counties
bade you farewell with songs.
Serving three emperors
you walked in and out with honors.
I shall return alone to
my river village
and live out my remaining years
in solitude.

杜甫　奉濟驛重送嚴公四韻

遠△送△
yuǎn sòng
long way to see you off

從○此△別△
cóng cǐ bié
parting from here

青○山○
qīng shān
blue mountain

空○復△情●
kōng fù qíng
with empty feeling

幾△時○
jǐ shí
when

盃○重○把△
bēi chóng bǎ
to hold cup again

昨△夜△
zuó yè
last night

月△同○行●
yuè tóng xíng
we strolled in moonlight

列△郡△
liè jùn
list of counties

謳○歌○惜△
ōu gē xī
singing songs to bid farewell

三○朝○[1]
sān cháo
three reigns

出△入△榮●
chū rù róng
in and out with honor

江○村○
jiāng cūn
river village

獨△歸○處△
dú guī chù
to return alone

寂△寞△
jì mò
in solitude

養△殘○生●
yǎng cán shēng
to live the remaining years

---

[*] Yan Wu, a governor in charge of military and civil affairs, often offered Du Fu both emotional and financial support.

[1] The three emperors: Xuanzong, Suzong, and Daizong.

Du Fu 杜甫

别房太尉墓

他乡复行役　　　他鄉復行役
驻马别孤坟　　　駐馬別孤墳
近泪无干土　　　近淚無乾土
低空有断云　　　低空有斷雲
对棋陪谢傅　　　對碁陪謝傅
把剑觅徐君　　　把劍覓徐君
唯见林花落　　　唯見林花落
莺啼送客闻　　　鶯啼送客聞

On Leaving the Tomb of Marshall Fang

In a strange land,
on a mission,
I halt my horse
to bid your lonely tomb farewell.
My tears keep
moistening the soil below.
The sky hangs low
with a few broken clouds.
I wish I could play chess
with Grand Tutor Xie.
Or look for the King of Xu
with a sword in my hand.
But what I see
is the fallen forest flowers,
as the orioles
cry good-bye.

杜甫　別房太尉墓

他○鄉○
tā xiāng
foreign land

復△行○役△
fù xíng yì
also go on a mission

駐△馬△
zhù mǎ
dismounted

別△孤○墳●[1]
bié gū fén
bid farewell to the lonely grave

近△淚△
jìn lèi
close to the tears

無○乾○土△
wú gān tǔ
no dry soil

低○空○
dī kōng
low altitude

有△斷△雲●
yǒu duàn yún
with broken clouds

對△碁○
duì qí
facing checkered board

陪○謝△傅△[2]
péi xiè fù
played with Grand Tutor Xie

把△劍△
bǎ jiàn
holding a sword

覓△徐○君●[3]
mì xú jūn
looked for King of Xu

唯○見△
wéi jiàn
only see

林○花○落△
lín huā luò
forest flowers falling

鶯○啼○
yīng tí
oriole crying

送△客△聞●
sòng kè wén
good-bye to a visitor

[1] The grave of Fang Guan, the Prime Minister of Emperor Xuanzong.

[2] Xie refers to Xie An, a prime minister of the East Jin Dynasty. Xie was known for his composure in the face of great danger. He once even calmly played chess the night before a major battle.

[3] An allusion to Jizha, who, on his way to the kingdom of Jin on a mission, learned that the king of Xu fell in love with his sword. He planned to give the sword to the king as a gift on his return. By the time he returned to Xu, the king had already died. In memory of the king, Jizha hung the sword on a tree next to the tomb.

Du Fu　　　　　　　　　杜甫

旅夜书怀

細草微风岸　　　　細草微風岸
危檣独夜舟　　　　危檣獨夜舟
星垂平野阔　　　　星垂平野闊
月涌大江流　　　　月湧大江流
名岂文章著　　　　名豈文章著
官因老病休　　　　官因老病休
飘飘何所似　　　　飄飄何所似
天地一沙鸥　　　　天地一沙鷗

Lodging for the Night

A breeze strokes
the thin grass on the shore.
A boat with a tall mast
stands at night, alone.
As the stars sink,
the field looks wide open;
the moon rises
on the waves of the great river.
Would writings ever
bring me fame?
Old and sick,
is it time to retire from my rank?
Drifting, drifting,
what am I like?
A sea gull
between Heaven and Earth.

杜甫　旅夜書懷

細△草△
xì cǎo
thin grass

微○風○岸△
wēi fēng àn
on shore with a breeze

危○檣○
wēi qiáng
tall mast

獨△夜△舟●
dú yè zhōu
a lonely boat at night

星○垂○
xīng chuí
stars sinking

平○野△闊△
píng yě kuò
open field expands

月△湧△
yuè yǒng
moon rushes on

大△江○流●[1]
dà jiāng liú
great river flowing

名○豈△
míng qǐ
can fame arise

文○章○著△
wén zhāng zhù
from writings that excel

官○因○
guān yīn
an officeholder

老△病△休●
lǎo bìng xiū
to retire due to illness and age

飄○飄○
piāo piāo
drifting, drifting

何○所△似△
hé suǒ sì
am I like what

天○地△
tiān dì
sky and earth

一△沙○鷗●
yī shā ōu
one sand gull

---

[1]　Great river here refers to the Yangtze River.

Du Fu   杜甫

登岳阳楼

昔闻洞庭水　　　　昔聞洞庭水
今上岳阳楼　　　　今上岳陽樓
吴楚东南坼　　　　吳楚東南坼
乾坤日夜浮　　　　乾坤日夜浮
亲朋无一字　　　　親朋無一字
老病有孤舟　　　　老病有孤舟
戎马关山北　　　　戎馬關山北
凭轩涕泗流　　　　憑軒涕泗流

Going up the Yueyang Tower

I have long heard of
the Lake Dongting;
only now have I climbed
the Yueyang Tower.
On the east and south,
Wu and Chu lie across the lake.
Day and night
the sun and moon float on the water.
From my relatives and friends
not a single word can be heard;
old and sick,
a boat is all I can have.
On the northern land
warhorses still trample.
I see my tears
dripping down on the windowsill.

杜甫　登岳陽樓

昔△聞○ xí wén heard in the past	洞△庭○水△ [1] dòng tíng shuǐ Dong Ting waters
今○上△ jīn shàng now coming up to	岳△陽○樓● [2] yuè yáng lóu Yue Yang Tower
吳○楚△ [3] wú chǔ Wu and Chu	東○南○坼△ dōng nán chè set apart on the east and south
乾○坤○ [4] qián kūn heaven and earth	日△夜△浮● rì yè fú float day and night
親○朋○ qīn péng relatives and friends	無○一△字△ wú yī zì without a single word
老△病△ lǎo bìng aging and ill	有△孤○舟● yǒu gū zhōu have only a boat
戎○馬△ róng mǎ army and horse	關○山○北△ guān shān běi north of Guan Mountain
憑○軒○ píng xuān leaning on the window	涕△泗△流● tì sì liú tears and snivels to fall

[1] Dongting or Lake Donting is in northern Hunan Province.
[2] The Yueyang Tower, which overlooks the Lake Dongting, is in Hunan Province.
[3] Refers to the southeastern region of China; the east side of Lake Dongting is Wu and the south side is Chu.
[4] Male and female; heaven and earth; sun and moon.

Du Mu 杜牧

旅宿

旅馆无良伴	旅館無良伴
凝情自悄然	凝情自悄然
寒灯思旧事	寒燈思舊事
断雁警愁眠	斷雁警愁眠
远梦归侵晓	遠夢歸侵曉
家书到隔年	家書到隔年
沧江好烟月	滄江好煙月
门系钓鱼船	門繫釣魚船

Hotel

Without a companion
at a tavern,
I felt a deep sense
of loneliness.
By a cold lamp,
I thought of the past.
A stray wild goose
roused me from my sleep.
Though it took more than a year
for my home mail to reach me,
I returned to my faraway home
in a dream just before dawn.
The dark blue river was
under a misty moonlight.
I saw my fishing boat
tied to the gate outside.

杜牧　旅宿

旅△ 館△
lǚ guǎn
at the tavern

無○ 良○ 伴△
wú liáng bàn
no good companions

凝○情○
níng qīng
feeling

自△悄△然●
zì qiǎo rán
sad about myself

寒○燈○
hán dēng
by the cold lamp

思○舊△事△
sī jiù shì
think of past events

斷△雁△
duàn yàn
a stray wild goose

警△愁○眠●
jǐng chóu mián
roused me from sleep

遠△夢△
yuǎn mèng
dreaming to go far

歸○侵○曉△
guī qīn xiǎo
returned home at dawn

家○書○
jiā shū
letter from home

到△隔△年●
dào gé nián
received one year later

滄○江○
cāng jiāng
dark blue river

好△煙○月△
hǎo yān yuè
nice view of mist and moon

門○繫△
mēn jì
moored outside of door

釣△魚○船●
diào yú chuán
a fishing boat

Du Xunhe   杜荀鶴

春宫怨

早被蝉娟误	早被蟬娟誤
欲妆临镜慵	欲妝臨鏡慵
承恩不在貌	承恩不在貌
教妾若为容	教妾若為容
风暖鸟声碎	風暖鳥聲碎
日高花影重	日高花影重
年年越溪女	年年越溪女
相忆采芙蓉	相憶採芙蓉

Spring Complaints in the Palace

Beauty with grace has
brought me misfortunes.
I want to doll up but
feel listless before the mirror.
If the emperor's grace
is not based on looks,
how can I do my
makeup in a good mood?
Birds twitter continuously
when the wind is warm;
too many flower shadows
when the sun is at its height.
Year after year, girls
of the Yue stream
still remember the time
of picking lotus.

杜荀鶴　春宮怨

早△被△　　　　　蟬○娟○誤△
zǎo bèi　　　　　chán juān wù
already was　　　hurt by beauty and grace

欲△妝○　　　　　臨○鏡△慵●
yù zhuāng　　　　lín jìng yōng
wishing to doll up　face mirror listlessly

承○恩○　　　　　不△在△貌△
chéng ēn　　　　bù zài mào
emperor's visit　　depends not on look

教△妾△　　　　　若△為○容●
jiào qiē　　　　ruò wéi róng
how can I　　　apply make-up

風○暖△　　　　　鳥△聲○碎△
fēng nuǎn　　　niǎo shēng suì
wind is warm　　birds twitter continuously

日△高○　　　　　花○影△重●
rì gāo　　　　　huā yǐng chóng
when sun is high　flower shadows superimpose

年○年○　　　　　越△溪○女△[1]
nián nián　　　　yuè xī nǚ
year after year　girls of Yue stream

相○憶△　　　　　採△芙○蓉●
xiāng yì　　　　cǎi fú róng
each remembers　picking lotus

[1] The girls who washed clothes in the Yue stream with Xi Shi, a beauty in the Period of Spring and Autumn (770—476, B. C.).

Han Hong 韩翃

酬程延秋夜即事见赠

长簟迎风早	長簟迎風早
空城澹月华	空城澹月華
星河秋一雁	星河秋一雁
砧杵夜千家	砧杵夜千家
节候看应晚	節候看應晚
心期卧亦赊	心期臥亦賒
向来吟秀句	向來吟秀句
不觉已鸣鸦	不覺已鳴鴉

Responding to Chen Yan's Poem "Autumn Night"

Tall bamboos greet
the early breeze in autumn.
Bright moonlight
bathes the tranquil town.
A lonely wild goose
is flying under the Milky Way.
From a thousand homes,
comes the washing-stone sound.
The season is
now deep in autumn.
I am willing to put off sleep
so as to respond to your poem.
I keep chanting
your beautiful lines,
not realizing the crows
have already started to caw.

韓翃　酬程延秋夜即事見贈

長○簟△ [1]
cháng diàn
tall bamboos

迎○風○早△
yíng fēng zǎo
greet the early wind

空○城○
kōng chéng
empty city

澹△月△華●
dàn yuè huá
tranquil in bright moonlight

星○河○
xīng hé
Milky Way

秋○一△雁△
qiū yī yàn
one autumn wild goose

砧○杵△ [2]
zhēn chǔ
stone block and club

夜△千○家●
yè qiān jiā
a thousand homes at night

節○候△
jié hòu
seasons

看○應○晚△
kān yīng wǎn
should be late by now

心○期○
xīn qī
keep thinking it

臥△亦△賒●
wò yì shē
borrow time from sleep

向△來○
xiàng lái
all along

吟○秀△句△
yín xiù jù
chanting beautiful lines

不△覺△
bù jué
unaware

已△鳴○鴉●
yǐ míng yā
crows already start to caw

[1] A long bamboo mat. It is used here to mean a variety of giant bamboo.
[2] A stone block and a wooden club were used to wash clothes in ancient times.

Jiao Ran, the Monk　　　僧皎然

寻陆鸿渐不遇

移家虽带郭　　　　移家雖帶郭
野径入桑麻　　　　野徑入桑麻
近种篱边菊　　　　近種籬邊菊
秋来未著花　　　　秋來未著花
叩门无犬吠　　　　叩門無犬吠
欲去问西家　　　　欲去問西家
报道山中去　　　　報道山中去
归时每日斜　　　　歸時每日斜

Not Finding Lu Hongjian at Home

Although you had moved
to the vicinity of the city wall,
I had to follow a wild path
to find your house among mulberry trees.
I saw newly planted
chrysanthemums by the fence.
They were not yet in bloom
though autumn was here.
Knocking at your door,
I heard no dog barking.
I then asked your
neighbor to the west.
I was told that you were
somewhere in the hills.
You wouldn't return each day
until the sun was about to set.

僧皎然　尋陸鴻漸不遇

移○家○
yí jiā
home moving

雖○帶△郭△
suī dài guō
though by the city wall

野△徑△
yě jìng
wild path

入△桑○麻●
rù sāng má
leads to mulberry field

近△種△
jìn zhòng
recently planted

籬○邊○菊△
lí biān jú
chrysanthemums by fence

秋○來○
qiū lái
autumn has come

未△著△花●
wèi zhúo huā
not yet in bloom

叩△門○
kòu mén
knocking at door

無○犬△吠△
wú quǎn fèi
no dog barking

欲△去△
yù qù
about to

問△西○家●
wèn xī jiā
ask neighbor to the west

報△道△
bào dào
responded by saying

山○中○去△
shān zhōng qù
gone to the hills

歸○時○
guī shí
time of return

每△日△斜●
měi rì xié
at sunset every day

Li Bai

李白

赠孟浩然

吾爱孟夫子
风流天下闻
红颜弃轩冕
白首卧松云
醉月频中圣
迷花不事君
高山安可仰
徒此揖清芬

吾愛孟夫子
風流天下聞
紅顏棄軒冕
白首臥松雲
醉月頻中聖
迷花不事君
高山安可仰
徒此揖清芬

For Meng Haoran

How could I not love you,
Master Meng!
The whole world knows about
your charm and elegance.
In your youth,
you gave up carriage and gown.
Now a white-haired man,
you lie beneath pines and clouds.
You drink with the moon
like a drunken saint;
you serve no ruler
for flowers are your main concern.
Who can look up to
so high a mountain?
Your virtues
I can only emulate with awe.

李白　贈孟浩然

吾○愛△ wú ài I love	孟△夫○子△ mèng fū zǐ Master Meng
風○流○ fēng liú charming and elegant	天○下△聞● tiān xià wén known in the whole world
紅○顏○ hóng yán rosy cheek	棄△軒○冕[1] qì xuān miǎn gave up carriage and hood
白△首△ bái shǒu white head	臥△松○雲● wò sōng yún lie under pines and clouds
醉△月△ zuì yuè drinking in moonlight	頻○中○聖△[2] pín zhōng shèng often gets drunk
迷○花○ mí huā fascinated by flowers	不△事△君● bù shì jūn unwilling to serve the ruler
高○山○ gāo shān lofty mountain	安○可△仰△ ān kě yǎng too high to look up to
徒○此△ tú cǐ can only	揖△清○芬● yī qīng fēn bow to pure virtue

[1] Carriages and hoods for officials in high position, a symbol of rank and accomplishments.
[2] Refers to a person who gets drunk.

Li Bai　　　　　　　　李白

渡荆门送别

渡远荆门外　　　　　渡遠荊門外
来从楚国游　　　　　來從楚國遊
山随平野尽　　　　　山隨平野盡
江入大荒流　　　　　江入大荒流
月下飞天镜　　　　　月下飛天鏡
云生结海楼　　　　　雲生結海樓
仍怜故乡水　　　　　仍憐故鄉水
万里送行舟　　　　　萬里送行舟

Saying Good-bye Beyond Mount Thorn-Gate

From a ferry faraway,
to the rear of Mt. Jingmen,
here we have come,
to the former Chu State.
The mountains fall behind
as the open field begins;
the river enters
the wilderness and surges ahead.
The moon descends
like a flying mirror;
the clouds emerge
to form a sea tower.
I still love
the water from my hometown.
For several thousand miles,
it carries a boat down.

李白　渡荊門送別

渡△遠△
dù yuǎn
from afar on boat

荊○門○外△[1]
jīng mén wài
outside of Jingmen Mountain

來○從○
lái cóng
coming to

楚△國△遊●
chǔ guó yóu
tour the State of Chu

山○隨○
shān suí
mountains follow

平○野△盡△
píng yě jìn
to be ended in open field

江○入△
jiāng rù
river enters

大△荒○流●
dà huāng liú
wilderness and flows

月△下△
yuè xià
moon descends

飛○天○鏡△
fēi tiān jìng
sky-flying mirror

雲○生○
yún shēng
clouds emerge

結△海△樓●
jié hǎi lóu
to form a sea tower

仍○憐○
réng lián
still love

故△鄉○水△
gù xiāng shuǐ
hometown waters

萬△里△
wàn lǐ
ten thousand *li*

送△行○舟●
sòng xíng zhōu
to see off a moving boat

---

[1] Jingmen Mountain, literally, Thorn-gate, is in modern-day Hubei Province. It was so named because it resembled a door.

Li Bai   李白

送友人

青山横北郭	青山橫北郭
白水绕东城	白水繞東城
此地一为别	此地一為別
孤蓬万里征	孤蓬萬里征
浮云游子意	浮雲游子意
落日故人情	落日故人情
挥手自兹去	揮手自茲去
萧萧班马鸣	蕭蕭班馬鳴

Farewell to a Friend

Blue mountains
lie across the northern outskirts;
white water
circles around the eastern town.
Once we part
from this place,
a lone thistledown
will be on a thousand-mile journey.
A floating cloud is
what you want to be like;
the setting sun is how
your old friend feels.
A wave of the hand,
and we go our own way.
Whinny, whinny,
the horses neigh.

李白　送友人

青○山○　　　　　　横○北△郭△
qīng shān　　　　héng běi guō
blue mountains　　lie across northern outskirts

白△水△　　　　　　繞△東○城●
bái shuǐ　　　　　rào dōng chéng
white water　　　　circles around eastern town

此△地△　　　　　　一△為○別△
cǐ dì　　　　　　　yī wéi bié
from this place　　once we part

孤○蓬○　　　　　　萬△里△征●
gū péng　　　　　wàn lǐ zhēng
a lone thistledown　ten-thousand-li journey

浮○雲○　　　　　　游○子△意△
fú yún　　　　　　yóu zǐ yì
floating clouds　　traveler's desire

落△日△　　　　　　故△人○情●
luò rì　　　　　　gù rén qíng
setting sun　　　old friend's feeling

揮○手△　　　　　　自△茲○去△
huī shǒu　　　　　zì zī qù
waving hand　　　go own way from here

蕭○蕭○　　　　　　班○馬△鳴●
xiāo xiāo　　　　　bān mǎ míng
"Whinny, whinny"　the parting horse neighs

Li Shangyin 李商隐

蝉

本以高难饱
徒劳恨费声
五更疏欲断
一树碧无情
薄宦梗犹泛
故园芜已平
烦君最相警
我亦举家清

本以高難飽
徒勞恨費聲
五更疏欲斷
一樹碧無情
薄宦梗猶汎
故園蕪已平
煩君最相警
我亦舉家清

The Cicada

To begin with, being clean
does not free you from hunger.
Why then keep
uttering bitterness?
By the fifth hour,
your voice becomes weak and husky.
But the green tree remains
indifferent and unmoved.
As a low-ranking official,
I am but a drifting twig.
The fields at home
are wasted with overgrown weeds.
Thank you for
alerting me, my friend.
My family and I are
just like you: pure and clean.

李商隱　蟬

本△以△
běn yǐ
from beginning

高○難○飽△[1]
gāo nán bǎo
lofty can't satisfy hunger

徒○勞○
tú láo
it is futile

恨△費△聲●
hèn fèi shēng
to utter bitterness

五△更○
wǔ gēng
the fifth watch

疏○欲△斷△
shū yù duàn
voice gets husky

一△樹△
yī shù
one tree

碧△無○情●
bì wú qíng
green but heartless

薄△宦△
bó huàn
low-ranking official

梗○猶○汎△
gěng yóu fàn
like a drifting twig

故△園○
gù yuán
old fields

蕪○已△平●
wú yǐ píng
wasted with overgrown weeds

煩○君○
fán jūn
thank you for

最△相○警△
zuì xiāng jǐng
warning me once again

我△亦△
wǒ yì
I am also

舉△家○清●
jǔ jiā qīng
clean in the whole family

[1] The cicada was praised for its purity in character as it was supposedly fed only on dew and wind.

Li Shangyin

李商隐

风雨

凄凉宝剑篇	淒涼寶劍篇
羁泊欲穷年	羈泊欲窮年
黄叶仍风雨	黃葉仍風雨
青楼自管弦	青樓自管絃
新知遭薄俗	新知遭薄俗
旧好隔良缘	舊好隔良緣
心断新丰酒	心斷新豐酒
消愁斗几千	消愁斗幾千

Wind and Rain

Sadly, what good does
a poem like "Precious Sword" ?
I still wander about,
year after year.
Yellow leaves still must
face the wind and rain.
Blue Chamber continues
to play the pipes and strings.
My new acquaintances
are unkindly treated.
Old friends are pressured to
sever ties.
No longer do I yearn for
the wine of Xinfeng
for it cannot reduce my sadness
even with a thousand jugs.

李商隱　風雨

淒○涼○ qī liáng very sad	寶△劍△篇●[1] bǎo jiàn piān the piece: Precious Sword
羈○泊△ jī bó wandering about	欲△窮○年● yù qióng nián year after year
黃○葉△ huáng yè yellow leaves	仍○風○雨△ réng fēng Yǔ still face wind and rain
青○樓○[2] qīng lóu blue chamber	自△管△絃● zì quǎn xián source of piping and fiddling
新○知○ xīn zhī new acquaintances	遭○薄△俗△ zāo bó sú being unkindly treated
舊△好△ jiù hǎo old friends	隔△良○緣● gé liáng yuán asked to sever friendship
心○斷△ xīn duàn stop thinking of	新○豐○酒△[3] xīn fēng jiǔ Xinfeng wine
消○愁○ xiāo chōu to get rid of sorrow	斗△幾△千● dǒu jǐ qiān need numerous jugs

[1] Guo Yuan Zhen, of the Tang Dynasty, impressed Empress Wu Zhao with his poem "The Precious Sword." He was subsequently rewarded with a high position job in the government.

[2] The Blue Chambers were places where singing girls entertained their male customers.

[3] Xinfeng, a place known for good wine, was in what is now Shanxi Province.

Li Shangyin　　　　　　　李商隐

落花

高阁客竟去　　　　　　高閣客竟去
小园花乱飞　　　　　　小園花亂飛
参差连曲陌　　　　　　參差連曲陌
迢递送斜晖　　　　　　迢遞送斜暉
肠断未忍扫　　　　　　腸斷未忍掃
眼穿仍欲归　　　　　　眼穿仍欲歸
芳心向春尽　　　　　　芳心向春盡
所得是沾衣　　　　　　所得是沾衣

Fallen Flowers

From the high pavilion,
guests are all gone.
Falling petals in the small garden
are whirling in the air.
Some are drifting down aimlessly
on the winding path;
some are following the setting sun
into the distance.
I cannot sweep them away
as it will break my heart.
Spring is leaving
despite my earnest wish for it to stay.
Gone with it is my
youthful heart.
All I am left with is my robe
stained with tears.

李商隱　落花

高○閣△	客△竟△去△
gāo gé	kè jìng qù
high pavilion	guests are all gone

小△園○	花○亂△飛●
xiǎo yuán	huā luàn fēi
small garden	petals flying in all directions

參○差○	連○曲△陌△
cēn cī	lián qǔ mò
aimlessly	fall on winding path

迢○遞△	送△斜○暉●
tiáo dì	sòng xié huī
faraway	escort the slanting sun

腸○斷△	未△忍△掃△
cháng duàn	wèi rěn sǎo
heartbroken	can't bear to sweep

眼△穿○	仍○欲△歸●
yǎn chuān	réng yù guī
wait earnestly	still want to return

芳○心○	向△春○盡△
fāng xīn	xiàng chūn jìn
young heart	gone with spring

所△得△	是△沾○衣●
suǒ dé	shì zhān yī
all I got	are wet clothes

Li Shangyin　　　　　　李商隐

涼思

客去波平檻
蝉休露满枝
永怀当此节
倚立自移时
北斗兼春远
南陵寓使迟
天涯占梦数
疑误有新知

客去波平檻
蟬休露滿枝
永懷當此節
倚立自移時
北斗兼春遠
南陵寓使遲
天涯占夢數
疑誤有新知

Thoughts in the Cold

With your departure,
the river has risen as high as my doorsill.
Cicadas cease chirping;
the branches are full of dew.
You are always in my heart
on such an occasion.
Time has passed,
while I am standing still.
The spring is far away,
but the Big Dipper is farther.
I have received no news from
Nanling, where you live.
At this corner of the world,
I can only figure things out from my dreams.
Am I wrong if I concluded that
you have found a new friend?

李商隱　涼思

客△去△
kè qù
guests gone

波○平○檻△
bō píng jiàn
waves rising to doorsill

蟬○休○
chán xiū
cicadas cease chirping

露△滿△枝●
lù mǎn zhī
branches full of dew

永△懷○
yǒng huái
always in my heart

當○此△節△
dāng cǐ jié
on this occasion

倚△立△
yǐ lì
standing still

自△移○時●
zì yí shí
unaware time has passed

北△斗△²
běi dǒu
The Big Dipper

兼○春○遠△
jiān chūn yuǎn
twice as far as spring

南○陵○¹
nán líng
Nanling

寓△使△遲●
yù shǐ chí
messenger to come late

天○涯○
tiān yá
edge of sky

占○夢△數△³
zhān mèng shòu
to divine dreams repeatedly

疑○誤△
yí wù
mistakenly assume

有△新○知●
yǒu xīn zhī
to have a new friend

¹ Nanling was in present-day Anhui Province, where the poet resided.
² The Big Dipper is used here to suggest the distance from his friend.
³ To divine by interpreting dreams.

Li Shangyin 李商隐

北青萝

残阳西入崦
茅屋访孤僧
落叶人何在
寒云路几层
独敲初夜磬
闲倚一枝藤
世界微尘里
吾宁爱与憎

殘陽西入崦
茅屋訪孤僧
落葉人何在
寒雲路幾層
獨敲初夜磬
閑倚一枝藤
世界微塵裡
吾寧愛與憎

At the North Green-Vine Cottage

The setting sun shines on
the mountain from the west.
I come to see a lonely monk
at a thatched cottage.
Where is he
amid the falling leaves?
The footpath
is lost in cloud upon cloud.
At dusk, he alone
beats a stone bell,
while I lean idly
against a rattan cane.
The universe
is contained in the fine dust.
How can I have
room for love and hate?

李商隱　北青蘿

殘○陽○
cán yáng
setting sun

茅○屋△
máo wū
thatched cottage

落△葉△
luò yè
falling leaves

寒○雲○
hán yún
cold clouds

獨△敲○
dú qiāo
beating alone

閑○倚△
xián yǐ
idly lean on

世△界△
shì jiè
the universe

吾○寧○
wú néng
how can I

西○入△崦△
xī rù yān
entered mountain from the west

訪△孤○僧●
fǎng gū sēng
visited a solitary monk

人○何○在△
rén hé zài
where was the man?

路△幾△層●
lù jǐ céng
layers of footpath

初○夜△磬△
chū yè qìng
evening stone bell

一△枝○藤●
yī zhī téng
a rattan cane

微○塵○裡△[1]
wéi chén lǐ
inside the fine dust

愛△與△憎●
ài yǔ zēng
have love and hate

[1] According to Buddhishm, the whole world is contained in the fine dust, suggesting that human affairs are so insignificant.

Li Yi 李益

喜见外弟又言别*

十年离乱后　　　十年離亂後
长大一相逢　　　長大一相逢
问姓惊初见　　　問姓驚初見
称名忆旧容　　　稱名憶舊容
别来沧海事　　　別來滄海事
语罢暮天钟　　　語罷暮天鐘
明日巴陵道　　　明日巴陵道
秋山又几重　　　秋山又幾重

Meeting with My Cousin Before Parting

For ten years during wartime,
We have been separated.
Not until we were grown-up
did we see each other again.
I was in shock at first
to be told your surname.
The image of your youthful face surfaced
upon my hearing your given name.
We talked about the vicissitudes
of life since we parted.
We kept talking until the
evening bell was heard.
Tomorrow you will be
on your way to Baling.
How many autumn mountains
will divide us once again?

李益　喜見外弟又言別

十△年。
shí nián
ten years

離。亂△後△
lí luàn hòu
after separation in war times

長△大△
zhǎng dà
growing up

一△相。逢●
yī xiāng féng
to meet for the first time

問△姓△
wèn xìng
asking surname

驚。初。見△
jīng chū jiàn
shocked at first

稱。名。
chēng míng
saying given name

憶△舊△容●
yì jiù róng
recalled old appearance

別△來。
bié lái
since parting

滄。海△事△
cāng hǎi shì
vicissitudes of life

語△罷△
yǔ bà
finished talking

暮△天。鐘●
mù tiān zhōng
evening bell from temple

明。日△
míng rì
tomorrow

巴。陵。道△
bā líng dào
on the way to Baling

秋。山。
qiū shān
autumn mountains

又△幾△重●
yòu jǐ chóng
one upon another again

---

* Cousin, the son of the father's sister, was thought to be Lu Lun (盧綸).
1 Baling was the modern-day Jueyang County in Hunan Province.

Liu Changqing 刘长卿

秋日登吴公台上寺远眺

古台摇落后	古臺搖落後
秋日望乡心	秋日望鄉心
野寺人来少	野寺人來少
云峰水隔深	雲峰水隔深
夕阳依旧垒	夕陽依舊壘
寒磬满空林	寒磬滿空林
惆怅南朝事	惆悵南朝事
长江独至今	長江獨至今

Climbing Lord Wu's Terrace in Autumn for a Distant View

On this ancient terrace,
desolated and deteriorated,
I stand on an autumn day
with a homesick heart.
In the wilds, the temple
has attracted few visitors.
The peaks, across the stream,
are deep in the clouds.
The setting sun
lingers on the ancient rampart.
The bare forest is filled
with the sound of *qing*.
It saddens me to recount things
of the Southern Dynasties.
Only the Long River
still flows as ever.

劉長卿　秋日登吳公台上寺遠眺

古△臺○[1]
gǔ tái
ancient terrace

搖○落△後△
yáo luò hòu
having been deteriorated and desolated

秋○日△
qiū rì
autumn day

望△鄉○心●
wàng xiāng xīn
with homesick heart

野△寺△
yě sì
temple in the wilds

人○來○少△
rén lái shǎo
visitors are rare

雲○峰○
yún fēng
cloudy peak

水△隔△深●
shuǐ gé shēn
looks deep across water

夕△陽○
xī yáng
setting sun

依○舊△壘△
yī jiù lěi
leans on old rampart

寒○磬△[2]
hán qìng
cold inverted bell

滿△空○林●
mǎn kōng lín
fills the empty grove

惆○悵△
chóu chàng
saddened by

南○朝○事△[3]
nán zháo shì
affairs of the Southern Dynasties

長○江○
cháng jiāng
Long River

獨△至△今●
dú zhì jīn
still flows alone

[1] Lord Wu's Terrace, in modern-day Jiangsu Province.
[2] Qing, an inverted bell used as a percussion instrument by the Buddhists.
[3] The Southern Dynasties (420—589 A.D.)

Liu Changqing 刘长卿

送李中丞归汉阳别业

流落征南将	流落征南將
曾驱十万师	曾驅十萬師
罢归无旧业	罷歸無舊業
老去恋明时	老去戀明時
独立三边静	獨立三邊靜
轻生一剑知	輕生一劍知
茫茫江汉上	茫茫江漢上
日暮复何之	日暮復何之

Seeing off Grand Censor Li on His Return to Hanyang

Now a wanderer,
the former South Expedition general
once commanded
a hundred thousand troops.
Dismissed and
without a professional job,
he cherishes, in old age,
his years of glory.
His mere presence ensured
peace at the three borders.
How dauntless he was,
only his sword could tell.
On the boundless
Jiang-Han waters at sunset,
where did he want to go?

劉長卿　送李中丞歸漢陽別業

流○落△
liú luò
wander away from home

曾○驅○
zēng qū
once commanded

罷△歸○
bà guī
removed and returned

老△去△
lǎo qù
getting old

獨△立△
dú lì
standing alone

輕○生○
qīng shēng
making light of life

茫○茫○
máng máng
boundless

日△暮△
rì mù
at dusk

征○南○將△
zhēng nán jiàng
a Southern expedition general

十△萬△師●
shí wàn shī
a hundred thousand troops

無○舊△業△
wú jiù yè
without old job

戀△明○時●
liàn míng shí
remenbered glorious years

三○邊○靜△
sān biān jìng
three sides were quiet

一△劍△知●
yī jiàn zhī
only a sword knew

江○漢△上△[1]
jiāng hàn shàng
on the Han River

復△何○之●
fù hé zhī
where to go

[1] Jiang-Han: the area where the Han River joins the Yangtse River.

79

Liu Changqing　　　刘长卿

饯别王十一南游

望君烟水阔	望君煙水闊
挥手泪沾巾	揮手淚霑巾
飞鸟没何处	飛鳥沒何處
青山空向人	青山空向人
长江一帆远	長江一帆遠
落日五湖春	落日五湖春
谁见汀洲上	誰見汀洲上
相思愁白苹	相思愁白蘋

Seeing Wang the Eleventh Leave for the South

Watching you disappear
in the boundless misty water,
I wave my hand to you
with tears on my kerchief.
Where are you going,
flying bird?
Only the blue mountain
stands before me.
Your sail is now
far away on the Long River.
The setting sun
shines brilliantly on the Five Lakes.
Who will notice that
on this islet
someone is staring blankly
at the white duckweed?

劉長卿　餞別王十一南遊

望△君○
wàng jūn
looking at you

揮○手△
huī shǒu
waving hand

飛○鳥△
fēi niǎo
flying birds

青○山○
qīng shān
blue mountain

長○江○
cháng jiāng
The Long River

落△日△
luò rì
setting sun

誰○見△
shuí jiàn
who can see

相○思○
xiāng sī
in yearning

煙○水△闊△
yān shuǐ kuò
vast expanse of misty water

淚△霑○巾●
lèi zhān jīn
tears moisten kerchief

沒△何○處△
mò hé chù
where do you end up

空○向△人●
kōng xiàng rén
blankly faces the person

一△帆○遠△
yī fān yuǎn
lone sail far away

五△湖○春●[1]
wǔ hú chūn
Five Lakes revive

汀○洲○上△
tīng zhōu shàng
on the islet

愁○白△蘋●
chóu bái píng
stare at the white duckweed

[1] Refers to the Tai Lake that lies across Jiansu and Zhejiang provinces.

Liu Changqing　　　　刘长卿

尋南溪常道人隱居

一路经行处
莓苔见履痕
白云依静渚
芳草闭闲门
過雨看松色
随山到水源
溪花与禅意
相对亦忘言

一路經行處
莓苔見履痕
白雲依靜渚
芳草閉閑門
過雨看松色
隨山到水源
溪花與禪意
相對亦忘言

Looking for Taoist Priest Chang at South Stream

Where I passed through
on my way here,
I saw on the green moss
traces of wooden shoes.
Above the quiet islet,
white clouds stayed afloat.
The sweet scent of the grass
seals your doorway.
After the rain,
pines looked fresher.
Along the mountain path
I walked to the water's source.
The stream, the flowers, and
a meditative mind
facing each other,
I was lost in words.

劉長卿　尋南溪常道人隱居

一△路△
yī lù
all the way

經○行○處△
jīn xíng chù
places where I walked through

莓○苔○
méi tái
moss

見△履△痕●
jiàn lǚ hén
showed traces of wooden shoe

白△雲○
bái yún
white clouds

依○靜△渚△
yī jìng zhǔ
leaned on quiet islet

芳○草△
fāng cǎo
scented grass

閉△閑○門●
bì xián mén
hid idle door

過△雨△
guò yǔ
after the rain

看○松○色△
kān sōng sè
looked at pine color

隨○山○
suí shān
following the hill

到△水△源●
dào shuǐ yuán
reached the water source

溪○花○
xī huā
stream flowers

與△禪○意△[1]
yǔ chán yì
and a meditative mind

相○對△
xiāng duì
face to face

亦△忘○言●
yì wàng yán
words were forgotten

[1] The purified state of the mind in Buddhism.

Liu Changqing 刘长卿

新年作

乡心新岁切	鄉心新歲切
天畔独潸然	天畔獨潸然
老至居人下	老至居人下
春归在客先	春歸在客先
岭猿同旦暮	嶺猿同旦暮
江柳共风烟	江柳共風煙
已似长沙傅	已似長沙傅
从今又几年	從今又幾年

Composed at New Year

My homesickness increases
as the new year grows near.
In a remote place alone,
can tears not be shed?
At my age, I am still
subordinate to others.
Spring is returning,
but I am still here.
Mountain monkeys
are with me day and night;
riverside willows
share with me the same wind and mist.
I am just like the
Imperial Tutor of Changsha.
How many more years
do I have to bear?

劉長卿　新年作

鄉○心○　　新○歲△切△
xiāng xīn　　xīn suì qiè
homesick heart　　new year is pressing

天○畔△　　獨△潸○然●
tiān pàn　　dú shān rán
at sky's end　　alone with tears falling

老△至△　　居○人○下△
lǎo zhì　　jū rén xià
at old age　　subordinate to others

春○歸○　　在△客△先●
chūn guī　　zài kè xiān
spring returns　　ahead of the visitor

嶺△猿○　　同○旦△暮△
lǐng yuán　　tóng dàn mù
mountain monkeys　　share day and night with me

江○柳△　　共△風○煙●
jiāng liǔ　　gòng fēng yān
riverside willows　　and I together face wind and mist

已△似△　　長○沙○傅△[1]
yǐ sì　　cháng shā fù
already like　　the grand-tutor of Changsha

從○今○　　又△幾△年●
cóng jīn　　yòu jǐ nián
from now on　　how many more years

[1] Jia Yi, a distinguished scholar and official in Han Dynasty, was
banished to serve as a tutor for the prince of Changsha.

Liu Shenxu 刘慎虚

阙题

<table>
<tr><td>道由白云尽</td><td>道由白雲盡</td></tr>
<tr><td>春与青溪长</td><td>春與青溪長</td></tr>
<tr><td>时有落花至</td><td>時有落花至</td></tr>
<tr><td>远随流水香</td><td>遠隨流水香</td></tr>
<tr><td>闲门向山路</td><td>閑門向山路</td></tr>
<tr><td>深柳读书堂</td><td>深柳讀書堂</td></tr>
<tr><td>幽映每白日</td><td>幽映每白日</td></tr>
<tr><td>清辉照衣裳</td><td>清輝照衣裳</td></tr>
</table>

A Poem Without a Title*

The road reaches
the white clouds.
The entire clean brook
is filled with spring.
At times, the petals
fall and drift down.
Their fragrance follows
them all the way.
My quiet door
faces the mountain path.
My study
is deep among the willow trees.
When I read in this secluded place
on a sunny day,
the sun will shed
its clear light on my clothes.

劉慎虛　闕題

道△由○ dào yóu road beginning here	白△雲○盡△ bái yún jìn all the way to the white clouds
春○與△ chūn yǔ spring is as	青○溪○長● qīng xī cháng long as the clean brook
時○有△ shí yǒu at times there are	落△花○至△ luò huā zhì fallen petals passing through
遠△隨○ yuǎn suí follow into the distance	流○水△香● liú shuǐ xiāng scented flowing water
閑○門○ xián mén idling door	向△山○路△ xiàng shān lù faces mountain path
深○柳△ shēn liǔ deep into willows	讀△書○堂● dú shū táng finds (my) study there
幽○映△ yōu yìng secluded and shaded	每△白△日△ měi bái rì each sunny day
清○輝○ qīng huī clear sunlight	照△衣○裳● zhào yī cháng shines on my clothes

* The title of this poem was either lost or not given by the poet.

Note that this poem deviates significantly from the established tonal patterns. It is interesting to note that parallelism applies to all four couplets.

Liu Yuxi 刘禹锡

蜀先主庙

天地英雄气
千秋尚凛然
势分三足鼎
业复五铢钱
得相能开国
生儿不像贤
凄凉蜀故妓
来舞魏宫前

天地英雄氣
千秋尚凛然
勢分三足鼎
業復五銖錢
得相能開國
生兒不像賢
凄涼蜀故妓
來舞魏宮前

The Temple of the First King of Zhu

His heroic spirit still pervades
heaven and earth.
For a thousand years,
he continued to inspire.
His historic rise completed
the tripod of powers in the land.
His great task was to
restore the coinage of Han.
With the help of his prime minister
he founded a kingdom.
But the son he raised
was not a worthy heir.
How sad and pitiful
are the singing girls of the former Shu,
who came dancing
in front of the Wei palaces!

劉禹錫　蜀先主廟

天○地△ tiān dì heaven and earth	英○雄○氣△ yīng xióng qì full of heroic spirit
千○秋○ qiān qiū a thousand years	尚△凜△然● shàng lǐn rán still awe-inspiring
勢△分○ shì fēn power divided into	三○足△鼎△[1] sān zú dǐng three-legged caldron
業△復△ yè fù task of restoring	五△銖○錢●[2] wú zhū qián coinage of Han
得△相△[3] dé xiàng obtaining a prime minister	能○開○國△ néng kāi guó who could found a state
生○兒○[4] shēng ér having a son	不△像△賢● bù xiàng xián unlike a worthy person
淒○涼○ qī liáng sad and pitiful	蜀△故△妓△ shǔ gù jì former singing girls of Shu
來○舞△ lái wǔ came to dance	魏△宮○前● wèi gōng qián in front of the Wei palaces

[1] A tripartite balance of power of the Three Kingdoms (220—280), which consisted of the Wei, Shu, and Wu. Liu Bei was the first king of Shu, which was eventually conquered by Wei.

[2] The system of coinage used during the Han Dynasty, which Liu Bei wanted to restore.

[3] Liu Bei was assisted by Zhuge Liang, a brilliant prime minister and military strategist.

[4] Liu Chan, Liu Bei's son, was weak and incompetent.

Lu Lun   卢纶

送李端

故关衰草遍
离别正堪悲
路出寒云外
人归暮雪时
少孤为客早
多难识君迟
掩泣空相向
风尘何处期

故關衰草遍
離別正堪悲
路出寒雲外
人歸暮雪時
少孤為客早
多難識君遲
掩泣空相向
風塵何處期

Seeing Li Duan Off

Grass is dying everywhere
at this ancient pass.
It is indeed sad
for us to part.
You will follow your way
beyond the chilly clouds;
I will return home,
walking into the evening snow.
Orphaned when young,
I became an early wanderer.
After numerous hardships,
I came to know you late.
Hiding my tears,
I look blankly in your direction.
In this turbulent time,
when can we meet again?

盧綸　送李端

故△關○　　衰○草△遍△
gù guān　　shuāi cǎo biàn
ancient pass　　grass is dying everywhere

離○別△　　正△堪○悲●
lí bié　　zhèng kān bēi
at parting　　it is sad indeed

路△出△　　寒○雲○外△
lù chū　　hán yún wài
your road extends　　beyond chilly clouds

人○歸○　　暮△雪△時●
rén guī　　mù xuě shí
I return　　into the snow at dusk

少△孤○　　為○客△早△
shào gū　　wéi kè zǎo
fatherless when young　　I left home early

多○難△　　識△君○遲●
duō nàn　　shí jūn chí
numerous hardships　　came to know you late

掩△泣△　　空○相○向△
yǎn qì　　kōng xiāng xiàng
hiding tears　　look at you blankly

風○塵○　　何○處△期●
fēng chén　　hé chù qī
wind and dust　　when to meet again

91

Ma Dai 马戴

灞上秋居

灞原风雨定　　　　灞原風雨定
晚见雁行频　　　　晚見雁行頻
落叶他乡树　　　　落葉他鄉樹
寒灯独夜人　　　　寒燈獨夜人
空园白露滴　　　　空園白露滴
孤壁野僧邻　　　　孤壁野僧鄰
寄卧郊扉久　　　　寄臥郊扉久
何年致此身　　　　何年致此身

My Stay in Baling in Autumn

Here in the Ba plain
the wind and rain have stopped.
In the twilight, the wild geese
can be seen line after line.
Leaves fall from the trees
of an alien land;
I sit alone at night
by a cold lamp.
In the empty garden,
the white dew is dripping;
behind the lonely wall,
a monk is my neighbor next door.
I have stayed too long
in the wilds.
When will I be able
to do something worthwhile?

馬戴　灞上秋居

灞△原○[1]
bà yuán
the plain of Ba River

晚△見△
wǎn jiàn
seen at night

落△葉△
luò yè
fallen leaves

寒○燈○
hán dēng
cold lamp

空○園○
kōng yuán
empty garden

孤○壁△
gū bì
lonely walls

寄△臥△
jì wò
temporary stay

何○年○
hé nián
which year

風○雨△定△
fēng yǔ dìng
wind and rain have stopped

雁△行○頻●
yàn háng pín
wild geese line upon line

他○鄉○樹△
tā xiāng shù
trees of alien land

獨△夜△人●
dú yè rén
man alone at night

白△露△滴△
bái lù dī
white dew drips

野△僧○鄰●
yě sēng lín
a monk next door

郊○扉○久△
jiāo fēi jiǔ
in wilds for long time

致△此△身●
zhì cì shēn
do something worthwhile

[1] The plain at both sides of Ba River, near Changan, the ancient capital.

93

Ma Dai 马戴

楚江怀古

露气寒光集　　　　露氣寒光集
微阳下楚丘　　　　微陽下楚丘
猿啼洞庭树　　　　猿啼洞庭樹
人在木兰舟　　　　人在木蘭舟
广泽生明月　　　　廣澤生明月
苍山夹乱流　　　　蒼山夾亂流
云中君不见　　　　雲中君不見
竟夕自悲秋　　　　竟夕自悲秋

Remembering the Past on the Xiang River

The dew-filled air
blends with the cold sunlight.
Weak rays slip
below the mountains of Xiang.
Monkeys are screeching from
the trees of Dongting.
I am steering my way in
a magnolia boat.
As the bright moon rises
over the vast water,
the stream runs turbulently
through the gray mountains.
I cannot find you,
Gentleman in the Cloud.
All night long,
I mourn the autumn alone.

馬戴　楚江懷古

露△氣△　　　　　　寒○光○集△
lù qì　　　　　　　hán guāng jí
dew-filled air　　　blends with cold light

微○陽○　　　　　　下△楚△丘●[1]
wéi yáng　　　　　xià chǔ qiū
weak rays　　　　　go down to Chu hills

猿○啼○　　　　　　洞△庭○樹△
yuán tí　　　　　　dòng tíng shù
monkeys screech　trees of Dongting

人○在△　　　　　　木△蘭○舟●
rén zài　　　　　　mù lán zhōu
a person is in　　　magnolia boat

廣△澤△　　　　　　生○明○月△
guǎng zé　　　　　shēng míng yuè
vast water　　　　a bright moon emerges

蒼○山○　　　　　　夾△亂△流●
cāng shān　　　　jiā luàn liú
dark green mountains　water running wild in between

雲○中○君○[2]　　不△見△
yún zhōng jūn　　bù jiàn
a gentleman in the clouds　not seen

竟△夕△　　　　　　自△悲○秋●
jìng xī　　　　　　zì bēi qiū
whole night　　　I mourn the autumn

[1] The mountains at both sides of the Xiang River.
[2] In the poem "Nine Song," Qu Yuan refers to the Gods of the Cloud as " a gentleman in the clouds." Here in this poem, the term alludes to Qu Yuan, who drowned himself in the Xiang River.

Meng Haoran 孟浩然

望洞庭湖赠张丞相

八月湖水平
涵虚混太清
气蒸云梦泽
波撼岳阳城
欲济无舟楫
端居耻圣明
坐观垂钓者
徒有羡鱼情

八月湖水平
涵虛混太清
氣蒸雲夢澤
波撼岳陽城
欲濟無舟楫
端居恥聖明
坐觀垂釣者
徒有羨魚情

To Prime Minister Zhang* by the Lake Dongting

In the eighth lunar month
the lake is full to the brim.
Boundless waters
blend with the sky's rim.
Over the Cloud-Dream Marsh
vaporous air rises;
against the Yueyang City wall
the roaring waves strike.
I wish to cross the river,
but there is no boat.
To live an easy life
would disappoint the wise ruler.
As I sit and watch
the angler casting his fish hook,
I can only
envy him for his joyful look.

孟浩然　望洞庭湖贈張丞相

八△月△
bā yuè
the eighth month

湖○水△平●
hú shuǐ píng
lake water is full

涵○虛○
hán xū
vastness of clear water

混△太△清●
hún tài qīng
mixed with the sky

氣△蒸○
qì zhēng
vapors rise over

雲○夢△澤△ [1]
yún mèng zé
Cloud Dream Mash

波○撼△
bō hàn
waves shake

岳△陽○城● [2]
yuè yáng chéng
Yueyang City

欲△濟△
yù jì
wanting to cross

無○舟○楫△
wú zhōu jí
there is no boat

端○居○
duān jū
to live a quiet life

恥△聖△明●
chǐ shèng míng
may embarrass the wise ruler

坐△觀○
zuò guān
sit and look at

垂○釣△者△
chuí diào zhě
the anglers

徒○有△
tú yǒu
be left with

羨△魚○情●
xiàn yú qíng
an envious feeling

*　Prime Minister Zhang refers to Zhang Jiuling.
[1] The low-lying ground that includes the southern Hubei Province and the northern Hunan Province.
[2] Yue Yang City wall was to the east of Lake Dongting.

97

Meng Haoran 孟浩然

与诸子登岘山

人事有代谢　　　　　人事有代謝
往来成古今　　　　　往來成古今
江山留胜迹　　　　　江山留勝跡
我辈复登临　　　　　我輩復登臨
水落鱼梁浅　　　　　水落魚梁淺
天寒梦泽深　　　　　天寒夢澤深
羊公碑尚在　　　　　羊公碑尚在
读罢泪沾襟　　　　　讀罷淚沾襟

Climbing Xian Mountain* with Friends

In all human affairs,
the new supersedes the old.
From past to present,
what comes must go.
Our land is left with
scenic spots and relics,
so our generation can still
come view them.
In low tide,
Yu Liang turns shallow;
in cold weather,
the Dream Marsh looks deep.
What still remains is
the Lord Yang Monument.
As I read the inscription,
my tears fell on my garment.

孟浩然　與諸子登峴山

人○事△
rén shì
human affairs

往△來○
wǎng lái
coming and going

江○山○
jiāng shān
our land

我△輩△
wǒ bèi
our generation

水△落△
shuǐ luò
water level falling

天○寒○
tiān hán
weather turning cold

羊○公○碑○[2]
yáng gōng bēi
Lord Yang Monument

讀△罷△
dú bà
upon reading it

有△代△謝△
yǒu dài xiè
new superseding the old

成○古△今●
chéng gǔ jīn
become past and present

留○勝△跡△
liú shèng jī
leaves historical marks

復△登○臨●
fù dēng lín
can come up again

魚○梁○淺△[1]
yú liàng qiǎn
Yu Liang is shallow

夢△澤△深●
mèng zé shēn
Dream Marsh looks deep

尚△在△
shàng zài
still here

淚△沾○襟●
lèi zhān jīn
tears soak garment

* Xian Mountain is in present-day Hubei Province.
[1] Yu Liang was a place known for its fish.
[2] A monument on the Xian Mountain to honor Yang Gu, an able and caring officer in the Jin Dynasty.

Meng Haoran 孟浩然

岁暮归南山

北阙休上书	北闕休上書
南山归敝卢	南山歸敝盧
不才明主弃	不才明主棄
多病故人疏	多病故人疏
白发催年老	白髮催年老
青阳逼岁除	青陽逼歲除
永怀愁不寐	永懷愁不寐
松月夜窗虚	松月夜窗虛

Returning to South Mountain at the Year's End

No more petitions
to the north palace now that I am
back to my humble cottage
in the South Mountain.
A courtier without talent
no wise ruler would want to keep.
A man frequently sick,
old friends would stop coming to visit.
Gray hair
has hastened the aging process.
A new spring
presses hard to replace the old year.
A heart full of sorrow
how can I fall asleep?
The moon above the pine trees
shines on my empty window.

孟浩然　歲暮歸南山

北△闕△ [1]
běi què
(to) north palace

休○上△書△
xiū shàng shū
stop submitting petition

南○山○ [2]
nán shān
South Mountain

歸○敝△盧●
guī bì lú
return to my humble cottage

不△才○
bù cái
(me) without talent

明○主△棄△
míng zhǔ qì
a wise ruler would abandon

多○病△
duō bìng
frequently sick

故△人○疏●
gù rén shū
old friends become distant

白△髮△
bái fǎ
white hair

催○年○老△
cuī nián lǎo
hastens aging process

青○陽○
qīng yáng
springtime

逼△歲△除●
bī suì chú
presses hard to replace old year

永△懷○愁○
yǒng huái chóu
a heart full of sorrow

不△寐△
bù mèi
unable to fall asleep

松○月△
sōng yuè
pine moon

夜△窗○虛●
yè chuāng xū
shines on empty window

---

[1] The tower at the north side of the palace where officials had to wait to be summoned by the court.
[2] South Mountain is another name for Mount Zhongnan.

Meng Haoran 孟浩然

过故人庄

故人具鸡黍　　故人具雞黍
邀我至田家　　邀我至田家
绿树村边合　　綠樹村邊合
青山郭外斜　　青山郭外斜
开轩面场圃　　開軒面場圃
把酒话桑麻　　把酒話桑麻
待到重阳日　　待到重陽日
还来就菊花　　還來就菊花

Stopping at a Friend's Farm-house

A friend has prepared
dishes of chicken and millet
and invited me
to his farm house.
Green trees
surround the village;
blue hills
are behind the outer wall.
With windows opened,
we face the rice field and garden.
With wine cups in our hands,
we talk about mulberry and hemp.
By the time
the Double Ninth Festival arrives,
I will be back
to enjoy your chrysanthemums.

孟浩然　過故人庄

故△人○
gù rén
old friend

邀○我△
yāo wǒ
invited me

綠△樹△
lǜ shù
green trees

青○山○
qīng shān
blue mountain

開○軒○
kāi xuān
open the window

把△酒△
bǎ jiǔ
hold a wine cup

待△到△
dài dào
wait until

遷○來○
hái lái
then come

具△雞○黍△
jù jī shǔ
prepared chickens and millet

至△田○家●
zhì tián jiā
to his farm house

村○邊○合△
cūn biān hé
surround the village

郭△外△斜●
guō wài xié
behind the outer wall

面△場△圃△
miàn cháng pǔ
and face grain field and garden

話△桑○麻●
huà sāng má
and chat about mulberry and hemp

重○陽○日△[1]
chóng yáng rì
the Double Ninth Festival

就△菊△花●
jiù jú huā
to enjoy the chrysanthemum

[1] The Chinese custom of climbing to a high place to celebrate the Double Ninth Festival on the 9th of the 9th lunar month each year.

Meng Haoran 孟浩然

秦中寄远上人

一丘尝欲卧　　　　一丘嘗欲臥
三径苦无资　　　　三徑苦無資
北土非吾愿　　　　北土非吾願
东林怀我师　　　　東林懷我師
黄金燃桂尽　　　　黃金燃桂盡
壮志逐年衰　　　　壯志逐年衰
日夕凉风至　　　　日夕涼風至
闻蝉但益悲　　　　聞蟬但益悲

To Buddhist Priest Yuan from Qinzhong*

A wooded hill
is where I want to retire.
But how could I afford
a place with three trails?
I have no desire to
stay in the North.
My teacher at East Wood
is often in my thoughts.
Money runs out fast
like cassia on fire.
My ambitions
are declining with age.
I must face the cold wind,
morning and night.
Listening to cicadas shrilling,
I feel even sadder.

孟浩然　秦中寄遠上人

一△丘○
yī qiū
a wooded hill

三○徑△[1]
sān jìng
three paths

北△土△
běi tǔ
northern land

東○林○
dōng lín
Dong Lin

黃○金○
huáng jīn
gold

壯△志△
zhuàng zhì
ambitions

日△夕△
rì xī
day and night

聞○蟬○
wén chán
listening to cicada

嘗○欲△臥△
cháng yù wò
often want to retire

苦△無○資●
kǔ wú zī
troubled by lack of money

非○吾○願△
fēi wú yuàn
not a place I want to stay

懷○我△師●
huái wǒ shī
reminds me of my teacher

燃○桂△盡△
rán guì jìn
gone like cassia twigs on fire

逐△年○衰●
zhú nián shuāi
in decline as years go by

涼○風○至△
liáng fēng zhì
cold wind arrives

但△益△悲●
dàn yì bēi
only to increase sadness

*　Qinzhong refers to the area of capital Chang'an.
[1]　In the Western Han Dynasty, Jiang Yu resigned from his position as a prefectural governor. When he lived in reclusion, he opened up three paths in the wood.

105

Meng Haoran　　　　孟浩然

宿桐庐江广陵旧游

山暝听猿愁	山暝聽猿愁
沧江急夜流	滄江急夜流
风鸣两岸叶	風鳴兩岸葉
月照一孤舟	月照一孤舟
建德非吾土	建德非吾土
维阳忆旧游	維陽憶舊遊
还将两行泪	還將兩行淚
遥寄海西头	遙寄海西頭

To My Friend in Yangzhou from a Boat on Tonglu River

Monkeys' whines
from the dark mountain sadden my heart.
The dark blue river
rushes its way forward at night.
The wind rustles
the leaves on both sides of the bank;
the moon shines upon
a solitary boat.
Jiande is not
my native land;
Yangzhou reminds me
fondly of my old friends.
Let me send
these two streams of tears
to you, far away
at the sea's western head.

孟浩然　宿桐廬江廣陵舊游

山○暝△ shān míng mountain at dark	聽△猿○愁● tīng yuán chóu sad to listen to apes
滄○江○ cāng jiāng Dark green river	急△夜△流● jí yè liú rushes to flow at night
風○鳴○ fēng míng wind rustles	兩△岸△葉△ liǎng àn yè leaves on both banks
月△照△ yuè zhào moon shines upon	一△孤○舟● yī gū zhōu one solitary boat
建△德△[1] jiàn dé Jiande	非○吾○土△ fēi wú tǔ not my native land
維○陽○ wéi yáng Yangzhou	憶△舊△遊● yì jiù yóu reminds me of old friends
還○將○ huán jiāng why not let	兩△行○淚△ liǎng háng lèi two streams of tears
遙○寄△ yáo jì send faraway to	海△西○頭●[2] hǎi xī tóu sea's western head

[1] Jiande was in present-day Zhejiang Province.
[2] Sea's western head refers to the area west of the Yellow Sea.

Meng Haoran 孟浩然

留别王维

寂寂竟何待　　　　寂寂竟何待
朝朝空自归　　　　朝朝空自歸
欲寻芳草去　　　　欲尋芳草去
惜与故人违　　　　惜與故人違
当路谁相假　　　　當路誰相假
知音世所稀　　　　知音世所稀
只应守寂寞　　　　祇應守寂寞
还掩故园扉　　　　還掩故園扉

Bidding Farewell to Wang Wei

Why wait for
something only in the air?
Every morning
I come home empty-handed.
I wish to go looking for
the fragrant grass,
but hate to part
with my old friends.
Who in power
would render a hand?
One who knows my heart
in this world is rare.
Shouldn't I be content with
a solitary life
and return home,
shutting my old garden gate?

孟浩然　留別王維

寂△寂△ jì jì quiet and still	竟△何○待△ jìng hé dāi waiting for what
朝○朝○ zhāo zhāo every morning	空○自△歸● kōng zì guī return alone empty-handed
欲△尋○ yù xún wish to look for	芳○草△去△ fāng cǎo qù fragrant grass
惜○與△ xī yù feel sorry to	故△人○違● gù rén wéi bid farewell to my old friends
當○路△ dāng lù those in power	誰○相○假△ shuí xiāng jiǎ who would offer help
知○音○ zhī yīn a bosom friend	世△所△稀● shì suǒ xī so rare in the world
祇△應○ zhǐ yīng ought to be	守△寂△寞△ shǒu jì mò content with a lonely life
還○掩△ huán yǎn and close	故△園○扉● gù yuán fēi my old garden gate

109

Meng Haoran 孟浩然

早寒有怀

木落雁南渡　　　　　木落雁南渡
北风江上寒　　　　　北風江上寒
我家襄水曲　　　　　我家襄水曲
遥隔楚云端　　　　　遙隔楚雲端
乡泪客中尽　　　　　鄉淚客中盡
孤帆天际看　　　　　孤帆天際看
迷津欲有问　　　　　迷津欲有問
平海夕漫漫　　　　　平海夕漫漫

Reflections on Early Winter

Leaves are falling;
wild geese fly south.
Wind blowing from the north
turns the river cold.
My home is
at the bend of Xiang River,
far away, below the
last clouds of Chu.
No more homesick tears
are left in a strange land.
In my solitary boat,
I see only the sky's rim.
I want to ask for
the correct direction,
but the sea at sunset
is so flat and boundless.

孟浩然　早寒有懷

木△落△
mù luò
leaves falling

雁△南○渡△
yàn nán dù
wild geese fly south

北△風○
běi fēng
north wind

江○上△寒●
jiāng shàng hán
chilly on the river

我△家○
wǒ jiā
my home

襄○水△曲△[1]
xiāng shuǐ qū
at the bend of Xiang River

遙○隔△
yáo gé
separating in distance

楚△雲○端●
chǔ yún duān
the clouds of Chu

鄉○淚△
xiāng lèi
homesick tears

客△中○盡△
kè zhōng jìn
exhausted away from home

孤△帆○
gū fān
a solitary boat

天○際△看●
tiān jì kān
see only the sky's rim

迷○津○
mí jīn
losing my way

欲△有○問△
yù yǒu wèn
I want to ask

平○海△
píng hǎi
level sea

夕△漫○漫●
xī mán mán
boundless at sunset

[1] The section of Han River that was near Xiang Yang, the poet's hometown.

111

Qian Qi

钱起

送僧归日本

上国随缘住　　　　上國隨緣住
来途若梦行　　　　來途若夢行
浮天沧海远　　　　浮天滄海遠
去世法舟轻　　　　去世法舟輕
水月通禅寂　　　　水月通禪寂
鱼龙听梵声　　　　魚龍聽梵聲
惟怜一灯影　　　　惟憐一燈影
万里眼中明　　　　萬里眼中明

Seeing a Monk Off to Japan

You were foreordained
to come and stay in China.
The voyage was like
a dream all the way.
You came on a boat that drifted
with the sky on the blue sea.
The vessel that carries a monk
is lighter on his way home.
In your meditation, you can
communicate with the water and moon.
The sound of your chanting
both fish and dragon can enjoy.
Hold dear
the single lantern that forever shines.
For thousand miles away,
it can illuminate many eyes.

錢起　送僧歸日本

上△國○ shàng guó coming to China	隨○緣○住△ suí yuán zhù followed your destiny
來○途○ lái tú on your way here	若△夢△行● ruò mèng xíng like walking in a dream
浮○天○ fú tiān floating sky	滄○海△遠△ cāng hǎi yuǎn boundless blue sea
去△世△ qù shì leaving here	法△舟○輕● fǎ zhōu qīng on a light Buddhist boat
水△月△ shuǐ yuè water and moon	通○禪○寂△ tōng chán jì understand the quietness of Zen
魚○龍○ yú lóng fish and dragon	聽△梵△聲● tīng fàn shēng listen to chanting sound
惟○憐○ wéi lián I especially love	一△燈○影△ yī dēng yǐng one shining lamp
萬△里△ wàn lǐ several thousand *li*	眼△中○明● yǎn zhōng Míng with light in the eyes

113

Qian Qi 钱起

谷口书斋寄杨补阙

泉壑带茅茨	泉壑帶茅茨
云霞生薜帷	雲霞生薜帷
竹怜新雨后	竹憐新雨後
山爱夕阳时	山愛夕陽時
闲鹭栖常早	閒鷺棲常早
秋花落更迟	秋花落更遲
家童扫萝径	家童掃蘿徑
昨与故人期	昨與故人期

To Censor Yang, from My Study at Gukou*

My thatched house
joins the stream and valley.
Rosy clouds emerge
above my shrubs.
Bamboos look refreshing
right after the rain;
at sunset the mountain
appears more charming.
The carefree egrets
return early to roost.
Autumn flowers here
are slow to fade.
My young male servant
sweeps the overgrown path.
I am expecting an old friend,
whom I invited yesterday.

錢起　谷口書齋寄楊補闕

泉○壑△
quán huò
stream and valley

雲○霞○
yún xiá
rosy clouds

竹△憐○
zhú lián
bamboos look refreshing

山○愛△
shān ài
mountain is lovely

閒○鷺△
xián lù
idling egrets

秋○花○
qiū huā
autumn flowers

家○童○
jiā tóng
young male servant

昨△與△
zuó yǔ
yesterday I and

帶△茅○茨●
dài máo cí
with a thatched house

生○薜△帷●
shēng bì wéi
emerge over shrubs

新○雨△後△
xīn yǔ hòu
after new rain

夕△陽○時●
xī yáng shí
at sun setting

棲○常○早△
qī cháng zǎo
perch earlier than usual

落△更△遲●
luò gèng chí
wither much later

掃△蘿○徑△
sǎo luó jìng
sweeps overgrown path

故△人○期●
gù rén qī
an old friend promised to meet

* Gukou was in what is now Shanxi Province.

115

Sikong Shu 司空曙

云阳馆与韩绅宿别

故人江海别　　　故人江海別
几度隔山川　　　幾度隔山川
乍见翻疑梦　　　乍見翻疑夢
相悲各问年　　　相悲各問年
孤灯寒照雨　　　孤燈寒照雨
深竹暗浮烟　　　深竹暗浮煙
更有明朝恨　　　更有明朝恨
离杯惜共传　　　離杯惜共傳

A Farewell to Han Shen at the Yunyang* Tavern

Since we bade farewell
at Jianghai,
we tried to meet, but
mountains and rivers were in between.
Suddenly you appeared;
how could I not feel like a dream!
We lamented and asked each other
how the years had passed.
A solitary lamp shed
its chilling light on the rain.
Among the dim bamboos,
drifting mist could be seen.
Let sorrowful feelings
be left for tomorrow.
For now, cherish this moment,
and pass the cup of farewell wine.

司空曙　雲陽館與韓紳宿別

故△人○　　　　　江○海△別△
gù rén　　　　　jiāng hǎi bié
old friend　　　farewell at Jianghai

幾△度△　　　　　隔△山○川●
jǐ dù　　　　　　gé shān chuān
several times　separated by mountains and rivers

乍△見△　　　　　翻○疑○夢△
zhà jiàn　　　　fān yí mèng
suddenly seeing you　suspected it to be a dream

相○悲○　　　　　各△問△年●
xiāng bēi　　　gè wèn nián
both lamented　asked about years of the past

孤○燈○　　　　　寒○照△雨△
gū dēng　　　　hán zhào yǔ
single lamp　　chillingly shone on rain

深○竹△　　　　　暗△浮○煙●
shēn zhú　　　　àn fú yān
deep bamboos　mist was dimly arising

更△有△　　　　　明○朝○恨△
gèng yǒu　　　　míng zhāo hèn
with more　　　sorrow to be felt tomorrow

離○杯○　　　　　惜△共△傳●
lí bēi　　　　　xī gòng chuán
farewell cups　cherished and passed to each other

---

*　Yunyang, name of a county in what is now Shanxi Province.

Sikong Shu　　　　　　司空曙

喜外弟卢纶见宿

静夜四无邻　　　　　靜夜四無鄰
荒居旧业贫　　　　　荒居舊業貧
雨中黄叶树　　　　　雨中黃葉樹
灯下白头人　　　　　燈下白頭人
以我独沉久　　　　　以我獨沉久
愧君相见频　　　　　愧君相見頻
平生自有分　　　　　平生自有分
况是霍家亲　　　　　況是霍家親

Delighted that Cousin Lu Lun Comes for the Night

A very quiet night
with no neighbors,
I live in a poor old house
in this wasteland.
The yellow-leaf trees
stand in the rain;
a white-haired man sits
by a lamp.
Knowing that I have long been
down and lonely,
you often come to see me
for that I am thankful.
In this life we were born to
be kind to each other.
Let alone we are close relatives.

司空曙　喜外弟盧綸見宿

靜△夜△
jìng yè
quiet night

四△無○鄰●
sì wú lín
no neighbors around

荒○居○
huāng jū
living in wasteland

舊△業△貧●
jiù yè pín
a poor old house

雨△中○
yǔ zhōng
in the rain

黃○葉△樹△
huáng yè shù
yellow-leaf trees

燈○下△
dēng xià
under the lamp

白△頭○人●
bái tóu rén
white-haired man

以△我△
yǐ wǒ
as I have been

獨△沉○久△
dú chén jiǔ
lonely and down for a long time

愧△君○
kuì jūn
appreciate your

相○見△頻●
xiāng jiàn pín
coming to see me often

平○生○
píng shēng
in this life

自△有△分△
zì yǒu fèn
good will for each other

況△是△
kuàng shì
let alone we are

霍△家○親●
huò jiā qīn
related as kinsfolk

119

Sikong Shu 司空曙

贼平后送人北归

世乱同南去	世亂同南去
时清独北还	時清獨北還
他乡生白发	他鄉生白髮
旧国见青山	舊國見青山
晓月过残垒	曉月過殘壘
繁星宿故关	繁星宿故關
寒禽与衰草	寒禽與衰草
处处伴愁颜	處處伴愁顏

Seeing Off a Friend Who Is Returning to the North After the Rebellion

As the war broke out,
we went South together.
Now at peace,
you return to the North alone.
My hair will turn gray
in this alien land;
you will see the blue mountains
near your home.
By the waning moon at dawn,
you will pass the ruined ramparts.
Under the starry sky,
you will sleep at the familiar pass.
The shivering birds
and the withering grass
will follow my dispirited face
everywhere I go.

司空曙　賊平後送人北歸

世△亂△
shì luàn
in times of war

同○南○去△
tóng nán qù
together went to the South

時○清○
shí qīng
now at peace

獨△北△還●
dú běi huán
you alone are returning to the North

他○鄉○
tā xiāng
in an alien land

生○白△髮△
shēng bái fǎ
grow white hair

舊△國△
jiù guó
hometown

見△青○山●
jiàn qīng shān
see blue mountains

曉△月△
xiǎo yuè
moon at dawn

過△殘○壘△
guò cán lěi
pass ruined rampart

繁○星○
fán xīng
starry sky

宿△故△關●
sù gù guān
stay overnight at familiar pass

寒○禽○
hán qín
shivering birds

與△衰○草△
yǔ shuāi cǎo
and withering grass

處△處△
chù chù
everywhere

伴△愁○顏●
bàn chóu yán
accompany a sad face

Wang Wei 王维

辋川闲居赠裴秀才迪

寒山转苍翠	寒山轉蒼翠
秋水日潺媛	秋水日潺湲
倚杖柴门外	倚杖柴門外
临风听暮蝉	臨風聽暮蟬
渡头余落日	渡頭餘落日
墟里上孤烟	墟里上孤煙
复值接舆醉	復值接輿醉
狂歌五柳前	狂歌五柳前

Retirement at Wangchuan—To Pei Di

The cold mountain
changes color to dark green.
The autumn water
keeps flowing day after day.
Leaning on a cane
outside my brushwood door,
I listen to cicadas shrilling
in the evening wind.
Over the ferry
the setting sun lingers;
above the village,
a wisp of smoke rises.
Like Jie Yu,
you drink without restraint
and sing with wild joy
in front of this Mr. Five Willows.

王維　輞川閑居贈裴秀才迪

寒○山○ hán shān cold mountain	轉△蒼○翠△ zhuǎn cāng cuì turns dark green
秋○水△ qiū shuǐ autumn water	日△潺○湲● rì chán yuán flows day after day
倚△杖△ yǐ zhàng leaning on a cane	柴○門○外△ chái mén wài outside the brushwood
臨○風○ lín fēng in the wind	聽○暮△蟬● tīng mù chán to listen to evening cicadas
渡△頭○ dù tóu over the ferry	餘○落△日△ yú luò rì setting sun lingers
墟○里△ xū lǐ the village	上△孤○煙● shàng gú yān single smoke rises
復△值△ fù zhí it happens again	接△輿○醉△[1] jiē yú zuì Jie Yu became intoxicated
狂○歌○ kuáng gē singing with wild joy	五△柳△前●[2] wǔ liǔ qián in front of Mr. Five Willows

[1] Jie Yu, a recluse during the Epoch of Spring and Autumn, was known for his excessive drinking.
[2] Mr. Five Willows refers to the famous poet Tao Qian (365—427).

123

Wang Wei 王维

山居秋暝

空山新雨后	空山新雨後
天气晚来秋	天氣晚來秋
明月松间照	明月松間照
清泉石上流	清泉石上流
竹喧归浣女	竹喧歸浣女
莲动下渔舟	蓮動下漁舟
随意春芳歇	隨意春芳歇
王孙自可留	王孫自可留

Autumn Evening in a Mountain Retreat

After the rain,
the empty mountain
at dusk
is full of autumn air.
A bright moon
shines between the pines;
the clear spring water
glides over the rocks.
Bamboo leaves rustling—
the washer girls bound home.
Water lilies swaying—
a fishing boat goes down.
Never mind that
spring plants are no longer green.
I am here to stay,
my noble friends!

王維　山居秋暝

空○山○　　　　　新○雨△後△
kōng shān　　　　xīn yǔ hòu
empty mountain　　after new rain

天○氣△　　　　　晚△來○秋●
tiān qì　　　　　wǎn lái qiū
weather　　　　　autumn arrives at night

明○月△　　　　　松○間○照△
míng yuè　　　　sōng jiān zhào
bright moon　　　shines through the pines

清○泉○　　　　　石△上△流●
qīng quán　　　　shí shàng liú
clear spring　　　flows over the rocks

竹△喧○　　　　　歸○浣△女△
zhú xuān　　　　guī huàn nǚ
bamboos rustling　washer girls return

蓮○動△　　　　　下△漁○舟●
lián dòng　　　　xià yú zhōu
water lilies moving　fishing boat goes down

隨○意△　　　　　春○芳○歇△
súi yì　　　　　chūn fāng xiē
never mind　　　spring plants withering

王○孫○　　　　　自△可△留●
wáng sūn　　　　zì kě liú
noble friend　　　of course can stay

125

Wang Wei 王维

归嵩山作

清川带长薄　　　清川帶長薄
车马去闲闲　　　車馬去閒閒
流水如有意　　　流水如有意
暮禽相与还　　　暮禽相與還
荒城临古渡　　　荒城臨古渡
落日满秋山　　　落日滿秋山
迢递嵩高下　　　迢遞嵩高下
归来且闭关　　　歸來且閉關

On Returning to Mount Song*

Along a limpid stream
surrounded by grass and trees,
I ride on a carriage,
slowly and carefree.
The flowing water
seemingly knows how I feel;
at dusk birds
come home with me.
A desolate town
overlooks the old ferry.
The setting sun fully bathes
the autumn mountain.
Far away under the
lofty Mount Song,
I shall return home
and shut myself away from the world.

王維　歸嵩山作

清○川○　　　　　　帶△長○薄△
qīng chuān　　　　dài cháng bó
clear stream　　　 with trees on both sides

車○馬△　　　　　　去△閒○閒●
chē mǎ　　　　　　qù xián xián
cart and horse　　　go slow and carefree

流○水△　　　　　　如○有△意△
liú shuǐ　　　　　　rú yǒu yì
flowing water　　　 seemingly knows how I feel

暮△禽○　　　　　　相○與△還●
mù qín　　　　　　 xiāng yǔ huán
evening birds　　　 go home with me

荒○城○　　　　　　臨○古△渡△
huāng chéng　　　 lín gǔ dù
desolate city　　　　overlooks old ferry

落△日△　　　　　　滿△秋○山●
luò rì　　　　　　　mǎn qiū shān
setting sun　　　　 fills the autumn mountain

迢○遞△　　　　　　嵩○高○下△
tiáo dì　　　　　　 sōng gāo xià
far away　　　　　　under lofty Mount Song

歸○來○　　　　　　且△閉△關●
guī lái　　　　　　 qiě bì guān
returning　　　　　 close from outside world

* Mount Song is in Hunan Province.

127

Wang Wei   王维

终南山

太乙近天都　　　　太乙近天都
连山接海隅　　　　連山接海隅
白云回望合　　　　白雲迴望合
青霭入看无　　　　青靄入看無
分野中峰变　　　　分野中峰變
阴晴众壑殊　　　　陰晴眾壑殊
欲投人处宿　　　　欲投人處宿
隔水问樵夫　　　　隔水問樵夫

Mount Zhongnan*

The Tai Yi peak
is near the capital of heaven.
Its range stretches
all the way to the coast.
As I look back,
the white clouds are closing in.
As I look close up,
the blue mists suddenly disappear.
The middle ridge divides into
two ever-changing sceneries.
On dark or clear days
each valley has a different view.
Wanting to put up
at someone's place for the night,
I ask a woodcutter
on the other side of the stream.

王維　終南山

太△乙△[1]
tài yǐ
Tai Yi

連○山○
lián shān
mountain upon mountain

白△雲○
bái yún
white clouds

青○靄△
qīng ǎi
blue mist

分○野△
fēn yě
dividing line

陰○晴○
yīn qíng
overcast or clear

欲△投○
yù tóu
wishing to lodge

隔△水△
gé shuǐ
across the stream

近△天○都●
jìn tiān dū
near heaven's capital

接△海△隅●
jiē hǎi yú
join the coast

迴○望△合△
huí wàng hé
close in while looking back

入△看○無●
rù kān wú
disappears up close

中○峰○變△
zhōng fēng biàn
changes at central peak

眾△壑△殊●
zhōng hè shū
valleys look different from each other

人○處△宿△
rén chù sù
where people reside

問△樵○夫●
wèn qiáo fū
ask the woodcutter

---

* Mount Zhongnan is in Hunan Province.
[1] The central peak of Mount Zhongnan.

Wang Wei 王维

酬张少府

晚年惟好静　　　晚年惟好靜
万事不关心　　　萬事不關心
自顾无长策　　　自顧無長策
空知返旧林　　　空知返舊林
松风吹解带　　　松風吹解帶
山月照弹琴　　　山月照彈琴
君问穷通理　　　君問窮通理
渔歌入浦深　　　漁歌入浦深

Thanking Associate Prefect Zhang

I prefer to live a quiet life
in my later years.
I am indifferent to
all mundane affairs.
A long-term plan
is not in my thoughts.
Returning to my old woods
was the only thing I sought.
The piney wind
blows loose my sash;
the mountain moon
shines on my lute.
You ask about
the ultimate truth of life.
The fishermen's song
drifts far above the shore.

王維　酬張少府

晚△年○
wǎn nián
later years

惟○好△靜△
wéi hào jìng
prefer a quiet life

萬△事△
wàn shì
all things

不△關○心●
bù guān xīn
indifferent to

自△顧△
zì gù
ask myself

無○長○策△
wú cháng cè
have no long-term plan

空○知○
kōng zhī
know only

返△舊△林●
fǎn jiù lín
to return to old woods

松○風○
sōng fēng
pine wind

吹○解△帶△
chuī jiě dài
blows loose the sash

山○月△
shān yuè
mountain moon

照△彈○琴●
zhào tán qín
shines upon lute

君○問△
jūn wèn
you ask about

窮○通○理△
qióng tiān lǐ
ultimate truth of life

漁○歌○
yú gē
fishermen's songs

入△浦△深●
rù pǔ shēn
go deep into the shore

Wang Wei 王维

过香积寺

不知香积寺	不知香積寺
数里入云峰	數里入雲峰
古木无人径	古木無人徑
深山何处钟	深山何處鐘
泉声咽危石	泉聲咽危石
日色冷青松	日色冷青松
薄暮空潭曲	薄暮空潭曲
安禅制毒龙	安禪制毒龍

On the Way to the Incense-Storing Temple

Not knowing where the
Incense-Storing Temple was,
I walked several miles
to the cloudy summit.
No footpath was found
around the aged old trees.
Deep in the mountain,
where was the bell tolled?
Running spring water
choked the jarred rocks;
in the sunlight,
green pines still looked cool.
Around dusk,
by the clear and tortuous pool,
I practiced meditation
to restrain the poisonous dragon.

王維　過香積寺

不△知○　　　香○積△寺△[1]
bù zhī　　　xiāng jī sì
where is　　incense storing temple

數△里△　　　入△雲○峰●
shù lǐ　　　rù yún fēng
several miles　into the cloudy summit

古△木△　　　無○人○徑△
gǔ mù　　　wú rén jìng
aged old trees　no footpaths seen

深○山○　　　何○處△鐘●
shēn shān　　hé chù zhōng
deep mountain　where is the bell

泉○聲○　　　咽△危○石△
quán shēng　　yè wēi shí
sound of spring water　chokes the jagged rocks

日△色△　　　冷△青○松●
rì sè　　　lěng qīng sōng
sunlight　　cools the green pines

薄△暮△　　　空○潭○曲△
bó mù　　　kōng tán qū
around sunset　the serene and winding pool

安○禪○　　　制△毒△龍●
ān chán　　zhì dú lóng
meditating　subdue poisonous dragon

---

[1] The Incense-Storing Temple was in present-day Shanxi Province.

Wang Wei

王维

送梓州李使君

万壑树参天	萬壑樹參天
千山响杜鹃	千山響杜鵑
山中一夜雨	山中一夜雨
树杪百重泉	樹杪百重泉
汉女输橦布	漢女輸橦布
巴人讼芋田	巴人訟芋田
文翁翻教授	文翁翻教授
不敢倚先贤	不敢倚先賢

Farewell to Prefect Li of Zi Zhou*

Trees in countless valleys
reach into the skies.
Numerous mountains
echo the cuckoos' cries.
A heavy rain all night long
in the mountains
brings down from tree tops
hundreds of cascades.
The Han women
pay tax in tong cloth;
the Ba men
dispute over the taro fields.
Wen Weng innovated
methods of instruction.
Do not be content with
accomplishments by the ancient sages.

王維　送梓州李使君

萬△壑△ wàn huò ten thousand valleys	樹△參○天● shù cān tiān trees reach the sky
千○山○ qiān shān thousand mountains	響△杜△鵑● xiǎng dù juān cuckoos cry
山○中○ shān zhōng in the mountain	一△夜△雨△ yī yè yǔ one night rain
樹△杪△ shù miǎo tips of tree branches	百△重○泉● bǎi chóng quán hundred strings of spring water
漢△女△ hàn nǚ Han girls	輸○橦○布△[1] shū tóng bù pay tax in flower cloth
巴○人○[2] bā rén Ba people	訟△芋△田● sòng yù tián dispute over taro field
文○翁○[3] wén wēng Wen Weng	翻○教△授△ fān jiào shòu innovated methods of teaching
不△敢△ bù gǎn dare not to	倚△先○賢● yǐ xiān xián rely on ancient saints

* Zi Zhou was in what is now Sichuan Province.
[1] A kind of cloth that was made from the flowers from a species of tree called tong.
[2] Men and women who were natives of the kingdom of Shu, in what is now Sichuan Province.
[3] Wen Weng, a governor in the Han dynasty, did a lot to educate and civilize the people of Shu.

135

Wang Wei 王维

汉江临眺

楚塞三湘接	楚塞三湘接
荆门九脉通	荊門九脈通
江流天地外	江流天地外
山色有无中	山色有無中
郡邑浮前浦	郡邑浮前浦
波澜动远空	波瀾動遠空
襄阳好风日	襄陽好風日
留醉与山翁	留醉與山翁

A View of the Han River*

The three Xiangs
are close to the border of Chu.
At Jinmen, the Han River
connects the nine tributaries.
The river flows
beyond heaven and earth;
the colors of the peaks
come and go.
The towns and villages
float out to the shore.
Billows upon billows
shake the distant sky.
How enchanting is
the scenery of Xiangyang!
Let me enjoy this moment
with the old mountain man.

王維　漢江臨眺

楚△塞△
chǔ sài
Chu's border

三○湘○接△¹
sān xiāng jiē
connects to the three Xiangs

荊○門○²
jīng mén
Jing Men Mountain

九△脈△通●³
jiǔ mài tōng
nine arteries go through

江○流○
jiāng liú
river flows

天○地△外△
tiān dì wài
beyond heaven and earth

山○色△
shān sè
mountain colors

有△無○中●
yǒu wú zhōng
between visible and invisible

郡△邑△
jùn yì
towns

浮○前○浦△
fú qián pǔ
float beyond riverside

波○瀾○
bō lán
billows

動△遠△空●
tòng yuǎn kōng
move distant sky

襄○陽○⁴
xiāng yáng
Xiangyang

好△風○日△
hǎo fēng rì
beautiful scenery

留○醉△
liú zuì
stay intoxicated

與△山○翁●
yǔ shān wēng
with the mountain old man

*　The Han River runs from Shanxi Province to Hubei Province before it emerges with the Yangtze River.
[1] Three Xiangs refer to the three counties in Hunan Province: Xiangshang, Xiangtan, and Xiangying.
[2] Jinmen Mountain was in present-day Hubei Province.
[3] The nine tributaries of the Yangtze River.
[4] Xiangyang was in what is now Hubei Province.

Wang Wei 王维

终南别业

中岁颇好道	中歲頗好道
晚家南山陲	晚家南山陲
兴来每独往	興來每獨往
胜事空自知	勝事空自知
行到水穷处	行到水窮處
坐看云起时	坐看雲起時
偶然值林叟	偶然值林叟
谈笑无还期	談笑無還期

My Villa in Mount Zhongnan*

Since my middle-age years,
I have enjoyed practicing Buddhism.
Now I am old
I live by Mount Zhongnan.
When I am in the mood,
I go out wandering alone.
What pleases me
only I myself know.
I walk to
the end of the stream,
then sit and watch
the clouds rising.
By chance, I run into
an old fellow in the wood.
We will chat and laugh
and forget to return home.

王維　終南別業

中○歲△ zhōng suì middle-age years	頗△好△道△ pō hào dào quite fond of Buddhism
晚△家○ wǎn jiā in later years I reside	南○山○陲● nán shān chuí at the side of Mount Zhongnan
興△來○ xíng lái in good mood	每△獨△往△ méi dú wǎng often go out alone
勝△事△ shèng shì happy things	空○自△知● kōng zì zhī only I myself know
行○到△ xíng dào walking to	水△窮○處△ shiǔ qióng chù the end of water
坐△看○ zuò kān sitting to look at	雲○起△時● yún qǐ shí clouds to appear
偶△然○ ǒu rán by chance	值△林○叟△ zhí lín sǒu meet an old man in the wood
談○笑△ tán xiào chatting and laughing	無○還○期● wú huán qī forget time to return home

* Mount Zhongnan is in Shansi Province.

Wei Yingwu 韦应物

淮上喜会梁州故人

江汉曾为客	江漢曾為客
相逢每醉还	相逢每醉還
浮云一别后	浮雲一別後
流水十年间	流水十年間
欢笑情如旧	歡笑情如舊
萧疏鬓已斑	蕭疏鬢已斑
何因北归去	何因北歸去
淮上对秋山	淮上對秋山

Joyful Gathering with an Old Friend from Liangzhou* on the Huai

We once were fellow travelers
on the River Han.
Each time we met,
we always returned tipsy.
We parted like
the floating clouds.
Almost without notice,
ten years have slipped by.
We laugh heartily
as we did in old times.
Our hair, thinly scattered,
has now turned gray.
You asked why I don't
return to the North with you.
I can face the autumn mountain
on the River Huai.

韋應物　淮上喜會梁州故人

江○漢△　　　　曾○為○客△
jiāng hàn　　　zēng wéi kè
Han River　　　once were fellow travelers

相○逢○　　　　每△醉△還●
xiāng féng　　　měi zuì huán
whenever we met　often returned tipsy

浮○雲○　　　　一△別△後△
fú yún　　　　yī bié hòu
floating clouds　after we parted

流○水△　　　　十△年○間●
liú shuǐ　　　shí nián jiān
flowing water　a span of ten years

歡○笑△　　　　情○如○舊△
huān xiào　　　qīng rú jiù
laugh heartily　as in old times

蕭○疏○　　　　鬢△已△斑●
xiāo shū　　　bìn yǐ bān
scattered thinly　hair spotted with gray

何○因○　　　　北△歸○去△
hé yīn　　　　běi guī qù
why not　　　return to the North

淮○上△　　　　對△秋○山●
huái shàng　　　duì qiū shān
on Huai River　face the autumn mountain

* Liangzhou was in modern-day southern Shanxi Province.

Wei Yingwu 韦应物

赋得暮雨送李胄

楚江微雨里	楚江微雨裡
建业暮钟时	建業暮鐘時
漠漠帆来重	漠漠帆來重
冥冥鸟去迟	冥冥鳥去遲
海门深不见	海門深不見
浦树远含滋	浦樹遠含滋
相送情无限	相送情無限
沾襟比散丝	沾襟比散絲

Seeing Li Zhou Off in the Evening Rain

It is raining
on the Yangtze River.
From Jian Ye comes
the sound of evening bells.
Amidst the misty fog,
sails approach sluggishly.
Beneath the gloomy sky,
birds delay their flight.
Sea Gate is
too deep to be seen.
Trees on the riverside
are sodden with rain.
I am too emotional
to bid you farewell.
Tears keep falling on my clothes
like threads of drizzle.

韋應物　賦得暮雨送李冑

楚△江○[1] chǔ jiāng Yangtze River	微○雨△裡△ wēi yǔ lǐ in the fine rain
建△業△[2] jiàn yè Jian Ye	暮△鐘○時● mù zhōng shí time of evening bells
漠△漠△ mò mò misty and foggy	帆○來○重△ fān lái zhòng sailing comes heavy
冥○冥○ míng míng dim and obscure	鳥△去△遲● niǎo qù chí birds fly away late
海△門○[3] hǎi mén Sea Gate	深○不△見△ shēn bù jiàn too deep to see
浦△樹△ pǔ shù riverside trees	遠△含○滋● yuǎn hán zī sodden with moisture
相○送△ xiāng sòng seeing off	情○無△限△ qíng wú xiàn feelings hard to control
沾○襟○ zhān jīn tears on clothes	比△散△絲● bǐ sàn sī like silk threads

[1] Chu River refers to the Yangtze River.
[2] Jianye was present-day Nanjing.
[3] Sea Gate, the estuary where the Yangtze River and the sea meet.

143

Wei Zhuang 韦庄

章台夜思

清瑟怨遥夜	清瑟怨遙夜
绕弦风雨哀	繞絃風雨哀
孤灯闻楚角	孤燈聞楚角
残月下章台	殘月下章臺
芳草已云暮	芳草已云暮
故人殊未来	故人殊未來
乡书不可寄	鄉書不可寄
秋雁又南回	秋雁又南迴

Night Thoughts on a Palace Tower

A clear note from a lute adds
bitterness to the long night.
It reverberates like
the mourning of wind and rain.
By the single lamp, I hear
the song of a bugle from the Chu land.
The waning moon is sinking
over the tower of the palace.
The time will soon come
for the fragrant grass to wither,
but my old friends
have yet to come.
A letter to my family
can no longer be delivered.
The autumn wild geese
have already turned south.

韋庄　章台夜思

清○瑟△
qīng sè
clear lute

繞△絃○
rào xiān
revolving around strings

孤○燈○
gū dēng
single lamp

殘○月△
cán yuè
waning moon

芳○草△
fāng cǎo
fragrant grass

故△人○
gù rén
old friends

鄉○書○
xiāng shū
letters to home

秋○雁△
qiū yàn
autumn wild geese

怨△遙○夜△
yuàn yáo yè
complains long night

風○雨△哀●
fēng yǔ āi
mourning of wind and rain

聞○楚△角△
wén chǔ jué
hear Chu's bugle sound

下△章○臺●[1]
xià zhāng tái
sinks behind the terrace

已△云○暮△
yǐ yún mù
close to withering

殊○未△來●
shū wèi lái
have yet to come

不△可△寄△
bù kě jì
cannot be mailed

又△南○迴●
yòu nán huí
return to the south again

[1] Zhangtai, a palace tower in what is now Shanxi Province.

145

Wen Tingyun   温庭筠

送人东游

荒成落黄叶	荒戍落黃葉
浩然离故关	浩然離故關
高风汉阳渡	高風漢陽渡
初日郢门山	初日郢門山
江上几人在	江上幾人在
天涯孤棹还	天涯孤櫂還
何当重相见	何當重相見
樽酒慰离颜	樽酒慰離顏

Farewell to a Friend Going East

Yellow leaves are falling
at this deserted fort.
In high spirits,
you will leave the old pass.
With the autumn wind blowing,
you will pass Hanyang Ferry.
By sunrise, you will
reach Yingmen Mountain.
Several people will
stand by the river
to greet your lonely boat
when it appears on the horizon.
When will we
see each other again?
Only a jar of wine
can console my parting grief.

溫庭筠　送人東遊

荒○戍△
huāng shù
deserted fort

浩△然○
hào rán
in high spirits

高○風○
gāo fēng
autumn wind

初○日△
chū rì
sun rising

江○上△
jiāng shàng
on the river

天○涯○
tiān yá
edge of sky

何○當○
hé dāng
when will

樽○酒△
zūn jiǔ
a jar of wine

落△黃○葉△
luò huáng yè
yellow leaves falling

離○故△關●
lí gù guān
leaving old pass

漢△陽○渡△
hàn yáng dù
Hanyang Ferry

郢△門○山●[1]
yǐng mén shān
Yingmen Mountain

幾△人○在△
jǐ rén zài
several people there

孤○櫂△還●
gū zhào huán
lonely boat returning

重△相○見△
zhòng xiāng jiàn
see each other again

慰△離○顏●
wèi lí yán
to console parting grief

---

[1] Yingmen Mountain, in Hubei Province, is also called Jinmen Mountain.

Xu Hun 许浑

秋日赴阙题潼关驿楼

红叶晚萧萧　　　　　紅葉晚蕭蕭
长亭酒一瓢　　　　　長亭酒一瓢
残云归太华　　　　　殘雲歸太華
疏雨过中条　　　　　疏雨過中條
树色随关回　　　　　樹色隨關迴
河声入海遥　　　　　河聲入海遙
帝乡明日到　　　　　帝鄉明日到
犹自梦渔樵　　　　　猶自夢漁樵

Inscribed on the Post House at Tong Pass* on an Autumn Day

The red leaves
rustling at dusk,
I stopped at a small pavilion
for a ladle of wine.
Evening clouds
sail back to Mt. Hua;
light rain passes through
the Zhongtiao Ridge.
The colorful trees
circle around the pass;
the loud river rushes
its way to the distant sea.
Tomorrow I shall reach
the Imperial City.
For now, I only dream
of fishing or woodcutting.

許渾　秋日赴闕題潼關驛樓

紅○葉△ hóng yè red leaves	晚△蕭○蕭● wǎn xiāo xiāo rustling at night
長○亭○ cháng tíng small pavilion	酒△一△瓢● jiǔ yī piáo one gourd ladle of wine
殘○雲○ cán yún evening clouds	歸○太△華△¹ guī tài huà return to Tai Hua
疏○雨△ shū yǔ fine rain	過△中○條●² guò zhōng tiáo passes through Zhongtiao
樹△色△ shū sè tree colors	隨○關○迴△ suí guān huí follow the winding pass
河○聲○ hé shēng river sounds	入△海△遙● rù hǎi yáo enter the distant sea
帝△鄉○ dì xiāng imperial capital	明○日△到 míng rì dào will reach there tomorrow
猶○自△ yóu zì I still	夢△漁○樵● mèng yú qiáo dream of fishing and woodcutting

* In what is now Tong Pass County, Shanxi Province.
¹ Tai Hua or Mt. Hua, a sacred mountain in Shanxii Province, west of Tong Pass.
² Zhong Tiao, a mountain in Shanxi Province.

Xu Hun 许浑

早秋

遥夜泛清瑟	遙夜汎清瑟
西风生翠萝	西風生翠蘿
残萤委玉露	殘螢委玉露
早雁拂银河	早雁拂銀河
高树晓还密	高樹曉還密
远山晴更多	遠山晴更多
淮南一叶下	淮南一葉下
自觉洞庭波	自覺洞庭波

Early Autumn

Night is longer
with autumn sounds in the air.
West wind blows against
the green vines.
The last glowworm
rests on the jade-white dew.
Early wild geese
fly across the Milky Way.
Tall trees
still look dim at dawn.
On a clear day,
the distant mountains are in full view.
Seeing a single leaf falling
south of River Huai,
I can feel Lake Dongting's
autumn waves.

許渾　早秋

遙○夜△
yáo yè
long night

汎△清○瑟△
fàn qīng sè
autumn sound in the air

西○風○
xī fēng
west wind

生○翠△蘿●
shēng cuì luó
blows green vines

殘○螢○
cán yīng
last glowworm

委△玉△露△
wěi yù lù
rests on jade-white dew

早△雁△
zǎo yàn
early wild geese

拂△銀○河●
fú yín hé
fly across Milky Way

高○樹△
gāo shù
tall trees

曉△還○密△
xiǎo hái mì
still dense at dawn

遠△山○
yuǎn shān
distant mountains

晴○更△多●
qíng gèng duō
full view on a fair day

淮○南○[1]
huái nán
south of Huai

一△葉△下△
yī yè xià
one leaf has fallen

自△覺△
zì júe
I can feel

洞△庭○波●
dòng tíng bō
the waves of Lake Dongting

[1] From the book Huai Nan Zi: A single fallen leaf tells of the oncoming autumn.

Zhang Ji 张籍

没番故人

<table>
<tr><td>前年戍月支</td><td>前年戍月支</td></tr>
<tr><td>城下没全师</td><td>城下沒全師</td></tr>
<tr><td>番汉断消息</td><td>番漢斷消息</td></tr>
<tr><td>死生长别离</td><td>死生長別離</td></tr>
<tr><td>无人收废帐</td><td>無人收廢帳</td></tr>
<tr><td>归马识残旗</td><td>歸馬識殘旗</td></tr>
<tr><td>欲祭疑君在</td><td>欲祭疑君在</td></tr>
<tr><td>天涯哭此时</td><td>天涯哭此時</td></tr>
</table>

To an Old Friend Lost in Tibet

In battling against theYuezhi,
the year before last,
your whole army was lost
at a city wall.
Between Tibet and China,
communications were cut off.
We probably will not meet again
even if you are not dead.
No one was there to collect
your damaged tent;
horses that came back
recognized your tattered flag.
I want to offer you a sacrifice,
but you might still be alive.
At this moment, I cry
toward the edge of the sky.

張籍　沒番故人

前○年○　　戌△月△支●[1]
qián nián　　shù yuè zhī
year before last　　in battling against the Yuezhi

城○下△　　沒△全○師●
chéng xià　　mò quán shī
at the city gate　　whole army was lost

番○漢△　　斷△消○息△
fān hàn　　duàn xiāo xī
Tibet and Han　　cut off news

死△生○　　長○別△離●
sǐ shēng　　cháng bié lí
death or alive　　separate forever

無○人○　　收○廢△帳△
wú rén　　shōu fèi zhàng
no one　　collected torn tents

歸○馬△　　識△殘○旗●
guī mǎ　　shì cán qí
returning horses　　recognized damaged banners

欲△祭△　　疑○君○在△
yù jì　　yí jūn zài
to offer a sacrifice　　you might still be alive

天○涯○　　哭△此△時●
tiān yá　　kū cǐ shí
far, far away　　cry at this moment

[1] Name of a nomadic tribe in the Tibetan region of ancient China.

Zhang Qiao 张乔

书边事

调角断清秋　　　　　調角斷清秋
征人倚戍楼　　　　　征人倚戍樓
春风对青冢　　　　　春風對青冢
白日落梁州　　　　　白日落梁州
大漠无兵阻　　　　　大漠無兵阻
穷边有客游　　　　　窮邊有客遊
蕃情似此水　　　　　蕃情似此水
長願向南流　　　　　長願向南流

Written from the Frontier

No more bugles
blowing in the clear autumn.
A traveler can rest on
the garrison watchtower.
Spring winds attend to
the green tomb.
The pale sun sets
beyond Liangzhou.
Soldiers no longer bar
the way to the desert;
tourists can sightsee
at the borders.
I wish the goodwill of the Tibetans
was like this river,
flowing southward
forever and forever.

張喬　書邊事

調○角△
tiáo jiǎo
bugle blowing

斷△清○秋●
duàn qīng qiū
ceased in the clear autumn

征○人○
zhēng rén
a warrior

倚△戍△樓●
yǐ shù lóu
learns on garrison watchtower

春○風○
chūn fēng
spring wind

對△青○冢△[1]
duì qīng zhǒng
faces green tomb

白△日△
bái rì
the pale sun

落△梁○州●[2]
luò liáng zhōu
goes down at Liangzhou

大△漠△
dà mò
great desert

無○兵○阻△
wú bīng zǔ
no soldiers to guard

窮○邊○
qióng biān
beyond frontier

有△客△遊●
yǒu kè yóu
tourists come

蕃○情○
fán qíng
passion of barbarians

似△此△水△
sì cǐ shuǐ
is like this river

長○願△
cháng yuàn
always wish

向△南○流●
xiàng nán liu
to flow southward

[1] The grave of Wang Zhaojun, a court lady during the Han Dynasty, who was married to a chieftain of a northern tribe against her will. It was said that the grass around her grave remained green all year long.
[2] Liangzhou, the frontier in what is now Sichuan and the southwest area of Shanxi.

155

PART 3

Seven-Character Regulated Verses

七言律诗

Bai Juyi

白居易

望月有感

时难年荒世业空　　時難年荒世業空
弟兄羁旅各西东　　弟兄羈旅各西東
田园寥落干戈后　　田園寥落干戈後
骨肉流离道路中　　骨肉流離道路中
吊影分为千里雁　　吊影分為千里雁
辞根散作九秋蓬　　辭根散作九秋蓬
共看明月应垂泪　　共看明月應垂淚
一夜乡心五处同　　一夜鄉心五處同

Thoughts from Gazing at the Moon

Hard times, a year of famine;
gone is our ancestral estate.
My brothers are scattered apart
in the east and in the west.
Fields and gardens
are now deserted after the war.
Kinsfolk still wander from
place to place on the road.
A distant wild goose flies alone
with its own shadow;
an autumn weed is blown
aimlessly without its root.
Let tears fall when we all see
the moon tonight.
For in five different places,
we are all longing for home.

白居易　望月有感

時○難△ shí nàn disastrous times	年○荒○ nián huāng a famine year	世△業△空● shì yè kōng ancestral estate gone
弟△兄○ dì xiōng brothers	羈○旅△ jī lǚ wander about	各△西○東● gè xī dōng in the east or west
田○園○ tián yuán fields and gardens	寥○落△ liáo luò deserted	干○戈○後△ gān gē hòu after armed conflicts
骨△肉△ gǔ ròu kinsfolk	流○離○ liú lí homeless	道△路△中● dào lù zhōng on the road
吊△影△ diào yǐng with own shadow	分○為○ fēn wéi separated	千○里△雁△ qiān lǐ yǎn long-distant wild geese
辭○根○ cí gēn rootless	散△作△ sàn zuò dispersed	九△秋○蓬● jiǔ qiū péng a loose weed in autumn
共○看○ gòng kān all looking at	明○月△ míng yuè bright moon	應○垂○淚△ yīng chuí lèi tears should fall
一△夜△ yī yè this night	鄉○心○ xiāng xīn homesickness	五△處△同● wǔ chù tóng same in five places

[1] Bai Juyi wrote this poem after the unrest in Henan and the famine in Guannei. His brothers and sisters were scattered in five different districts.

○ = ping (level) tone
△ = ze (deflected) tone
● = rhyme (ping tone)
▲ = rhyme (ze tone)

Cen Shen 岑参

和贾至舍人早朝大明之作

鸡鸣紫陌曙光寒	雞鳴紫陌曙光寒
莺啭皇州春色阑	鶯囀皇州春色闌
金阙晓钟开万户	金闕曉鐘開萬戶
玉阶仙仗拥千宫	玉階仙仗擁千宮
花迎剑佩星初落	花迎劍珮星初落
柳拂旌旗露未乾	柳拂旌旗露未乾
独有凤凰池上客	獨有鳳凰池上客
阳春一曲和皆难	陽春一曲和皆難

In Reply to Court Official Jia Zhi's Poem "Morning Audience at Daming Palace"

Roosters crowing, it is cool
at dawn on the imperial road.
Orioles twitter, and spring
in the capital is on the wane.
A myriad of doors open right after
the palace's morning bell.
On the jade stairs, numerous officials
are surrounded by the Guard of Honors.
Sword pendants glint upon flowers
as stars begin to sink.
Willows brush the banners
while dew remains on the twigs.
The poem of one official
from Phoenix Pool is especially
hard to match, for it is composed
in a "Sunny Spring" tune.

岑參　和賈至舍人早朝大明之作

雞○鳴○ **jī míng** roosters crow	紫△陌△ **zǐ mò** purple path	曙△光○寒● **shǔ guāng hán** feeling chill at dawn
鶯○囀△ **yīng zhuàn** orioles twitter	皇○州○¹ **huáng zhōu** Huang Zhou	春○色△闌● **chūn sè lán** spring is on the wane
金○闕△ **jīn què** golden palace	曉△鐘○ **xiǎo zhōng** morning bell	開○萬△戶△ **kāi wàn hù** numerous doors are open
玉△階○ **yù jiē** jade steps	仙○仗△ **xiān zhàng** guard of honor	擁△千○宮● **yōng qiān gōng** a thousand officials
花○迎○ **huā yíng** flowers greet	劍△珮△ **jiàn pèi** sword and jade pendants	星○初○落△ **xīng chū luò** stars begin to sink
柳△拂△ **liǔ fú** willows stroke	旌○旗○ **jīng qí** banners	露△未△乾● **lù wèi gān** dew not yet dry
獨△有△ **dú yǒu** there is only	鳳△凰○池○² **fèng huáng chí** Phoenix Pool	上△客△ **shàng kè** guest of
陽○春○³ **yáng chūn** "Sunny Spring"	一△曲△ **yī qǔ** a song	和△皆○難● **hè jiē nán** hard to match

¹ Huang Zhou refers to the capital city of Chang'an.
² Phoenix Pool was the name of the building in which Jia Zhi had his office.
³ "Yang Chun" (spring sunlight), an ancient song considered to be so elegant that it was beyond compare.

161

Cui Hao 崔颢

行经华阴

岩尧太华俯咸京
天外三峰削不成
武帝祠前雲欲散
仙人掌上雨初晴
河山北枕秦关险
驿路西连汉峙平
借问路傍名利客
无如此处学长生

岩嶢太華俯咸京
天外三峰削不成
武帝祠前雲欲散
仙人掌上雨初晴
河山北枕秦關險
驛路西連漢峙平
借問路傍名利客
無如此處學長生

Passing Hua Yin*

Overlooking the Xian capital,
the lofty Mt. Hua stands.
Its three peaks, the work of God,
extend beyond heaven.
In front of the Wu Emperor's Shrine,
clouds are about to disperse;
above the Immortal's Palm, the sky,
after a rain, has just turned clear.
To the north, mountain and river
lean against the perilous Qin Pass;
to the west, the courier road
connects to the level Emperor's Altar.
You, the roadside travelers,
who pursue fame and wealth,
why not come here to learn
about the secret of longevity?

崔顥　行經華陰

岩○嶢○ tiáo yáo lofty	太△華△ tài huà Mt.Hua	俯△咸○京● fǔ xián jīng overlooks Xian capital
天○外△ tiān wài beyond sky	三○峰○ sān fēng three peaks	削△不△成● xuè bù chéng can't be sharpened
武△帝△祠○ wǔ dì cí Wu Emperor's Shrine	前○ qián in front	雲○欲△散△ yūn yù sàn clouds will disperse
仙○人○掌△[1] xiān rén zhǎng The Immortal's Palm	上△ shàng over	雨△初○晴● yǔ chū qíng rain starts to clear
河○山○ hé shān river mountain	北△枕△ bèi zǎn north: to lean on	秦○關○險△ qíng guān xiǎn perilous Qin Pass
驛△路△ yì lù courier road	西○連○ xī lián west: connect to	漢△峙平●[2] hàn zhì píng Han temple on plain
借△問△ juè wèn may I ask	路△傍○ lù pán by road side	名○利△客△ míng lì kè fame-and profit-seekers
無○如○ wú rú might as well	此△處△ cǐ chù this place	學△長○生● xué cháng shēng learn about long life

*Hua Yin is now Hua Yin County in Shanxi Province.
[1] Immortal's Palm is one of Mt. Hua's peaks.
[2] A place where the emperor used to worship in the Han Dynasty.

Du Fu　　　　　　　　　　杜甫

蜀相

丞相祠堂何处寻　　　丞相祠堂何處尋
锦官城外柏森森　　　錦官城外柏森森
映阶碧草自春色　　　映階碧草自春色
隔叶黄鹂空好音　　　隔葉黃鸝空好音
三顾频频天下计　　　三顧頻頻天下計
两朝开济老臣心　　　兩朝開濟老臣心
出师未捷身先死　　　出師未捷身先死
长使英雄泪满襟　　　長使英雄淚滿襟

The Temple of the Prime Minister of Shu*

Where can I find the
prime minister's shrine?
Outside Jin Guan City,
where cypress densely grow.
The green grass brightens the steps
in spring color;
a yellow oriole behind the leaves
vainly sings its sweet song.
Three calls at the thatched cottage
to seek help in building a nation;
with two reigns of dedicated services,
he gave his heart and soul.
He died before he could see
his campaign turn into a success.
Since then, how many heroes
have shed their tears!

杜甫　蜀相

丞○相△
chéng xiàng
prime minister

祠○堂○
cí táng
ancestral temple

何○處△尋●
hé chù xún
where to find

錦△官○城○
jǐn guān chéng
Jin Guan city

外△
wài
outside

柏△森○森●
bǎi sēn sēn
cypress grow thick

映△階○
yìng jiē
reflecting on steps

碧△草△
bì cǎo
green grass

自△春○色△
zì chūn sè
with its spring color

隔△葉△
gé yè
between leaves

黃○鸝○
huáng lí
yellow orioles

空○好△音●
kōng hǎo yīn
nice sound in vain

三○顧△¹
sān gù
three visits

頻○頻○
pín pín
repeatedly

天○下△計△
tiān xià jì
plan for the world

兩△朝○²
liǎng cháo
two reigns

開○濟△
kāi jì
to serve and guide

老△臣○心●
lǎo chén xīn
unwavering loyalty

出△師○³
chū shī
dispatching troops

未△捷△
wèi jié
not yet succeeded

身○先○死△
shēn xiān sǐ
one already died

長○使△
cháng shǐ
always cause

英○雄○
yīng xióng
heroes

淚△滿△襟●
lèi mǎn jīn
tears fill garment

* Zhuge Liang, the prime minister of the Kingdom of Shu during the Epoch of the Three Kingdoms, was known for his great talent and wisdom.
¹ Liu Bei, the emperor of Zhu, made three visits to Zhuge Llang's thatched cottage in an effort to obtain his service.
² Zhuge Liang had served Liu Bei and his son, Liu Chan.
³ Zhuge Liang passed away before his plan to defeat the states of Wei and Wu.

Du Fu

杜甫

客至

舍南舍北皆春水	舍南舍北皆春水
但见群鸥日日来	但見群鷗日日來
花径不曾缘客扫	花徑不曾緣客掃
蓬门今始为君开	蓬門今始為君開
盘餐市远无兼味	盤餐市遠無兼味
樽酒家贫只旧醅	樽酒家貧只舊醅
肯与邻翁相对饮	肯與鄰翁相對飲
隔篱呼取尽余杯	隔籬呼取盡餘杯

Welcoming a Guest*

The southern and northern sides
of my cottage are flooded with spring rains.
Every day, no one but the gulls
come visiting.
The flowery path
has not been swept for a guest;
my thatched door
is opened just for you.
Far away from the market,
I cannot offer dishes of fish and meat.
Poor as I am,
I can only afford a jar of old home-brewed wine.
If you are willing to drink
with my old neighbor,
I will call him over the fence
to empty our cups!

杜甫　客至

舍△南○ **shè nán** south of house	舍△北△ **shè běi** north of house	皆○春○水△ **jiē chūn shuǐ** all spring waters
但△見△ **dàn jiàn** but see	群○鷗○ **qún ōu** flock of gulls	日△日△來● **rì rì lái** come every day
花○徑△ **huā jìng** flowery path	不△曾○ **bù zēng** has not been	緣○客△掃△ **yuán kè sǎo** swept for guest
蓬○門○ **péng mén** thorn-wood gate	今○始△ **jīn shǐ** begins only now	為△君○開● **wèi jūn kāi** to open for you
盤○餐○ **pán cān** dishes of food	市△遠△ **shì yuǎn** market far away	無○兼○味△[1] **wú jiān wèi** no two tastes
樽○酒△ **zūn jiǔ** a jar of wine	家○貧○ **jiā pín** poor family	只△舊△醅● **zhǐ jiù pēi** old unstrained only
肯△與△ **kěn yǔ** willing to	鄰○翁○ **lín wēng** with neighbor	相○對△飲△ **xiāng duì yǐn** drink together
隔△籬○ **gé lí** over the fence	呼○取△ **hū qǔ** call and ask	盡△餘○杯● **jìn yú bēi** to finish the cup

* The guest was country magistrate Cui, Du Fu's uncle.
[1] A meal that includes dishes with fish and meat.

167

Du Fu

杜甫

野望

西山白雪三城戍
南浦清江万里桥
海内风尘诸弟隔
天涯涕泪一身遥
唯将迟暮供多病
未有涓埃答圣朝
跨马出郊时极目
不堪人事日萧条

西山白雪三城戍
南浦清江萬里橋
海內風塵諸弟隔
天涯涕淚一身遙
唯將遲暮供多病
未有涓埃答聖朝
跨馬出郊時極目
不堪人事日蕭條

A View of the Countryside

Snow covers the western ranges
while troops are guarding the three cities.
Across the clear river at the south bank,
the Ten-Thousand-Li Bridge stands.
Because of the civil war, I have lost
contact with my younger brothers.
Alone in a remote corner,
I can't help shedding tears.
Old and disease prone,
I cannot make any contribution
to the present dynasty.
On horseback to the countryside,
I often look as far as I can.
How can I bear to see
the condition of human suffering?

杜甫　野望

西○山○ [1]
xī shān
western mountain

白△雪△
bái xuě
white snow

三○城○戍△ [2]
sān chéng shù
three cities on guard

南○浦△
nán pǔ
south bank

清○江○
qīng jiāng
clear river

萬○里△橋●
wàn lǐ qiáo
Ten-Thousand-Li Bridge

海△內△
hǎi nèi
within four seas

風○塵○
fēng chén
wind and dust

諸○弟△隔△
zhū dì gé
brothers are separated

天○涯○
tiān yá
sky's end

涕△淚△
tì lèi
shedding tears

一△身○遙●
yī shēn yáo
one person far away

唯○將○
wéi jiāng
only because

遲○暮△
chí mù
later years

供○多○病△
gōng duō bìng
and disease prone

未△有△
wèi yǒu
not having

涓○埃○
juān āi
a tiny fragment

答△聖△朝●
dá shèng cháo
to offer to present
dynasty

跨△馬△
kuà mǎ
mounting a horse

出△郊○
chū jiāo
to go to outskirts

時○極△目△
shí jí mù
often look very far

不△堪○
bù kān
can't bear

人○事△
rén shì
human affairs

日△蕭○條●
rì xiāo tiáo
getting worse day by
day

---

[1] Refers to the Mountain located to the west of Chengdu, in Sichuan
Province.
[2] Three ancient cities—Song, Wei, Bao—were in present-day Sichuan
Province.
.

Du Fu 杜甫

闻官军收河南河北

剑外忽传收蓟北　　劍外忽傳收薊北
初闻涕泪满衣裳　　初聞涕淚滿衣裳
却看妻子愁何在　　卻看妻子愁何在
漫卷诗书喜欲狂　　漫卷詩書喜欲狂
白日放歌须纵酒　　白日放歌須縱酒
青春作伴好还乡　　青春作伴好還鄉
即从巴峡穿巫峡　　即從巴峽穿巫峽
便下襄阳向洛阳　　便下襄陽向洛陽

On Hearing of the Recovery of Both Henan and Hebei by the Imperial Army

Suddenly, from outside Jianmen,
came a word about the recovery of Ji Bei.
On hearing the news, I could not
help shedding tears all over my clothes.
Turning around and looking at my wife,
I saw no more sadness on her face.
Rolling up my poetry books mindlessly,
I turned my joy into ecstasy.
Let's drink to our hearts' content
and sing loudly in daylight;
let's go home together
and enjoy the enchanting scene of spring.
Why not start our sail now,
from the Ba Gorge through the Wu Gorge,
downstream to Xiangyang,
and then go up toward Luoyang.

杜甫　聞官軍收河南河北

劍△外△[1] jiàn wài outside Jianmen	忽△傳○ hú chuān suddenly heard	收○薊△北△[2] shōu jì běi retaking of Ji Bei
初○聞○ chū wén first hear about	涕△淚△ tì lèi snivel and tears	滿△衣○裳● mǎn yī cháng wet entire clothes
卻△看○ què kān turning to look at	妻○子△ qī zǐ wife	愁○何○在△ chóu hé zài where is sadness
漫△卷△ màn jiǔn rolling up casually	詩○書○ shī shū poetry books	喜△欲△狂● xǐ yù kuáng be overjoyed
白△日△ bái rì daytime	放△歌○ fàng gē sing loudly	須○縱△酒△ xū zòng jiǔ must drink at will
青○春○ qīng chūn springtime	作△伴△ zuò bàn with companions	好△還○鄉● hǎo huán xiāng to return to native land
即△從○ jí cóng starting at once from	巴○峽△ bā xiá Ba Gorge	穿○巫○峽△ chuān wū xiá through Wu Gorge
便△下△ biàn xià then go down to	襄○陽○ xiāng yáng Xiangyang	向△洛△陽● xiàng luò yáng toward Luoyang

[1] South of Jianmen (Swordgate) was in present-day Sichuan Province.
[2] Ji Bei, the stronghold of the rebellion of An Lushan, was in what is now northern Hebei Province.

171

Du Fu 杜甫

登楼

花近高楼伤客心	花近高樓傷客心
万方多难此登临	萬方多難此登臨
锦江春色来天地	錦江春色來天地
玉垒浮云变古今	玉壘浮雲變古今
北极朝廷终不改	北極朝廷終不改
西山寇盗莫相侵	西山寇盜莫相侵
可怜后主还祠庙	可憐後主還祠廟
日暮聊为梁甫吟	日暮聊為梁甫吟

Ascending a Tower

It breaks my heart to see flowers
so close to this high tower.
I have come up here
amidst war ravages everywhere.
The spring scenery of Jin River
comes from heaven and earth.
The floating clouds of Jade Rampart
change through the ages.
The imperial court, like the North Star,
in the end will not falter.
The invasion of bandits from
the Western Mountain will fail.
How pitiable! There is still
a shrine of the last king of Shu.
At sunset, let me just chant
the Liangfu tune.

杜甫　登樓

花○近△ huā jìn flowers near	高○樓○ gāo lóu tall tower	傷○客△心● shāng kè xīn break my heart
萬△方○ wàn fāng everywhere	多○難△ duō nàn many hardships	此△登○臨● cǐ dēng lín to climb up here
錦△江○ jǐng jiāng Jin River	春○色△ chūn sè spring scenery	來○天○地△ lái tiān dì comes from heaven and earth
玉△壘△ yù lěi Jade Rampart	浮○雲○ fú yún floating clouds	變△古△今● biàn gǔ jīn change through the ages
北△極△ běi jí the North Pole	朝○廷○ cháo tíng imperial court	終○不△改△ zhōng bù gǎi will not falter
西○山○¹ xī shān Western Mountain	寇△盜△ kòu dào bandits and thieves	莫△相○侵● mò xiāng qīn won't try to invade
可△憐○ kě lián pitiable	後△主△² hòu zhǔ last ruler	還○祠○廟△ huán cí miào temple still remains
日△暮△ rì mù at dusk	聊○為○ liáo wéi just to	梁○甫△吟●³ liáng fǔ yín chant a Liangfu tune

¹ Refers to the Tibetan regime in ancient China.
² Liu Chan was the last ruler of the State of Shu during the Epoch of Three Kingdoms.
³ "Liangfuyin" was the name of a song that Zhuge Liang, Liu Chan's prime minister, enjoyed singing.

Du Fu   杜甫

宿府

岁暮阴阳催短景　　　歲暮陰陽催短景
天涯霜雪霁寒宵　　　天涯霜雪霽寒宵
五更鼓角声悲壮　　　五更鼓角聲悲壯
三峡星河影动摇　　　三峽星河影動搖
野哭千家闻战伐　　　野哭千家聞戰伐
夷歌几处起渔樵　　　夷歌幾處起漁樵
卧龙跃马终黄土　　　臥龍躍馬終黃土
人事音书漫寂寥　　　人事音書漫寂寥

A Night at the Pavilion

Yin and yang of the year's end
have cut the scenic view short.
On a cold night far away from home,
the snow has just stopped falling.
The drum and bugle sound solemn
and stirring at the fifth watch.
The shadows of stars and Milky Way
tremble over the Three Gorges.
As thousands of families wail in the field,
the noises of fighting continue.
Fishermen and woodcutters start to hum
the barbarian songs here and there.
Sleeping Dragon and Horse Leaper
became yellow dust in the end.
Why do they still matter—
personal affairs and loss of contact?

杜甫　宿府

歲△暮△ suì mù end of the year	陰○陽○ yīn yáng yin and yang	催○短△景△ cuī duǎn jǐng shorten time of scene
天○涯○ tiān yá edge of the world	霜△雪△ shuāng xuě frost and snow	霽△寒○宵● jì hán xiāo clear up cold night
五△更○[1] wǔ gēng the fifth watch	鼓△角△ gǔ jiǎo drum and bugle	聲○悲○壯△ shēng bēi zhuàng sound solemn and stirring
三○峽△ sān xiá three gorges	星○河○ xīng hé Milky Way	影△動△搖● yǐng dòng yáo shadows move
野△哭△ yě kū crying in the field	千○家○ qiān jiā thousand families	聞○戰△伐△ wén zhàn fá hear fighting
夷○歌○ yí gē barbarian song	幾△處△ jǐ chù several places	起△漁○樵● qǐ yú qiáo from fishermen and woodcutters
臥○龍○[2] wò lóng Sleeping Dragon	躍△馬△[3] yuè mǎ Horse Leaping	終○黃○土△ zhōng huáng tǔ ended up yellow soil
人○事△ rén shì human affairs	音○書○ yīn shū news and letters	漫△寂△寥● màn jì liáo of less importance

[1] The fifth watch of the night was the time just before dawn.
[2] Sleeping Dragon refers to Zhuge Liang, the brilliant military
Strategist in the Epoch of the Three Kingdoms.
[3] Horse Leaping refers to Gongsun Shu, who declared himself
 king on a horse.

Du Fu 杜甫

咏怀古迹 (其一)

支离东北风尘际　　　　支離東北風塵際
漂泊西南天地间　　　　漂泊西南天地間
三峡楼台淹日月　　　　三峽樓臺淹日月
五溪衣服共云山　　　　五溪衣服共雲山
羯胡事主终无赖　　　　羯胡事主終無賴
词客哀时且未还　　　　詞客哀時且未還
庾信平生最萧瑟　　　　庾信平生最蕭瑟
暮年诗赋动江关　　　　暮年詩賦動江關

Reflections on the Historical Sites (First of Five Poems)

Ravaged by the war,
I fled from the Northeast.
I ended up wandering in the
Southwest of the country.
The sun and moon shine upon
the balconies at the Three Gorges.
People of different customs share
the clouds and mountains at Five Streams.
The rumor that the Jie-Hu rebels
would surrender was simply unfounded.
The poets who lament
over the situation have yet to return.
What a lonely and sorrowful life
Yu Xin must have lived.
Composed at his evening years,
his poetry had created a sensation in Jiangling.

杜甫　詠懷古跡（其一）

支○離○ zhī lí wander about	東○北△ dōng běi northeast	風○塵○際△ fēng chén jì in times of war
漂○泊△ piāo bó drifting	西○南○ xī nán Southeast	天○地△間● tiān dì jiān that part of the world
三○峽△ sān xiá The Three Gorges	樓○臺○ lóu tái balcony	淹○日△月△ yān rì yuè submerged under sun and moon
五△溪○[1] wǔ xī The Five Brooks	衣○服△ yī fú clothes	共△雲○山● gòng yún shān share clouds and mountains
羯△胡○ jié hú non-Han tribes	事△主△ shì zhǔ serving the master	終○無○賴△ zhōng wú lài can't be trusted
詞○客△ cí kè poets	哀○時○ āi shí feel sad for the times	且△未△還● qiě wèi huán still not yet returned
庾△信△[2] yǔ xìn Yu Xin	平○生○ pín shēng whole life	最△蕭○瑟△ zuì xiāo sè most lonely and sorrowful
暮△年○ mù nián evening years	詩○賦△ shī fù poetry	動△江○關● dòng jiāng guān excited Jiangling

[1] The Five Streams, where minority people once lived, are in present-day Hunan Province.
[2] Yu Xin, an envoy of the Liang Dynasty, was forced to stay in the north for twenty-seven years after Liang was defeated by the State of Wei.
He composed a poem lamenting Jiangnan—an area to the south of the Yangtze River.

Du Fu 杜甫

咏怀古迹（其二）

摇落深知宋玉悲　　搖落深知宋玉悲
风流儒雅亦吾师　　風流儒雅亦吾師
怅望千秋一洒泪　　悵望千秋一灑淚
萧条异代不同时　　蕭條異代不同時
江山故宅空文藻　　江山故宅空文藻
云雨荒台岂梦思　　雲雨荒臺豈夢思
最是楚宫俱泯灭　　最是楚宮俱泯滅
舟人指点到今疑　　舟人指點到今疑

Reflections on the Historical Sites (Second of Five Poems)

I know how sad was Song Yu
at the sight of falling leaves.
Elegant in style and words,
he is my teacher as well.
A thousand years later,
I long pensively for him with tears.
Though in a different era,
I am just as depressed.
Near river and mountain, does his old house
exist only to store his refined writings?
In a shroud of clouds and rain,
was the desolated terrace merely an idea
from his dream?
What a pity! The palace of the Chu State
has vanished without a trace.
A boatman pointed to me the alleged site,
but I still have some doubt in my mind.

杜甫　詠懷古跡（其二）

搖○落△[1]
yáo luò
desolation

深○知○
shēn zhī
deeply understand

宋△玉△悲●[2]
sòng yù bēi
how sad was Song Yu

風○流○
fēng liú
elegance in style

儒○雅△
rú yǎ
scholarly and refined

亦△吾○師●
yì wú shī
also my teacher

悵△望△
chàng wàng
longing pensively

千○秋○
qiān qiū
a thousand years

一△灑△淚△
yī sǎ lèi
one shedding of tears

蕭○條○
xiāo tiáo
lonely and depressed

異△代△
yì dài
different era

不△同○時●
bù tóng shí
at different times

江○山○
jiāng shān
river and mountain

故△宅△
gù zhè
former residence

空○文○藻△
kōng wén zǎo
only to display elegant words

雲○雨△
yún yǔ
cloud and rain

荒○臺○
huāng tái
deserted terrace

豈△夢△思●
qǐ mèng xī
could it be a dream

最△是△
zuì shì
moreover

楚△宮○[3]
chǔ gōng
Chu palace

俱○泯△滅△
ju mǐn miè
completely vanished

舟○人○
zhōu rén
a boatman

指△點△
zhī diǎn
give direction

到△今○疑●
dào jīn yī
until now with doubt

[1] A phrase used by Song Yu to describe the falling and withering of grass and trees.
[2] Song Yu was a student of the patriot poet Qu Yuan of the Chu State during the Epoch of Warring States.
[3] The Chu palace was in present-day Jianglin County, Hubei Province.

Du Fu   杜甫

咏怀古迹 (其三)

群山万壑赴荆门	群山萬壑赴荊門
生长明妃尚有村	生長明妃尚有村
一去紫台连朔漠	一去紫臺連朔漠
独留青冢向黄昏	獨留青塚向黄昏
画图省识春风面	畫圖省識春風面
环佩空归月夜魂	環珮空歸月夜魂
千载琵琶作胡语	千載琵琶作胡語
分明怨恨曲中论	分明怨恨曲中論

Reflections on the Historical Sites (Third of Five Poems)

A myriad of mountains and valleys
extend downward to Jinmen.
The village in which Court Lady Ming
grew up is still there.
She left the Purple Terrace
for the distant northern desert.
All that remains is her evergreen
tomb facing the setting sun.
From her portrait, one can tell
that she had a beautiful face.
With her pendant tingling,
she returns in spirit in moonlight.
A thousand years henceforth,
the *pipa* is played in a Tartar tune.
Obviously it conveys
her feelings of regret and bitterness.

杜甫　詠懷古跡 (其三)

群○山○
qún shān
mountain ranges

萬△壑△
wàn hè
myriad valleys

赴△荊○門●
fù jīng mén
go to Jingmen Mountain

生○長△
shēng zhǎng
grow up

明○妃○[1]
míng fēi
imperial concubine

尚△有△村●
shàng yǒu cūn
still there is a village

一△去△
yī qù
once gone

紫△臺○[2]
zǐ tái
purple terrace

連○朔△漠△
lián shuò mò
join northern desert

獨△留○
dú liú
alone to stay

青○塚△
qīng zhǒng
green grave

向△黃○昏●
xiàng huáng hūn
face toward dusk

畫△圖○
huà tú
(from) the portrait

省△識△
xǐng zhì
detect

春○風○面△[3]
chūn fēng miàn
spring-wind face

環○珮△
huán pèi
ornaments

空○歸○
kōng guī
return in vain

月△夜△魂●
yuè yè hún
moonlit spirit

千○載△
qiān zǎi
thousand year

琵○琶○
pí pá
pipa

作△胡○語△
zuò hú yǔ
mix with Hu language

分○明○
fēn míng
obviously

怨△恨△
yuàn hèn
complain and regret

曲△中○論●
qǔ zhōng lún
tune of the song

[1] Another name of Wang Zhaojun, a court lady during the Han Dynasty, who was sent to the north to marry the head of a barbarian tribe as a diplomatic condition.
[2] Purple Terrace was the private quarters in the palace in which Wang Zhaojun once lived.
[3] The beautiful face of Wang Zhaojun. The artist who drew her Portrait deliberately distorted her look because she refused to pay him money. As a result, the emperor never saw her until she was about to leave the palace.

Du Fu　　　　　　杜甫

咏怀古迹(其四)

蜀主窥吴幸三峡	蜀主窺吳幸三峽
崩年亦在永安宫	崩年亦在永安宮
翠华想像空山里	翠華想像空山裡
玉殿虚无野寺中	玉殿虛無野寺中
古庙杉松巢水鹤	古廟杉松巢水鶴
岁时伏腊走村翁	歲時伏臘走村翁
武侯祠屋常邻近	武侯祠屋常鄰近
一体君臣祭祀同	一體君臣祭祀同

Reflections on the Historical Sites (Fourth of Five Poems)

The ruler of Shu came to the
Three Gorges to invade Wu.
He died in the Yongan Palace
in which he was enthroned.
I can visualize the emerald banners,
still here in this quiet mountain.
I can also vaguely see his former
palace in the deserted temple.
By the ancient temple, cranes
build their nests on firs or pines.
When the time comes, village old men
come to make annual offerings.
The temple of Zhuge Liang
is quite close to that of Liu Bei.
So both the ruler and the minister
receive sacrifices at the same time.

杜甫　詠懷古跡(其四)

蜀△主△[1]
shǔ zhǔ
ruler of Shu

窺○吳○
kuī wú
invaded Wu

幸△三○峽△
xìng shān xiá
came to the Three Gorges

崩○年○
bēng nián
year of death

亦△在△
yì zài
also was in

永△安○宮●[2]
yǒng ān gōng
the Yongan Palace

翠△華○
cuì huá
imperial banner

想△像△
xiǎng xiàng
to visualize

空○山○裡△
kōng shān lǐ
in empty mountains

玉△殿△
yú diàn
Jade Palace

虛○無○
xū wú
to vaguely imagine

野△寺△中●
yě sì zhōng
in a deserted temple

古△廟△
gǔ miào
ancient shrine

杉○松○
shān sōng
firs and pines

巢○水△鶴△
cháo shuǐ hè
cranes to build nests

歲△時○
suì shí
annual

伏△臘△
fú là
sacrificial ceremony

走△村○翁●
zǒu cūn wēng
village old men have come

武△侯○
wǔ hóu
Count of Wu

祠○屋△
cí wū
temple

常○鄰○近△[3]
cháng lín jìn
is nearby

一△體△
yī tǐ
both

君○臣○
jūn chén
ruler and his official

祭△祀△同●
jì sì tóng
receive sacrifices at the
same time

[1] Liu Bei was the ruler of Shu in the period of the Three Kingdoms.
[2] In Yongan (Forever Peace) Palace, Liu Bei declared himself the ruler of
the state of Shu. He died in the same palace in 223 B.C.
[3] Zhuge Liang's shrine was close to Liu's ancestral temple.

Du Fu 杜甫

咏怀古迹（其五）

诸葛大名垂宇宙	諸葛大名垂宇宙
宗臣遗像肃清高	宗臣遺像肅清高
三分割据纡筹策	三分割據紆籌策
万古云霄一羽毛	萬古雲霄一羽毛
伯仲之间见伊吕	伯仲之間見伊呂
指挥若定失萧曹	指揮若定失蕭曹
运移汉祚终难复	運移漢祚終難復
志决身歼军务劳	志決身殲軍務勞

Reflections on the Historical Sites (Fifth of Five Poems)

Zhuge's great name will last
as long as the universe.
His portrait invites
reverence to this morally lofty man.
He devised a complicated strategy
to share power in a tripartite standoff.
High in the clouds, he remains
immortal with his unique feather fan.
Among his equals,
one can only think of Yi and Lu.
In commanding, he surpassed
Cao Shen and Xiao He.
Circumstances changed;
the dynasty of Han could not be restored.
With tireless dedication, he gave up
his life to military affairs.

杜甫　詠懷古跡（其五）

諸○葛△ zhū gě Zhuge	大△名○ dà míng great name	垂○宇△宙△ chuí yǔ zhòu stays in the world
宗○臣○ zōng chén high officials	遺○像△ yí xiàng portrait of the dead	蕭△清○高● sù qīng gāo revere his lofty morality
三○分○¹ sān fēn divided into three	割△據△ gē jù separatist regimes	紆○籌○策△ yū chóu cè complicated strategy
萬△古△ wàn gǔ through the ages	雲○霄○ yún xiāo the skies	一△羽△毛● yī yǔ máo one feather
伯△仲△ bó zhòng equals	之○間○ zhī jiān among	見△伊○呂△² jiàn yī lǚ see Yi and Lu
指△揮○ zhǐ huī in directing	若△定△ ruò dìng so calm	失△蕭○曹●³ zhī xiāo cáo better than Xiao and Cao
運△移○ yùn yí luck changed	漢△祚△ hàn zuò Han's blessing	終○難○復△ chōng nán fù not be recovered
志△決△ zhì jué determined	身○殲○ shēn jiān gave up life	軍○務△勞● jūn wù láo dedicated to military affairs

[1] Shu, Wei, and Wu, the three kingdoms, were about equal in strength.
[2] Yi Yin and Lu Shang were both great prime ministers of the Shang and Zhou dynasties.
[3] Xiao He and Cao Shen were military strategists of the Han Dynasty.

Du Fu   杜甫

登高

风急天高猿啸哀　　　　　風急天高猿嘯哀
渚清沙白鸟飞回　　　　　渚清沙白鳥飛迴
无边落木萧萧下　　　　　無邊落木蕭蕭下
不尽长江滚滚来　　　　　不盡長江滾滾來
万里悲秋常作客　　　　　萬里悲秋常作客
百年多病独登台　　　　　百年多病獨登臺
艰难苦恨繁霜鬓　　　　　艱難苦恨繁霜鬢
潦倒新停浊酒杯　　　　　潦倒新停濁酒杯

Ascending Heights

Sharp wind, high sky,
gibbons howl sadly.
Clear islet, white sand,
birds fly in circles.
Endless trees,
leaves keep rustling and falling.
Rapid water of the long river
never ceases flowing my way.
A wanderer often feels sad in autumn
three thousand miles away.
Chronically sick year after year,
I climb up alone to the terrace.
A life with continuous hardship and bitterness
has added frost to my temples.
Down on my luck, I have just put aside
my cup of unstrained wine.

杜甫　登高

風○急△ fēng jí wind: hurrying	天○高○ tiān gāo sky: high	猿○嘯△哀● yuán xiào āi apes howling sadly
渚△清○ zhǔ qīng islet: clear	沙○白△ shā bái sand: white	鳥△飛○迴● niǎo fēi huí birds flying around
無○邊○ wú biān endless	落△木△ luò mù falling leaves	蕭○蕭○下△ xiāo xiāo xià come down rustlingly
不△盡△ bù jìn never ending	長○江○ cháng jiāng long river	滾△滾△來● gǔn gǔn lái surging ahead
萬△里△ wàn lǐ ten thousand *lis*	悲○秋○ bēi qiū feeling sad with the coming of autumn	常○作△客△ cháng zuò kè frequently travel as a guest
百△年○ bǎi nián one hundred years	多○病△ duō bìng suffering from chronic illnesses	獨△登○臺● dú dēng tái ascend heights alone
艱○難○ jiān nán hardship	苦△恨△ kǔ hèn bitterly hate	繁○霜○鬢△ fán shuāng bìn white temples
潦△倒△ liáo dǎo frustrated	新○停○ xīn tíng just stopped	濁△酒△杯● zhuó jiǔ bēi unstrained wine cup

Gao Shi　　　　　高适

送李少府贬峡中王少府贬长沙

嗟君此别意何如	嗟君此別意何如
驻马衔杯问谪居	駐馬衘杯問謫居
巫峡啼猿数行泪	巫峽啼猿數行淚
衡阳归雁几封书	衡陽歸雁幾封書
青枫江上秋帆远	青楓江上秋帆遠
白帝城边古木疏	白帝城邊古木疏
圣代即今多雨露	聖代即今多雨露
暂时分手莫踌躇	暫時分手莫躊躇

Seeing Off Prefect Li and Prefect Wang Who Are Degraded to Xiazhong and Changsha

Alas! How do you feel
to bid farewell like this?
Stay your horse for a drink
and tell me where to be banished.
At Wu Gorge, tears
will fall at the howling of monkeys;
from Hengyang, the wild geese
will bring back but a few letters.
Autumn's sail will carry you
far away on Green Maple River;
old trees will be sparse
around White Emperor Town.
Imperial favor will soon fall
like rain and dew.
Take it easy, for our separation
will not last very long.

高適　送李少府貶峽中王少府貶長沙

嗟○君○ jiē jūn alas, you	此△別△ cǐ bié at parting	意△何○如● yì hé rú think what
駐△馬△ zhù mǎ halt the horse	銜○杯○ xián bēi hold a cup	問△謫△居● wèn zhé jū ask where to be banished
巫○峽△ wū xiá Wu Gorge	啼○猿○ tí yuán howling monkeys	數△行○淚△ shù háng liè a few lines of tears
衡○陽○ héng yáng Hengyang	歸○雁△ guī yàn returning wild geese	幾△封○書● jǐ fēng shū several letters
青○楓○江△¹ qíng féng jiāng Green Maple River	上△ shàng on	秋○帆○遠△ qiū fán yuǎn autumn sail is far
白△帝△城○² bái dì chéng White Emperor Town	邊○ biān side	古△木△疏● gǔ mù shū old trees are sparse
聖△代△ shēng dài sacred dynasty	即△今○ jí jīn right now	多○雨△露△³ duō yǔ lù sufficient rain and dew
暫△時○ zhàn shí temporary	分○手△ fēn shǒu farewell	莫△躊○躇● mò chóu chú don't waver

¹ Green Maple River was in Changsha, Hunan Province.
² White Emperor Town was in Sichuan Province.
³ Rain and dew symbolize imperial favor or grace.

Han Hong 韩翃

同题仙游观

仙台初见五城楼	仙臺初見五城樓
风物凄凄宿雨收	風物淒淒宿雨收
山色遥连秦树晚	山色遙連秦樹晚
砧声近报汉宫秋	砧聲近報漢宮秋
疏松影落空坛静	疏松影落空壇靜
细草香生小洞幽	細草香生小洞幽
何用别寻方外去	何用別尋方外去
人间亦自有丹丘	人間亦自有丹丘

An Inscription for the Temple of the Immortals

I first see the Five-City Tower
at the Immortals' Terrace.
After a night rain,
the scenes appear bleak.
Mountain colors at dusk
blend in with the Qin's woods afar.
The sound of stone blocks signals
the arrival of autumn in the Han Palace.
The shadows of thin pines
fall on the quiet altar.
The fragrance of the slender grass
is felt in the serene cave.
No need to search for the
fairyland in the other world.
Here on earth, you can find
the human paradise too.

韓翃　同題仙游觀

仙○臺○	初△見△	五△城○樓●[1]
xiān tái	chū jiàn	wǔ chéng lóu
Immortal terrace	first see	Five-City Tower
風○物△	淒○淒○	宿△雨△收●
fēng wù	qī qī	sù yǔ shōu
scenes	so desolate	night rain stopped
山○色△	遙○連○	秦○樹△晚△
shān sè	yáo lián	qín shù wǎn
mountain colors	join in distance	Qin's trees are late
砧○聲○	近△報△	漢△宮○秋●
zhēn shēng	jìn bào	hàn gōng qiū
stone block sounds	declare nearby	Han Palace in autumn
疏○松○	影△落△	空○壇○靜△
shū sōng	yǐng lòu	kōng tán jìng
scattered pines	shadows fall	empty altar is quiet
細△草△	香○生○	小△洞△幽●
xì cǎo	xiāng shēng	xiǎo dòng yōu
slender grass	with fragrance	little cave is serene
何○用△	別△尋○	方○外△去△
hé yòng	bié xún	fāng wài qù
no need to	search elsewhere	beyond this world
人○間○	亦△自△有△	丹○丘●
rén jiān	yì zì yǒu	dān qiū
on earth	there is also	immortals' place

[1] Five-City Tower was the place where immortals were believed to have resided.

Huangfu Ran 皇甫冉

春思

莺啼燕语报新年　　　鶯啼燕語報新年
马邑龙堆路几千　　　馬邑龍堆路幾千
家住层城邻汉苑　　　家住層城鄰漢苑
心随明月到胡天　　　心隨明月到胡天
机中锦字论长恨　　　機中錦字論長恨
楼上花枝笑独眠　　　樓上花枝笑獨眠
为问元戎窦车骑　　　為問元戎竇車騎
何时返旆勒燕然　　　何時返旆勒燕然

Spring Thoughts

Orioles singing, swallows chattering,
another new year has arrived.
So far away from here to
Horse Town and Dragon Mound!
My home is in the capital city
adjacent to the Han Palace.
My heart follows the bright moon
all the way to the Tartar's sky.
At my loom, I weave a palindrome
to express my long grief;
upstairs, the flowery branches
jeer at me for sleeping alone.
May I ask you, General Dou,
the commander of the expedition,
when will you return in triumph and
engrave your mark on Mount Yanran?

皇甫冉　春思

鶯○啼○
yīng tí
orioles cry

燕△語△
yàn yǔ
swallows talk

報△新○年●
bào xīn nián
announcing the new year

馬△邑△[1]
mǎ yì
Horse Town

龍○堆○[2]
lóng duī
Dragon Mound

路△幾△千●
lù jǐ qiān
far away from here

家○住△
jiā zhù
home is in

層○城△
céng chéng
two-tier city

鄰○漢△苑△
lín hàn yuàn
near the Han garden

心○隨○
xīn suí
heart follows

明○月△
míng yuè
bright moon

到△胡○天●
dào hú tiān
reaching the Tartar sky

機○中○
jī zhōng
spinning wheel

錦△字△[3]
jǐng zì
brocade words

論○長○恨△
lún cháng hèn
express long regret

樓○上△
lóu shàng
upstairs

花○枝○
huā zhī
flower branches

笑△獨△眠●
xiào dú mián
jest at me for sleeping alone

為△問△
wèi wèn
may I ask

元○戎○
yún róng
commander of the expedition

竇△車○騎△
dòu chē qí
General Dou

何○時○
hén shí
when

返△旆△
fǎn pèi
return in triumph

勒△燕○然●[4]
lè yàn rán
engrave on Yanran

[1] Horse Town (Ma Yi), a military stronghold during the Han dynasty, was in what is now Shanxi Province.
[2] Dragon Mount (Long Dui), a desert in what is now Xinjiang Province.
[3] A silk brocade that contains a palindrome.
[4] Yanran Mountain was in what is now Mongolia.

Li Bai   李白

登金陵凤凰台

凤凰台上凤凰游	鳳凰臺上鳳凰遊
凤去台空江自流	鳳去臺空江自流
吴宫花草埋幽径	吳宮花草埋幽徑
晋代衣冠成古丘	晉代衣冠成古丘
三山半落青天外	三山半落青天外
二水中分白鹭洲	二水中分白鷺洲
总为浮云能蔽日	總為浮雲能蔽日
长安不见使人愁	長安不見使人愁

On the Phoenix Terrace in Jin Ling

The phoenixes used to play
on the Phoenix Terrace.
The birds are gone;
only the river keeps flowing.
Flowers and grass of the Wu Palace
were buried beneath a solitary path;
persons of nobility in the Jin Dynasty
are now the ancient dirt.
One half of the three peaks
is beyond the blue sky;
the river is divided in the middle
by the White Egret Islet.
The sun is often hidden
behind the floating clouds.
How can I not be sad
when Chang'an is out of sight?

李白　登金陵鳳凰台

鳳△凰○臺○¹	上△	鳳△凰○遊●
fèng huáng tái	shàng	fèng huáng yóu
Phoenix Terrace	on	phoenix play

鳳△去△	臺○空○	江○自△流●
fèng qù	tái kōng	jiāng zì liú
phoenix left	terrace empty	river itself flows

吳○宮○²	花○草△	埋○幽○徑△
wú guān	huā cǎi	mái yōu jìng
Wu palace	flower and grass	buried in quiet path

晉△代△	衣○冠○³	成○古△丘●
jìn dài	yī guān	chēng gǔ qiū
Jin dynasty	clothes and caps	became ancient mounds

三○山○	半△落△	青○天○外△
sān shān	bàn luò	qīng tiān wài
three mountains	half fall	beyond blue sky

二△水△	中○分○	白△鷺△洲●
èr shuǐ	zhōng fēn	bái lù zhōu
two waters	divided in middle	White Egret Island

總△為△	浮○雲○	能○蔽△日△
zǒng wèi	fú yún	néng bì rì
always	floating clouds	can hide the sun

長○安○	不△見△	使△人○愁●
cháng ān	bú jiàn	shǐ rén chóu
Chang'an	can't be seen	make people sad

¹ Phoenix Terrace: in what is now Nanjing. It was so named because the phoenixes were believed to fly over and rest above the terrace.
² Wu Palace: a palace in the state of Wu during the Epoch of the Three Kingdoms.
³ Refers to the wealthy and powerful families in the Jin Dynasty.

Li Qi　　　　李颀

送魏万之京

朝闻遊子唱離歌	朝聞遊子唱離歌
昨夜微霜初度河	昨夜微霜初度河
鸿雁不堪愁里听	鴻雁不堪愁裡聽
云山况是客中过	雲山況是客中過
关城曙色催寒近	關城曙色催寒近
御苑砧声向晚多	御苑砧聲向晚多
莫是长安行乐处	莫是長安行樂處
空令岁月易蹉跎	空令歲月易蹉跎

Seeing Wei Wan* Off to the Capital

The first frost reached
this side of the river last night.
This morning I heard you
singing the parting song.
I can't bear to hear
wild geese honking in sadness.
Moreover, there is a
cloudy mountain for you to climb.
The light at dawn in Hangu Pass
foretells that winter is near;
towards evening around the royal garden
stone-beating sounds can be clearly heard.
Don't regard Chang'an as a
playground for pleasure,
and let months and seasons slip away
with no accomplishment at all.

李頎　送魏萬之京

朝○聞○ zhāo wén hear in morning	遊○子△ yóu zǐ a traveler	唱△離○歌● chàng lí gē singing parting song
昨△夜△ zuó yè last night	微○霜○ wéi shuāng light frost	初○度△河● chū dù hé began to cross river
鴻○雁△ hón yàn wild geese	不△堪○ bù kān can't bear	愁○裡△聽△ chōu lǐ tìng to hear in sorrow
雲○山○ yún shān cloudy mountain	況△是△ kuàng shì moreover	客△中○過● kè zhōng guō you must cross
關○城○¹ guān chéng Hangu Pass	曙△色△ shū sè light at daybreak	催○寒○近△ chuī hán jìng winter is very near
御△苑△ yù yuàn imperial garden	砧○聲○² zhēn shēn stone-beating sounds	向△晚△多● xiàng wǎn duō increase towards evening
莫△是△ mò shì don't consider	長○安○ cháng ān Chang'an	行○樂△處△ xíng lè chù a place for pleasure
空○令○ hōng líng in vain let	歲△月△ suì yuè times and seasons	易△蹉○跎● yì cuō tuó to easily slip away

* Wei Wan, a poet in the Tang Dynasty.
¹ Hangu Pass, a frontier city through which Wei Wan had to pass.
² The sound of beating clothes against a flat rock top.

197

Li Shangyin　　　　　李商隐

锦瑟

锦瑟无端五十弦	錦瑟無端五十絃
一弦一柱思华年	一絃一柱思華年
庄生晓梦迷蝴蝶	莊生曉夢迷蝴蝶
望帝春心托杜鹃	望帝春心託杜鵑
沧海月明珠有泪	滄海月明珠有淚
蓝田日暖玉生烟	藍田日暖玉生煙
此情可待成追忆	此情可待成追憶
只是当时已惘然	只是當時已惘然

The Painted Zither

Is it a coincidence that the zither
has fifty strings?
Each string and each pin
reminds me of my youth.
Zhuangzi's morning dream
of a butterfly left him confused.
King Wang's lustful thoughts
relied on the help of the cuckoos.
In moonlight, pearls shed tears
under the dark blue sea.
In warm sun, jade emits smoke
on the Blue Field Hill.
These feelings could be recalled
at some later time,
but I was in a daze then,
unaware of their existence.

李商隱　錦瑟

錦△瑟△¹ jǐ sè a painted zither	無○端○ wú duān without reason	五△十△絃● wǔ shí xián has fifty strings
一△絃○ yī xián each string	一△柱△ yī zhù each pin	思△華○年● sī huá nián remind of my youth
莊○生○² zhuāng shēng Zhuang Zhou	曉△夢△ xiǎo mèng dreaming at dawn	迷○蝴○蝶△ mí hú dié confused with a butterfly
望△帝△³ wàng dì Emperor Wang	春○心○ chūn xīn lustful thoughts	託△杜△鵑● tuō dù jiān rely on the cuckoo
滄○海△ cāng hǎi dark blue sea	月△明○ yuè míng bright moon	珠○有△淚△⁴ zhū yǒu lèi pearls shed tears
藍○田○⁵ lán tián Blue Field	日△暖△ rì nuǎn warm sun	玉△生○煙● yù shēng yān jades emit smoke
此△情○ cǐ qíng these feelings	可△待△ kě dài can wait	成○追○憶△ chéng zhuī yì to be recalled
只△是△ zhǐ shì but then	當○時○ dāng shí at the time	已△惘△然● yǐ wǎng rán already in a daze

¹ An ancient Chinese musical instrument with fifty strings.
² Zhuangzi, a philosopher who advocated Taoism, woke up from an early morning dream with a feeling of confusion: Did he himself dream of being a butterfly or did the butterfly dream of being him?
³ Wang Di, the king of an ancient kingdom in what is Sichuan today. It was said that he became a cuckoo after his death. The cuckoo cried its heart out in an attempt to bring back springtime.
⁴ It was said that pearls came from the tears of mermaids.
⁵ Lantian (Blue Field), the name of a county and a hill in Shanxi Province, is known for producing jades.

Li Shangyin   李商隐

无题

昨夜星辰昨夜风	昨夜星辰昨夜風
画楼西畔桂堂东	畫樓西畔桂堂東
身无彩凤双飞翼	身無綵鳳雙飛翼
心有灵犀一点通	心有靈犀一點通
隔座送钩春酒暖	隔座送鉤春酒暖
分曹射覆蜡灯红	分曹射覆蠟燈紅
嗟余听鼓应官去	嗟余聽鼓應官去
走马兰台类断蓬	走馬蘭臺類斷蓬

Untitled

Last night's stars,
last night's wind.
By the west of the painted tower,
to the east of Cassia Hall.
Though we did not have the
phoenix's two flying wings,
we had the *lingxi*
to connect our two hearts.
While the spring wine was warm,
we passed the hook from seat to seat.
In red candle light,
we guessed objects in groups.
Alas! I heard the sound of a drum
and had to go to the morning court.
I hurried to the Orchid Terrace
on a horse like a rootless tumbleweed

李商隱　無題

昨△夜△	星○辰○	昨△夜△風●
zuó yè	xīng chén	zuó yè fēng
last night	stars	last night wind

畫△樓○	西○畔△	桂△堂○東●
huà lóu	xī pàn	guì táng dōng
painted tower	west side	east of cassia hall

身○無○	綵△鳳△	雙△飛○翼△
shēng wú	cǎi fèng	shuāng fēi yì
body without	varicolored phoenix	twin flying wings

心○有△	靈○犀○¹	一△點△通●
xīn yǒu	lín xī	yī diǎn tōng
heart had	mental sensitivity	to connect one point

隔△座△	送△鉤○²	春○酒△暖△
gé zuò	sòng gōu	chūn jiǔ nuǎn
between seats	hook-passing	spring wine was warm

分○曹○	射△覆△³	蠟△燈○紅●
fēn cáo	shè fù	là dēng hóng
in groups	word-guessing	candle light was red

嗟○余○	聽△鼓△	應○官○去△⁴
jiē yú	tīng gǔ	yīng guān qù
I lamented at	hearing drumbeat	respond to official call

走△馬△	蘭○臺○⁵	類△斷△蓬●
zǒu mǎ	lán tái	lèi duàn péng
to ride a trot	Lan Tai	like broken tumbleweed

¹ Lingxi, a rhinoceros' horn, was believed to be very sensitive to external stimuli. Here it refers to a meeting of minds.
² A game in which a small hook was passed secretly over from seat to seat. The person who failed to guess its correct location would be imposed a drinking penalty
³ A game in which someone was asked to guess a covered object.
⁴ When a night watchman beat the drum, it was time to get ready for the morning court in the palace.
⁵ Lan Tai, or Orchid Terrace, was the building in which historical documents and books were kept.

Li Shangyin　　　　　李商隐

隋宫

紫泉宫殿锁烟霞　　　紫泉宮殿鎖煙霞
欲取芜城昨帝家　　　欲取蕪城昨帝家
玉玺不缘归日角　　　玉璽不緣歸日角
锦帆应是到天涯　　　錦帆應是到天涯
于今腐草无萤火　　　於今腐草無螢火
终古垂杨有暮鸦　　　終古垂楊有暮鴉
地下若逢陈后主　　　地下若逢陳後主
岂宜重问后庭花　　　豈宜重問後庭花

The Sui Palace

The Purple Spring Palace
is shrouded in mists and clouds.
Emperor Sui had a plan
to make Wu City his palace.
Had the imperial seal
not ended up in Li Yuan's hands,
the brocade sailboat would have taken
him to the edge of sky.
No more fireflies can be found
among the rotten weed.
At sunset, only crows perch on
the age-old weeping willows.
If you happen to see
Emperor Chen in the nether world,
try not to ask him again about
the "Song of the Courtyard Flowers."

李商隱　隋宮

紫△泉○	宮○殿△	鎖△煙○霞●
zǐ quán	gōng diàn	suǒ yān xiá
purple spring	palace	in mists and clouds

欲△取△	蕪○城△[1]	昨△帝△家●
yù qǔ	wú chéng	zuó dì jiā
wish to take	Wu City	as royal residence

玉△璽△	不△緣○	歸○日△角△[2]
yù xǐ	bù yuán	guī rì jué
imperial seal	had not	belonged to Sun's Corner

錦△帆○	應○是△	到△天○涯●
jǐn fān	yīng shì	dào tiān yá
brocade sail	would have been	to the sky's edge

於○今○	腐△草△	無○螢○火△[3]
yú jīng	fǔ cǎo	wú yíng huǒ
at present	decayed grass	without fireflies

終○古△	垂○楊○	有△暮△鴉●
zhōng gǔ	chuí yáng	yǒu mù yā
ancient	weeping willows	have evening crows

地△下△	若△逢○	陳○後△主△[4]
dì xià	ruò féng	chén hòu zhǔ
the nether world	if seeing	last monarch of Chen

豈△宜○	重○問△	後△庭○花●[5]
qǐ yí	chóng wèn	hòu tíng huā
is it fitting	to ask again about	The Courtyard Flowers

[1] Wu City or Jiangdu, in Jiangsu Province.
[2] The first emperor of the Tang Dynasty, Li Yuan, was referred to as Rijue (sun's corner) because his forehead resembled the shape of the sun.
[3] Yangdi, the last emperor of Sui Dynasty, ordered his officials to collect fireflies so that the entire valley could be seen at night.
[4] The last emperor of the Chen Dynasty, who was overthrown by Yangdi.
[5] "A Song of Courtyard Flowers" was the title of a popular song in Emperor's Chen's palace.

Li Shangyin　　　　　李商隐

无题 (其一)

来是空言去绝踪　　來是空言去絕蹤
月斜楼上五更钟　　月斜樓上五更鐘
梦为远别啼难唤　　夢為遠別啼難喚
书被催成墨未浓　　書被催成墨未濃
蜡照半笼金翡翠　　蠟照半籠金翡翠
麝薰微度绣芙蓉　　麝薰微度繡芙蓉
刘郎已恨蓬山远　　劉郎已恨蓬山遠
更隔蓬山一万重　　更隔蓬山一萬重

Untitled (1)

You never came as promised,
and left without a trace.
The moon shone obliquely on the floor
upstairs around four o'clock.
I couldn't keep hold of you in my dream
no matter how loud I cried;
I hurried to write you a letter
before the ink became thickened.
The candlelight partially illuminated
the golden kingfisher on the screen;
the musk scent was still mildly left on
the embroidered lotus quilt.
Master Liu complained that the distance
to Penglai Hill was too far.
But the distance between us is
ten thousand times farther.

李商隱　無題 (其一)

來○是△ lái shì coming to be	空○言○ kōng yán empty word	去△絕△蹤● qù jué zōng leaving with no trace
月△斜○ yuè xié slanting moon	樓○上△ lǒu shàng upstairs	五△更○鐘● wǔ gēng zhōng time: fifth watch
夢△為○ mèng wéi dreaming about	遠△別△ yuǎn bié distant parting	啼○難○喚△ tí nán huàn hard to call up by crying
書○被△ shū bèi letter was	催○成○ cuī chéng done in a hurry	墨△未△濃● mò wèi nóng ink not yet thick
蠟△照△ là zhào candle light	半△籠○ bàn lóng half coop up	金○翡△翠△ jīn fěi cuì gold kingfisher
麝△薰○ shè xūn musk fragrance	微○度△ wēi dù slightly extent	繡△芙○蓉● xiù fú róng embroidered lotus
劉○郎○[1] liú láng Master Liu	已△恨△ yǐ hèn complained	蓬○山○遠△ péng shān yuǎn Penglai too far away
更△隔△ gèng gé even further than	蓬○山○[2] péng shān Penglai	一△萬△重● yī wàn cóng a ten thousand times

[1] A reference to Liu Chen who was believed to have met a fairy in an enchanted mountain.
[2] Peng Mountain or Penglai was the name of an enchanted mountain on a fairy-tale island.

205

Li Shangyin　　　　　　李商隐

无题 (其二)

飒飒东风细雨来	颯颯東風細雨來
芙蓉塘外有轻雷	芙蓉塘外有輕雷
金蟾啮锁烧香入	金蟾齧鎖燒香入
玉虎牵丝汲井回	玉虎牽絲汲井迴
贾氏窥帘韩掾少	賈氏窺簾韓掾少
宓妃留枕魏王才	宓妃留枕魏王才
春心莫共花争发	春心莫共花爭發
一寸相思一寸灰	一寸相思一寸灰

Untitled (2)

Sa, Sa, the east wind
blows with a misty rain.
Beyond the lotus pool
a light thunder passes through.
She inserts joss sticks in
the lock-biting mouth of the golden toad
and draws water from the well by
pulling the jade tiger pulley.
Lady Jia peered behind the curtain at
Han Shou, the young assistant;
Concubine Mi left a pillow to
the talented Prince of Wei.
Don't let your spring heart
vie with the flowers in bloom,
for one inch of longing will be paid
with one inch of ash.

颯△颯△ sà sà swishing sound	東○風○ dōng fēng east wind	細△雨△來● xì yǔ lái comes a misty rain
芙○蓉○塘○ fú róng táng the lotus pool	外△ wài outside	有△輕○雷● yǒu qīng léi there is a slight thunder
金○蟾○ jīn chán golden toad censer	齧△鎖△ niè suǒ biting a lock	燒△香○入△ shāo xiāng rù insert joss sticks
玉△虎△ yù hǔ jade tiger (pulley)	牽○絲○ qiān sī pulling a rope	汲△井△迴● jí jǐng huí draw water from well repeatedly
賈○氏△[1] jiǎ shì Ms. Jia	窺○簾○ kuī lián peering behind curtain	韓△掾△少△ hán yuàn shào Assistant Official Han
宓△妃○[2] mì fēi concubine Mi	留○枕△ liú zhěn leaving a pillow to	魏△王○才● wèi wáng cái talented Prince Wei
春○心○ chūn xīn spring heart	莫△共△ mò gòng not to compete	花△爭○發△ huā zhēng fà with flowers for blooming
一△寸△ yī cùn one inch of	相○思○ xiāng sī longing	一△寸△灰● yī cùn huī one inch of ash

[1] Jia Wu, the daughter of Jia Chong, was attracted to her father's handsome assistant Han. She later married Han with her father's blessing.
[2] Alluding to Lady Zhen, a concubine of Cao Pi, the founder of the Wei Dynasty. Upon her death, he gave her personal belongings to his talented brother Cao Zhi, whom she truly loved.

Li Shangyin 李商隐

筹笔驿

猿鸟犹疑畏简书　　猿鳥猶疑畏簡書
风云常为护储胥　　風雲常為護儲胥
徒令上将挥神笔　　徒令上將揮神筆
终见降王走传车　　終見降王走傳車
管乐有才真不忝　　管樂有才真不忝
关张无命欲何如　　關張無命欲何如
他年锦里经祠庙　　他年錦里經祠廟
梁父吟成恨有余　　梁父吟成恨有餘

The Chou Bi Military Camp

Monkeys and birds are still
in awe of your bamboo order.
Winds and clouds often
shield your old fortress.
What a pity to see the commander's
magical brush brandished in vain.
The defeated ruler finally departed
on a prison cart.
You outshone Guan Zhong and Yue Yi
in talent and wisdom.
But what could you do after generals
Guan Yu and Zhang Fei were killed?
When I pass through your temple
in Jin City someday,
I will chant your poem "Liangfu"
with a lot of sadness, to be sure.

李商隱　籌筆驛

猿○鳥△ yuán niǎo apes and birds	猶○疑○ yóu yí hesitate	畏△簡△書●[1] wèi jiǎn shū for fear of bamboo order
風○雲○ fēng yún wind and clouds	常○為△ cháng wéi often serve to	護○儲○胥● hù chǔ xū protect fence
徒○令○ tú lìng acting in vain	上△將△ shàng jiàng commander-in-chief	揮○神○筆△ huī shén bǐ wave magical pen
終○見△ zhōng jiàn finally seeing	降○王○[2] xiáng wáng conquered king	走△傳△車● zǒu zhuàn jū away on a courier cart
管△樂△[3] guǎn yuè Guan and Yue	有△才○ yǒu cái to have talent	真○不△忝△ zhēn bù tiǎn really not ashamed
關○張○[4] guān zhāng Guan and Zhang	無○命△ wú mìng loss of life	欲△何○如● yù hé rú what to do?
他○年○ tā nián in the future	錦△里△ jǐn lǐ Jing Guan city	經○祠○廟△ jīng cí miào passed Zhuge's temple
梁○父△[5] liáng fù "Liang Fu"	吟○成○ yín chéng after chanting	恨△有△餘● hèn yǒu yú feeling more regret

[1] The orders from the court written on tablets of wood or bamboo.
[2] The defeated king was Liu Chan, the last ruler of the Kingdom of Shu.
[3] Guan and Yue refer to Guan Zhong, the prime minister of the state of Qi, and Yue Yi, a military strategist.
[4] Guan and Zhang refer to Guan Yu and Zhang Fei, the two generals in the Kingdom of Shu.
[5] "The Poem of Liang Fu" was composed by Zhuge Liang, in which he expressed his aspirations before he became the prime minister of Shu.

Li Shangyin　　　　　　　李商隐

无题

相见时难别亦难　　　相見時難別亦難
东风无力百花残　　　東風無力百花殘
春蚕到死丝方尽　　　春蠶到死絲方盡
蜡炬成灰泪始干　　　蠟炬成灰淚始乾
晓镜但愁云鬓改　　　曉鏡但愁雲鬢改
夜吟应觉月光寒　　　夜吟應覺月光寒
蓬莱此去无多路　　　蓬萊此去無多路
青鸟殷勤为探看　　　青鳥殷勤為探看

Untitled

It's hard to see each other
just as it is hard to part.
The east wind is weak;
all sorts of flowers have withered.
The silk won't stop
until the silkworm has died;
the melted wax won't dry
until the candle has become ashes.
Looking at the mirror at dawn,
you worry about changes in your hairdo;
when I chant poetry at night,
I feel the chill of moonlight.
From here to the Penglai mountain
isn't that far.
Blue bird, would you serve
as my diligent pathfinder?

李商隱　無題

相○見△時○	難○	別△亦△難●
xiāng jiàn shí	nán	bié yì nán
seeing each other	is hard	so is parting

東○風○	無○力△	百△花○殘●
dōng fēng	wú lì	bǎi huā cán
east wind	lack of strength	all sorts of flowers wither

春○蠶○	到△死△	絲¹方○盡△
chūn cán	dào sǐ	sī fāng jìn
spring silkworm	till death	silk then ceases

蠟△炬△²	成○灰○	淚△始△乾●
là jù	chéng huī	lèi shǐ gān
a wax candle	becomes ash	tears then dry

曉△鏡△	但△愁○	雲△鬢△改△
xiǎo jìng	dàn chóu	yún bìn gǎi
mirror at dawn	but worry	hairdo alters

夜△吟○	應○覺△	月△光○寒●
yè yín	yìng jué	yuè guāng hán
chanting at night	should feel	moonlight is cold

蓬○萊○³	此△去△	無○多○路△
péng lái	cǐ qù	wú duō lù
Penglai fairyland	from here	not very far

青○鳥△⁴	殷○勤○	為△探△看●
qīng niǎo	yīn qín	wèi tàn kān
blue bird	eager to	find out for me

¹ The Chinese character for silk is 絲, which sounds like the character 思, which means "think of" or "long for." Here, the silkworm's silk is compared to the depth of the poet's love.
² The melted wax of a guttering candle is here likened to human tears.
³ The name of a fairy mountain in a Chinese fairly tale.
⁴ A bird messenger of Fairy Godmother Xi Wangmu.

Li Shangyin　　　　　　李商隐

春雨

怅卧新春白袷衣	悵臥新春白袷衣
白门寥落意多违	白門寥落意多違
红楼隔雨相望冷	紅樓隔雨相望冷
珠箔飘灯独自归	珠箔飄燈獨自歸
远路应悲春晼晚	遠路應悲春晼晚
残宵犹得梦依稀	殘宵猶得夢依稀
玉珰缄札何由达	玉璫緘札何由達
万里云罗一雁飞	萬里雲羅一雁飛

Spring Rain

Dejectedly, I lie down in casual clothes
on this new spring day.
White Gate is dreary;
my wishes are unfulfilled.
The red chamber in the rain
looked so cold to me.
The raindrops fell on the wavering lamp
as I came back alone.
During your long journey, do you
regret the parting of spring?
Late in the night, I still hope to hold on to
your vague image in my dream.
The jade earrings and letter—
but where to send them?
Three thousand miles of clouds—
how can a wild goose fly across?

李商隱　春雨

悵△臥△ chàng wò lying dejectedly	新○春○ xīn chūn new spring	白△袷△衣● bái jiá yī white-lined garment
白△門○[1] bái mén White Gate	寥○落△ liáo luò desolate	意△多○違● yì duō wéi many wishes unfulfilled
紅○樓○[2] hóng lóu red pavilion	隔△雨△ gé yǔ between rain	相○望○冷△ xiāng wàng lěng look at each other in cold
珠○箔△[3] zhū bó screen of beads	飄○燈○ piāo dēng wavering lamp	獨△自△歸● dú zì guī return alone
遠△路△ yuǎn lù distant journey	應○悲○ yīng bēi should feel sad	春○晼△晚△ chūn wǎn wǎn spring at sunset
殘○宵○ cán xiāo night on the wane	猶○得△ yóu dé still get	夢△依○稀● mèng yī xī vague dream
玉△璫○ yù dāng jade earring	緘○札△ jiān zhá a letter	何○由○達△ hé yóu dá how to reach
萬△里△ wàn lǐ ten thousand *li*	雲○羅○ yún luó cloud nets	一△雁△飛● yī yàn fēi one wild goose flying

[1] White Gate (Baimen) was in what is now Nanjing.
[2] A general term for a residence of wealthy people. Here it refers to the house in which the poet's sweetheart used to live.
[3] A screen of beads. Here it refers to the rain drops that resemble a pearl screen.

Li Shangyin 李商隐

无题

凤尾香罗薄几重	鳳尾香羅薄幾重
碧文圆顶夜深缝	碧文圓頂夜深縫
扇裁月魄羞难掩	扇裁月魄羞難掩
车走雷声语未通	車走雷聲語未通
曾是寂寥金烬暗	曾是寂寥金燼暗
断无消息石榴红	斷無消息石榴紅
斑骓只系垂杨岸	斑騅只繫垂楊岸
何处西南任好风	何處西南任好風

Untitled

With phoenix tails sewn on it, the silk curtain
consisted of several thin layers.
She stitched the green-striped canopy
deep into the night.
The moon-shaped fan could not
hide her shyness.
The rattle of the carriage was too noisy
for me to convey my words.
How many dreary nights I sat and waited
for the candlewick to be consumed.
No news at all on this day
of red pomegranate blossoms.
For now let me tether the piebald horse
to a drooping willow
and wait for the southwest wind
to blow me to the right direction.

李商隱　無題

鳳△尾△ fèng wěi phoenix tail	香○羅○[1] xiāng luó scented net	薄△幾△重● bó jǐ cóng several thin layers
碧△文○ bì wén green stripes	圓○頂△[2] yuán dǐng round top	夜△深○縫● yè shēn féng stitched deep into the night
扇△裁○ shàn cái tailored a fan	月△魄△ yuè pò in moon shape	羞○難○掩△ xiū nán yǎn hard to cover shyness
車○走△ jū zǒu chariot running	雷○聲○ léi shēng sound of thundering	語△未△通● yǔ wèi tōng words didn't convey
曾○是△ zēng shì already to be	寂△寥○ jì liáo lonely	金○爐△暗△ jīn jìn àn candlewick dark
斷△無○ duàn wú cut off	消○息△ xiāo xī news	石△榴○紅● shí liú hóng pomegranate red
斑○騅○ bān zhuī a piebald horse	只△繫△ zhǐ jì only to be tied to	垂○楊○岸△ chuí yán àn drooping willow at the bank
何○處△ hé chù where	西○南○ xī nán southwest	任△好△風● rén hǎo fēng wait for the nice wind

[1] A curtain of thin silk with pictures of phoenix on it.
[2] The canopy of a curtain with green stripes on the top.

215

Li Shangyin 李商隐

无题 (其二)

重帷深下莫愁堂
卧后清宵细细长
神女生涯原是梦
小姑居处本无郎
风波不信菱枝弱
月露谁教桂叶香
直道相思了无益
未妨惆怅是清狂

重帷深下莫愁堂
臥後清宵細細長
神女生涯原是夢
小姑居處本無郎
風波不信菱枝弱
月露誰教桂葉香
直道相思了無益
未妨惆悵是清狂

Untitled (2)

Layers of the curtain
hang deep in her boudoir.
Lying in bed, minute by minute,
she finds the night slow and long.
The romance of the Goddess
of Wu Mountain was but a dream.
The little aunt of Blue Brook
turned out to be a spinster after all.
Winds and waves don't care how
frail are the water caltrop plants;
moon and dew heed not the
fragrance of the cassia leaves.
What's the use of confessing
my lovesickness?
I might as well let pure passion
drive me into melancholy.

李商隱　無題（其二）

重△帷○	深○下△	莫△愁○堂● [1]
chóng wéi	shēn xià	mò chóu táng
layers of curtain	hang deep	not-to-worry hall

臥△後△	清○宵○	細△細△長●
wò hòu	qīng xiāo	xì xì cháng
after lying down	clear night	lengthened minute by minute

神○女△ [2]	生○涯○	原○是△夢△
shén nǚ	shēng yá	yuán shì mèng
goddess	career	was but a dream

小△姑○ [3]	居○處△	本△無○郎●
xiǎo gū	jū chù	běn wú láng
little aunt	residence	simply no lover

風○波○	不△信△	菱○枝○弱△
fēng bō	bù xìn	líng zhī ruò
wind and wave	don't believe	water caltrop is frail

月△露△	誰○教○	桂△葉△香●
yuè lù	shuí jiāo	gui yè xiāng
moon and dew	who teaches	cassia leaves fragrant

直△道△	相○思○	了△無○益△
zhí dào	xiāng sī	liǎo wú yì
straight talk	lovesickness	useless

未△妨○	惆○悵△	是△清○狂
wèi fáng	chóu chàng	shì qīng kuáng
might as well	melancholy	be of pure passion

[1] Mo Chou—literally, *not to worry*— was a lengendary maiden. Here the private quarter refers to the boudoir of an unmarried girl.
[2] The Goddess of Wu Mountain was said to have an encounter with the emperor of the state of Chu in a dream.
[3] It refers to the girl of Blue Brook of the Sixth Dynasties, who was never married.

Liu Changqing 刘长卿

江州重别薛六柳八二员外

生涯岂料承优诏　　　生涯豈料承優詔
世事空知学醉歌　　　世事空知學醉歌
江上月明胡雁过　　　江上月明胡雁過
淮南木落楚山多　　　淮南木落楚山多
寄身且喜沧洲近　　　寄身且喜滄洲近
顾影无如白发何　　　顧影無如白髮何
今日龙钟人共弃　　　今日龍鍾人共棄
媿君犹遣慎风波　　　媿君猶遣慎風波

Bidding Farewell Again with Two Friends in Jiangzhou

At this stage of my career,
I no longer expect imperial favor.
The way human affairs are,
be content to get drunk and go singing.
In the bright moon light, the Tartar's wildgeese
fly across the river;
with leaves falling at Huai Nan,
I can see more of the Chu Mountains.
I am pleased to be near the water
during my sojourn in exile.
But it is so hard to see
white hair in the mirror!
Now that I am weak and old,
few want to associate with me.
But you, my friends, still advise me
to be cautious of winds and waves.

劉長卿　江州重別薛六柳八二員外

生○涯○ shēng yá career	豈△料△ qǐ liào why expect	承○優○詔△ chéng yōu zhào to receive imperial edict
世△事△ shì shì human affairs	空○知○ kōng zhī in vain know	學△醉△歌● xué zuì gē learn to drink and sing
江○上△ jiāng shàng on the river	月△明○ yuè míng moon bright	胡○雁△過△ hú yàn guò Tartar's geese pass
淮○南○ huái nán south of Huai River	木△落△ mù luò leaves falling	楚△山○多● chǔ shān duō see more of Chu Mountains
寄△身○ jì shēng to sojourn away	且△喜△ qiě xǐ but happy	滄○洲○近△ cāng zhōu jìn near the sea
顧△影△ gù yǐng looking at self	無○如○ wú rú nothing I can do	白△髮△何● bái fǎ hé with white hair
今△日△ jīn rì today	龍○鍾○ lóng zhōng sign of senility	人○共△棄△ rén gòng qì people leave me alone
媿△君○ kuì jūn thanking you for	猶○遣△ yóu qiǎn still sending	慎△風○波● shèn fēng bō caution of winds and waves

219

Liu Changqing 刘长卿

长沙过贾谊宅

三年谪宦此栖迟　　三年謫宦此棲遲
万古惟留楚客悲　　萬古惟留楚客悲
秋草独寻人去后　　秋草獨尋人去後
寒林空见日斜时　　寒林空見日斜時
汉文有道恩犹薄　　漢文有道恩猶薄
湘水无情吊岂知　　湘水無情弔豈知
寂寂江山摇落后　　寂寂江山搖落後
怜君何事到天涯　　憐君何事到天涯

Passing by the Place Where Jia Yi* Once Lived

For three years, you lived here
during your banishment.
For all posterity, this place brings back
the sorrow of a visitor from Chu.
When people are gone, I alone search
for any trace amidst autumn grass.
Only the slanting sun is seen
through the cold grove.
Emperor Wendi, though virtuous,
bestowed little favor upon you.
The water of Xiang was too
merciless to know your mourning.
Leaves falling, the mountain looks
so desolate, the stream so lonely.
I am puzzled at what brought you
to such a remote place!

劉長卿　長沙過賈誼宅

三○年○
sān nián
three years

謫△宦△[1]
zhé huàn
live in exile

此△棲○遲●
cǐ qī chí
this place to rest

萬△古△
wàn gǔ
through the ages

惟○留○
wéi liú
only to remain

楚△客△悲●[2]
chǔ kè bēi
sadness of a Chu guest

秋○草△
qiū cǎo
autumn grass

獨△尋○
dú xín
alone search

人○去△後△
rén qù hòu
after people all left

寒○林○
hán lín
cold woods

空○見△
kōng jiàn
only see

日△斜○時●
rì xié shí
time of sunset

漢△文○[3]
hàn wén
Emperor Han Wen

有△道△
yǒu dào
virtuous

恩○猶○薄△
ēn yóu bó
but not as gracious

湘○水△[4]
xiāng shuǐ
Hunan's water

無○情○
wú qíng
merciless

弔△豈△知●
diào qǐ zhī
how would he know your grief

寂△寂△
jì jì
solitary

江○山○
jiāng shān
rivers and mountains

搖○落△後△
yáo luò hòu
after desolation

憐○君○
lián jūn
sorry for you

何○事△
hé shì
for what reason

到△天○涯●
dào tiān yá
reach the edge of sky

---

* Jia Yi was an official in the Han Dynasty.

[1] Jia Yi was banished to Changsha, Hunan, for three years during the realm of Emperor Wendi.

[2] Refers to Qu Yuan (343—290 B.C.), the patriot poet of the state of Chu, who drowned himself in the river.

[3] Refers to Emperor Wendi of the Han Dynasty.

[4] Jia Yi wrote a poem to mourn for the death of Qu Yuan when he was crossing the Xiang River.

Liu Changqing　　　　　刘长卿

自夏口至鹦鹉洲夕望岳阳寄源中

汀洲无浪复无烟	汀洲無浪復無煙
楚客相思益渺然	楚客相思益渺然
汉口夕阳斜渡鸟	漢口夕陽斜渡鳥
洞庭秋水远连天	洞庭秋水遠連天
孤城背岭寒吹角	孤城背嶺寒吹角
独戍临江夜泊船	獨戍臨江夜泊船
贾谊上书忧汉室	賈誼上書憂漢室
长沙谪去古今怜	長沙謫去古今憐

A Sunset View of Yueyang on the Way to the Parrot Island—To a Friend

No waves nor mist near
the Parrot Island.
Here in the land of Chu,
I am especially reminded of you.
Birds fly obliquely over Hankou
under the slanting sun.
The sky merges in the distance with the
autumn water in Lake Dongting.
Below the ridges, the sound
of bugle from Yueyang is chillingly clear.
A lonely soldier is watching at the riverside
as I moor my boat at night.
Out of his concern for the House of Han,
Jia Yi submitted his royal plea.
His banishment to Changsha
has since saddened many hearts.

劉長卿　自夏口至鸚鵡洲夕望岳陽寄源中

汀○洲○[1]	無○浪△	復△無○煙●
tīng zhōu	wú làng	fù wú yān
Ting Islet	no waves	also no mist
楚△客△[2]	相○思○	益△渺△然●
chǔ kè	xiāng xī	yì miǎo rán
a Chu traveler	longing	even more endless
漢△口△[3]	夕△陽○	斜○渡△鳥△
hàn kǒu	xī yáng	xié dù niǎo
Hankou	setting sun	bird crossing obliquely
洞△庭○	秋○水△	遠△連○天●
dòng tíng	qiū shuǐ	yuǎn lián tiān
Dongting (lake)	autumn waters	join sky far away
孤○城○	背△嶺△	寒○吹○角△
gū chéng	bèi lǐng	hán chuī jiǎo
solitary city	behind ridge	blows a horn in the cold
獨△戍△	臨○江○	夜△泊△船●
dú shù	líng jiāng	yè bó chuān
single guard	facing river	mooring a boat at night
賈△誼△	上△書○	憂○漢△室△
jiǎ yì	shàng shū	yōu hàn shì
Jia Yi	submitted a plea	concerned about the House of Han
長○沙○[4]	謫△去△	古△今○憐●
chiáng shā	zhé qù	gǔ jīn lián
Changsha	to go in exile	sympathy through the ages

[1] Another name of Parrot Island.
[2] Hankou (Xiakou) is in Hubei Province.
[3] The traveler in the former state of Chu refers to the poet himself.
[4] Jia Yi was banished to Changsha in Hunan Province as a form of punishment.

Liu Yuxi 刘禹锡

西塞山怀古

王浚楼船下益州　　　王濬樓船下益州
金陵王气黯然收　　　金陵王氣黯然收
千寻铁锁沉江底　　　千尋鐵鎖沉江底
一片降幡出石头　　　一片降幡出石頭
人世几回伤往事　　　人世幾回傷往事
山形依旧枕寒流　　　山形依舊枕寒流
从今四海为家日　　　從今四海為家日
故垒萧萧芦荻秋　　　故壘蕭蕭蘆荻秋

Reflections on an Ancient Event at Mt. West Fort

As Wang Jun's towering warship
sailed eastward from Yizhou,
morale in the imperial city
suddenly was very low.
Eight thousand feet of iron chain
sank to the river bed,
while flags of surrender appeared
on the city of Stone Wall.
How often in this world
are we touched by a past event?
The mountains, as ever, pillow on
the cold, flowing river.
Henceforth, the country
is united as one nation.
The relics of old forts remain
in the midst of autumn reeds.

劉禹錫　西塞山懷古

王○濬△[1]	樓○船○	下△益△州●[2]
wáng jùn	lóu chuán	xià yī zhōu
Wang Jun	warships	get off Yizhou
金○陵○[3]	王○氣△	黯△然○收●
jīn líng	wáng qì	àn rán shōu
Jin Ling	imperial morale	in low spirit
千○尋○[4]	鐵△鎖△	沉○江○底△
qiān xún	tiě suǒ	chén jiāng dǐ
eight thousand feet	iron chains	sinking to river's bed
一△片△	降○旛○	出△石△頭●[5]
yī piàn	xiáng fān	chū shí tóu
a	white flag	put up above Stone Wall
人○世△	幾△回○	傷○往△事△
rén shì	jǐ huí	shāng wǎng shì
this world	how often	grief over past events
山○形○	依○舊△	枕△寒○流●
shān xíng	yī jiù	zhěn hán liú
mountain's shape	remains	resting on cold current
從○今○	四△海△	為○家○日△
cóng jīn	sì hǎi	wéi jiā rì
from now on	four seas	as one family
故△壘△	蕭○蕭○	蘆○荻△秋●
gù lěi	xiāo xiāo	lú dí qiū
ancient rampart	dreary	reeds in autumn

[1] Wang Jun, a prefectual governor of the Jin dynasty, was instructed by the emperor to build a towering ship big enough to accommodate two thousand people for the purpose of invading the state of Wu.

[2] Yizhou was in now Sichuan Province.

[3] Jin Ling, the capital of the state of Wu, is now Nanjing.

[4] Xun was an ancient measure of length equivalent to about eight feet.

[5] Stone Wall was in what is now Nanjing.

Liu Zhongyuan 柳宗元

登柳州城楼寄漳汀封连四州刺史

城上高楼接大荒	城上高樓接大荒
海天愁思正茫茫	海天愁思正茫茫
惊风乱飐芙蓉水	驚風亂颭芙蓉水
密雨斜侵薜荔墙	密雨斜侵薜荔牆
岭树重遮千里目	嶺樹重遮千里目
江流曲次九回肠	江流曲次九迴腸
共来百粤文身地	共來百粤文身地
犹是音书滞一乡	猶是音書滯一鄉

To Four Prefectural Governors, from the City Tower in Liuzhou*

From the lofty city tower,
I see the great wilderness.
My sorrowful thoughts
are as boundless as the sky and sea.
A sudden wind randomly stirs
the lotus pond.
A rapid rain obliquely strikes
the green vines on the wall.
Trees upon trees on the mountain ridge
shut out my distant view.
With its twists and turns,
the river looks like an ileum.
All of us came to this land
of the tattooers.
Still, it is so hard to communicate—
each in a different town.

柳宗元　登柳州城樓寄漳汀封連四州刺史

城○上△	高○樓○	接△大△荒●
chéng shàng	gāo lóu	jiē dà huāng
on the city wall	high tower	joins wilderness

海△天○	愁○思△	正△茫○茫●
hǎi tiān	chóu sì	chèng máng máng
sea and sky	sorrowful thoughts	are endless right now

驚○風○	亂△颭△	芙○蓉○水△
jīng fēng	luàn zhǎn	fú róng shuǐ
surprising wind	randomly blows	over lotus water

密△雨△	斜○侵○	薜△荔△牆●
mì yǔ	xié qīn	bì lì qiáng
dense rain	invades obliquely	climbing vine wall

嶺△樹△	重○遮○	千○里△目△
lǐng shù	chóng zhē	qiān lǐ mù
mountain trees	hide thick	distant view

江○流○	曲△次△	九△迴○腸●
jiāng liú	qǔ cì	jiǔ huí cháng
river flowing	like twisty	nine ileum

共△來○	百△粵△[1]	文○身○地△
gòng lái	bǎi yuè	wén shēn dì
come together	Yue region	land of tattooers

猶○是△	音○書○	滯△一△鄉●
yóu shì	yīn shū	zhì yī xiāng
still to be	letters	confined in one village

[*] Liuzhou was in present-day Guangxi Province.
[1] Refers to what is now Southern China.

227

Lu Lun 卢纶

晚次鄂州

云开远见汉阳城	雲開遠見漢陽城
犹是孤帆一日程	猶是孤帆一日程
估客昼眠知浪静	估客晝眠知浪靜
舟人夜语觉潮生	舟人夜語覺潮生
三湘愁鬓逢秋色	三湘愁鬢逢秋色
万里归心对月明	萬里歸心對月明
旧业已随征战尽	舊業已隨征戰盡
更堪江上鼓鼙声	更堪江上鼓鼙聲

A Night-Mooring at Ezhou*

With clouds dispersing,
Hanyang, in the distance, can be seen.
It is still one more day away
for our lonely sail.
When the water is calm,
the merchants take an afternoon nap;
in high tide, the boatmen
talk to each other at night.
In Three Xiangs, the autumn scene
reminds me of my thin temple hair.
Far, far away, the bright moon
intensifies my homesick heart.
Gone are all my possessions
with the ravages of war.
How can I bear to hear
the sound of war drums over the river?

盧綸　晚次鄂州

雲○開○ yún kāi clouds disperse	遠△見△ yuǎn jiàn see in the distance	漢△陽○城● hàn yáng chéng Han Yang City
猶○是△ yóu shì still is	孤○帆○ gū fān lone sail	一△日△程● yī rì chéng one-day journey
估○客△ gū kè merchants	晝△眠○ zhòu mián day nap	知○浪△靜△ zhī làng jìng know waves are calm
舟○人○ zhōu rén boatmen	夜△語△ yè yǔ night talk	覺△潮○生● jué cháo shēng feeling high tide
三○湘○[2] sān xiāng the Three Xiangs	愁○鬢△ chóu bìn worrisome temples	逢○秋○色△ féng qiū sè meet autumn scene
萬△里△ wàn lǐ ten thousand *li*	歸○心○ guī xīn eager to return	對△月△明● duì yuè míng face bright moon
舊△業△ jiù yè old estate	已△隨○ yǐ suí already gone with	征○戰△盡△ zhēng zhàn jìn fighting in a battle
更△堪○ gèng kān how can I bear	江○上△ jiāng shàng over the river	鼓△鼙○聲● gǔ pí shēng sound of war drums

*Ezhou: in what is now Wuchang area, Hubei Province.
[1] The Three Xiangs: three different areas in Hunan Province.

229

Qian Qi

钱起

赠阙下裴舍人

二月黄鹂飞上林　　二月黃鸝飛上林
春城紫禁晓阴阴　　春城紫禁曉陰陰
长乐钟声花外尽　　長樂鐘聲花外盡
龙池柳色雨中深　　龍池柳色雨中深
阳和不散穷途恨　　陽和不散窮途恨
霄汉长怀捧日心　　霄漢長懷捧日心
献赋十年犹未遇　　獻賦十年猶未遇
羞将白发对华簪　　羞將白髮對華簪

To Master Pei at the Palace

In the second month, the yellow orioles
fly over the imperial garden.
The Forbidden City looks dark
at dawn in spring.
The sound of bell at Long Joy Palace
dies away beyond the flowers.
By the Dragon Pool, the willows
are gloomy in the rain.
The warm sun can't drive away
the bitterness of a man in straits.
The firmament often embraces
a sun-glorifying heart.
For ten years, my written advice
has met with a deaf ear.
Too ashamed for a white-haired man
to face a gorgeous pin in the hair.

錢起　贈闕下裴舍人

二△月△ **èr yuè** the second month	黃○鸝○ **huáng lí** orioles	飛○上△林● **fēi shàng lín** fly over the imperial garden
春○城○ **chūn chéng** spring town	紫△禁△¹ **zī jìn** Purple Forbidden	曉△陰○陰● **xiǎo yīn yīn** in a somber morning
長○樂△ **cháng lè** Long Joy Palace	鐘○聲○ **zhōng shēng** sound of bell	花○外△盡△ **huā wài jìn** dies away beyond flowers
龍○池○ **lóng chí** Dragon Pool	柳△色△ **liǔ sè** willow scene	雨△中○深● **yǔ zhōng shēn** deep in the rain
陽○和○ **yáng hé** warm spring	不△散△ **bù sàn** can't break up	窮○途○恨△ **qióng tú hèn** poverty-stricken bitterness
霄○漢△ **xiāo hàn** the firmament	長○懷○ **cháng huái** always cherishes	捧△日○心●² **pěng rì xīn** sun-glorifying heart
獻△賦△ **xiàn fù** presenting verses	十△年○ **shí nián** ten years	猶○未△遇△ **yóu wèi yù** still no response
羞○將○ **xiū jiāng** ashamed to use	白△髮△ **bái fǎ** white hair	對△華○簪●³ **duì huā zān** to face a gorgeous hairpin

¹ The Forbidden City, where the emperor's family resided.
² The sun here is a metaphor for the emperor.
³ A person of nobility.

231

Qin Taoyu 秦韬玉

贫女

蓬门未识绮罗香　　蓬門未識綺羅香
拟托良媒益自伤　　擬託良媒益自傷
谁爱风流高格调　　誰愛風流高格調
共怜时世俭梳妆　　共憐時世儉梳妝
敢将十指夸针巧　　敢將十指誇鍼巧
不把双眉斗画长　　不把雙眉鬥畫長
苦恨年年压金线　　苦恨年年壓金線
为他人作嫁衣裳　　為他人作嫁衣裳

A Poor Girl*

A girl from a poor family
has never worn a fragrant silk dress.
To arrange a marriage would
induce her own self-pity.
Who would appreciate an
elegant style and noble taste?
With whom could she face
hard times in simple dress?
Without doubt, her sewing skill
is beyond compare.
She vies with no one for
the length of painted eyebrows.
With bitterness, she keeps
embroidering year after year.
For other people's wedding gowns
she must continue to sew.

秦韜玉　貧女

蓬○門○ péng mén poor family	未△識△ wèi zhì do not know	綺△羅○香● qǐ luó xiāng fragrant silk dress
擬△託△ nǐ tuō plan to request	良○媒○ liáng méi nice matchmaker	益△自△傷● yì zì shàng resulted in more self-pity
誰○愛△ shuí ài who would cherish	風○流○ fēng liú elegance	高○格△調△ gāo gé diào noble style and taste
共△憐○ gòng lián together share	時○世△ shí shì hard times	儉△梳○妝● jiǎn shū zhuāng simple dress and makeup
敢△將○ gǎn jiāng dare to let	十△指△ shí zhǐ ten fingers	誇○鍼○巧△ kuā zhēn qiǎo boast needle skill
不△把△ bù bǎ not to use	雙○眉○ shuāng méi both eyebrows	鬥△畫△長● dòu huà cháng to vie for length of painted eyebrows
苦△恨△ kǔ hèn bitterly hate	年○年○ nián nián year after year	壓△金○線△ yā jīn xiàn hold down golden thread
為△他○人○ wèi tā rén for others	作△ zuò to do	嫁△衣○裳● jià yī cháng wedding gowns

*On the surface, this poem is about a poor girl. At its deeper level, it reflects the poet's own feelings about a poor scholar, most likely himself, who has the talent but not the opportunity to be appreciated.

Shen Quanqi 沈全期

独不见

卢家少妇郁金堂　　　盧家少婦鬱金堂
海燕双栖玳瑁梁　　　海燕雙棲玳瑁梁
九月寒砧催木叶　　　九月寒砧催木葉
十年征戍忆辽阳　　　十年征戍憶遼陽
白狼河北音书断　　　白狼河北音書斷
丹凤城南秋夜长　　　丹鳳城南秋夜長
谁为含愁独不见　　　誰為含愁獨不見
更教明月照流黄　　　更教明月照流黃

Alone with No One in Sight*

The young wife of the Lu family
alone in her tulip-decorated chamber.
Petrels in pairs perch on
the hawksbill beam of her house.
In the ninth lunar month, the chilly sounds
of stone block hasten leaves falling.
For ten years, she keeps longing for
him, on military duty in Liaoyang.
No more news to the
north of the White Wolf River,
while the autumn night seems longer
south of the Red Phoenix City.
Who can see her feelings of sadness
for being alone?
Who would ask the bright moon to shine
on her yellow silk curtain?

沈全期　獨不見

盧○家○
lú jiā
the Lu family

海△燕△
hǎi yàn
petrels

九△月△
jiǔ yuè
ninth lunar month

十△年○
shí nián
ten years

白△狼○河○¹
bái láng hé
White Wolf River

丹○鳳△城○²
dān fèng chéng
Red Phoenix

誰○為△
shuí wèi
for whom

更△教○
gèng jiāo
furthermore

少△婦△
shào fù
young wife

雙○棲○
shuāng qī
both perched

寒○砧○
hán zhēn
cold stone block

征○戍△
zhēng shù
garrison on frontier

北△
běi
north

南○
nán
south

含○愁○
hán chóu
feeling sorrow

明○月△
míng yuè
bright moon

鬱△金○堂●
yù jīn táng
tulip-decorated boudoir

玳△瑁△梁●
dài mào liáng
hawksbill beam

催△木△葉△
cuī mù yé
hastened trees and leaves

憶△遼○陽●
yì liáo yáng
recalled Liao Yang

音○書○斷△
yīn shū duàn
news cut off

秋○夜△長●
qiū yè cháng
autumn night was long

獨△不△見△
dú bù jiàn
alone and no one in sight

照△流○黄●
zhào liú huáng
shone upon yellow silk curtain

* "Alone with No One in Sight" was originally the title of a poem written for singing.
¹ White Wolf River is now Daling River, in Shenyang, Liaoning Province.
² Red Phoenix City was another name for Chang'an.

Wang Wei   王维

和贾至舍人早朝大明宫之作

绛帻鸡人报晓筹	絳幘雞人報曉籌
尚衣方进翠云裘	尚衣方進翠雲裘
九天阊阖开宫殿	九天閶闔開宮殿
万国衣冠拜冕旒	萬國衣冠拜冕旒
日色才临仙掌动	日色纔臨仙掌動
香烟欲傍衮龙浮	香煙欲傍袞龍浮
朝罢须裁五色诏	朝罷須裁五色詔
佩声归向凤池头	珮聲歸向鳳池頭

In Reply to Court Official Jia Zhi's Poem "Morning Audience at Daming Palace"

The crimson-capped watchman
announces the arrival of dawn.
The wardrobe keepers
bring in emerald-cloud furs.
With all gates widely opened,
the palace is in full view.
Envoys from all nations
bow to the crown.
The aurora shines upon
the palm-shaped fan.
Fragrant incense floats
over the dragon robe.
A five-color edict must be done
right after the audience.
With pendants tinkling,
you walk back to the Phoenix Pool.

王維　和賈至舍人早朝大明宮之作

絳△幘△
jiàng zé
crimson headdress

雞○人○[1]
jī rén
cock-like person

報△曉△籌●[2]
bào xiǎo chóu
to announce dawn

尚△衣○
shàng yī
robe keepers

方○進△
fāng jìn
present

翠△雲○裘●
cuì yún qiú
emerald-cloud furs

九△天○
jiǔ tiān
nine sections

閶○闔△
chāng hé
all gates

開○宮○殿△
kāi gōng diàn
open the palace

萬△國△
wàn guó
envoys of all nations

衣○冠○
yī guán
in formal dress

拜△冕△旒●[3]
bài miǎn liú
bow to the crown

日△色△
rì sè
sunbeams

纔○臨○
cái lín
just arrive

仙○掌△動△[4]
xiān zhǎng dòng
Immortal palms move

香○煙○
xiāng yān
fragrant incense

欲△傍△
yù bàng
draws near

袞△龍○浮●
gǔn lóng fú
float over dragon robe

朝○罷△
cháo bà
after the audience

須○裁○
xū cái
must decide on

五△色△詔△
wǔ sè zhào
five-colored imperial edict

珮△聲○
péi shēng
pendants jingling

歸○向△
guī xiàng
return toward

鳳△池○頭●[5]
fèng chí tóu
Phoenix Poll

[1] A night watchman who wore a crimson cap that resembled a cockscomb.
[2] The watches of the night that corresponded to the hour of daybreak in ancient China.
[3] A crown with strings of jade beads that the emperor wore during the morning court session.
[4] A palm-shaped fan used to shield the emperor during the morning audience.
[5] Phoenix Pool: the headquarters for the cabinet of ministers in the Tang Dynasty.

Wang Wei   王维

奉和圣制从蓬莱向兴庆阁道中留春雨中春望之作应制

渭水自萦秦塞曲	渭水自縈秦塞曲
黄山旧绕汉宫斜	黃山舊繞漢宮斜
銮舆迥出千门柳	鑾輿迥出千門柳
阁道回看上苑花	閣道迴看上苑花
云里帝城双凤阙	雲裡帝城雙鳳闕
雨中春树万人家	雨中春樹萬人家
为乘阳气行时令	為乘陽氣行時令
不是宸游玩物华	不是宸遊翫物華

Responding to the Emperor's Call for Matching His Poem "Looking Down in a Spring Rain"

The Wei River coils itself around
the stronghold of Qin.
The Yellow Hill slantingly embraces
the former palace of Han.
The emperor's carriage
passes through willows upon willows.
On the high road, his majesty looks back
at the flowers in the imperial garden.
The twin phoenix towers of the capital
in the clouds stand tall;
spring trees of a thousand houses
appear verdantly in the rain.
To comply with the law of nature,
his Majesty is out to inspect in the spring.
He is not on a pleasure outing
just to enjoy the beautiful scenes.

王維　奉和聖制從蓬萊向興慶閣道中留春雨中春望
　　之作應制

渭△水△¹
wèi shuǐ
Wei River

自△縈○
zì yíng
coils itself

秦○塞△曲△
qín sài qū
around the twisty Qin
fortress

黃○山○²
huáng shān
Yellow Hill

舊△繞△
jiù rào
used to circle

漢△宮○斜●
hàn gōng xié
Han Palace obliquely

鑾○輿○
luán yú
imperial carriage

迥△出△
jiǒng chū
out for distant trip

千○門○柳△
qiān mén liǔ
pass numerous willows

閣△道△
gé dào
pavilion road

迴○看○
huí kān
turn back and look

上△苑△花●
shàng yuàn huā
flowers in imperial garden

雲○裡△
yún lǐ
in the clouds

帝△城○
dì chéng
capital city

雙○鳳△闕△
shuāng fèng què
twin-phoenix palace

雨△中○
yǔ zhōng
in the rain

春○樹△
chūn shù
spring trees

萬△人○家●
wàn rén jiā
ten thousand families

為△乘○
wèi chéng
to follow

陽○氣△
yáng qì
spring air

行○時○令△
xīng shí lìng
for seasonal inspection

不△是△
bù shì
not to be

宸○遊○
chén yóu
a pleasure trip

翫△物△華●
wàn wù huá
for enjoying splendid
scenery

¹ Wei River: a tributary of the Yellow River.
² Yellow Hill was in present-day Shanxi Province.

239

Wang Wei 王维

酬郭给事

洞门高阁霭余辉　　　　洞門高閣靄餘輝
桃李阴阴柳絮飞　　　　桃李陰陰柳絮飛
禁里疏钟官舍晚　　　　禁裡疏鐘官舍晚
省中啼鸟吏人稀　　　　省中啼鳥吏人稀
晨摇玉佩趋金殿　　　　晨搖玉珮趨金殿
夕奉天书拜琐闱　　　　夕奉天書拜瑣闈
强欲从君无那老　　　　強欲從君無那老
将因卧病解朝衣　　　　將因臥病解朝衣

Writing to Thank Counselor Guo

The setting sun shines on
the tall pavilions with arched doors.
Peach and plum trees look darker;
willow catkins fly.
A bell rings sporadically in the palace;
it is now evening time.
Birds cry in the court area;
few officials stay late.
With jade pendants swinging,
you rush to the palace at dawn;
with an imperial edict in the evening,
you bow at the palace gate.
Were it not for my old age,
I would have followed your footsteps.
Bedridden with sickness, I will have to
take off my court robe and retire.

王維　酬郭給事

洞△門○[1]
dòng mén
door after door

高○閣△
gāo gé
tall pavilion

靄△餘○輝●
ǎi yú huī
waning sunlight shines

桃○李△[2]
táo lǐ
peach and plum

陰○陰○
yīn yīn
gloomy

柳△絮△飛●
liǔ xù fēi
willow catkins fly

禁△裡△
jìn lǐ
forbidden area

疏○鐘○
shū zhōng
sparse bell

官○舍△晚△
guān shè wǎn
late in government house

省△中○[3]
shěng zhōng
in the court

啼○鳥△
tí niǎo
crying birds

吏△人○稀●
lì rén xī
very few civil officials

晨○搖○
chēn yáo
morning: swinging

玉△珮△
yù pèi
jade pendant

趨○金○殿△
qū jīn diàn
rush to the palace

夕△奉△
xī fèng
evening: attending to

天○書○
tiān shū
imperial order

拜△瑣△闈●[4]
bài suǒ wéi
bow at palace gate

強○欲△
qiáng yù
trying to

從○君○
cóng jūn
follow you

無○那△老△
wú nèi lǎo
if I were not that old

將○因○
jiāng yīn
because of

臥△病△
wò bìng
being sick in bed

解△朝○衣●
jiě cháo yī
untie court clothes

[1] A series of doors that were connected to each other.
[2] Peaches and plums—implies that Guo had a lot of disciples
[3] Refers to the administrative area in the imperial court.
[4] The gate of the palace with carved interlocked rings.

Wei Yingwu   韦应物

寄李儋元锡

去年花里逢君别	去年花裡逢君別
今日花开又一年	今日花開又一年
世事茫茫难自料	世事茫茫難自料
春愁黯黯独成眠	春愁黯黯獨成眠
身多疾病思田里	身多疾病思田裡
邑有流亡愧俸钱	邑有流亡愧俸錢
闻道欲来相问讯	聞道欲來相問訊
西楼望月几回圆	西樓望月幾回圓

To Li Dan

Last year we met and parted
among blossoming flowers.
Today, one year later,
flowers are once again in bloom.
Too changeable are the world affairs
for one to predict.
So gloomy is the spring sorrow
for me to fall asleep alone.
Physically in poor health,
I think of returning to my farmland;
seeing refugees in the city,
for my emoluments I feel ashamed.
I hear that you plan to come
visiting your friends.
At the West Tower, I will watch
how many times the moon becomes full.

韋應物　寄李儋元錫

去△年○
qù nián
last year

今○日△
jīn rì
today

世△事△
shì shì
human affairs

春○愁○
chūn chóu
spring sorrow

身○多○
shén duō
body with many

邑△有△
yì yǒu
city to have

聞○道△
wén dào
someone said

西○樓○[2]
xī lóu
west pavilion

花○裡△
huā lǐ
in the flowers

花○開○
huā kāi
in blossom

茫○茫○
máng máng
boundless

黯△黯△
àn àn
gloomy

疾△病△
jí bìng
illnesses

流○亡○[1]
liú wáng
wanderers

欲△來○
yù lái
wish to come

望△月△
wàng yuè
watching the moon

逢○君○別△
féng jūn bié
met you and parted

又△一△年●
yòu yī nián
another year

難○自△料△
nán zì liào
difficult to predict

獨△成○眠●
dú chéng mián
alone to fall asleep

思○田○裡△
sī tián lǐ
think of the field

愧△俸△錢●
kuì fèng qián
ashamed of emoluments

相○問△訊△
xiāng wèn xùn
inquire each other

幾△回○圓●
jǐ huí yuán
how often in full moon

---

[1] People forced to leave home as refugees.
[2] West Tower, also called Guanfeng Tower, in Suzhou, Jiangsu Province.

243

Wen Tingyun　　　　　　　温庭筠

利洲南渡

澹然空水对斜晖　　　澹然空水對斜暉
曲岛苍茫接翠微　　　曲島蒼茫接翠微
波上马嘶看棹去　　　波上馬嘶看棹去
柳边人歇待船归　　　柳邊人歇待船歸
数丛沙草群鸥散　　　數叢沙草群鷗散
万顷江田一鹭飞　　　萬頃江田一鷺飛
谁解乘舟寻范蠡　　　誰解乘舟尋范蠡
五湖烟水独忘机　　　五湖煙水獨忘機

Going South from Lizhou by a Ferryboat*

The wide river glistened
under the slanting sun.
The mountain mists joined
the vapor over the tortuous island.
A horse neighed as the boat
rowed away in ripples.
People rested beside the willows
waiting for the ferry to return.
Among several tufts of sand grass
a flock of gulls dispersed.
Over many acres of riverside fields,
a lone egret winged.
Who can understand the desire
to search for Fan Li on a boat?
Amid the misty waters of the five lakes,
one can forget the mundane affairs.

溫庭筠　利洲南渡

澹△然○
dàn rán
tranquil and calm

曲△島△
qū dǎo
tortuous islet

波○上△
bō shàng
above water

柳△邊○
liǔ biān
side of willow

數△叢○
shù cóng
several thickets

萬△頃△
wàn qǐng
huge area

誰○解△
shuí jiě
who understands

五△湖○[2]
wǔ hú
Five Lakes

空○水△
kōng shuǐ
wide water

蒼○茫○
cāng máng
vast expanse

馬△嘶○
mǎ sī
horse to neigh

人○歇△
rén xiē
people to rest

沙○草△
shā cǎo
sand and grass

江○田○
jiāng tián
river and field

乘○舟○
chéng zhōu
taking a boat

煙○水△
yān shuǐ
misty water

對△斜○暉●
duì xié huī
face slanting sun

接○翠△微●
jiē cuì wēi
join vapor of green mountain

看○棹△去△
kān zhào qù
seeing oar gone

待△船○歸●
dài chuán guī
waiting boat to return

群△鷗○散△
qún ōu sàn
a flock of gull breaking up

一△鷺△飛●
yī lù fēi
one egret is flying

尋○范△蠡[1]
xín fàn lǐ
to search for Fan Li

獨△忘○機●
dú wàng jī
alone to forget worldly affairs

---

* Li Zhou was in what is now Sichuan Province.
[1] Fan Li, who helped the king of Yue to defeat the kingdom of Wu, gave up a powerful position in order to enjoy life on the five lakes.
[2] The five lakes include the Tai Lake and four other lakes in the same area.

Wen Tingyun

温庭筠

苏武庙

苏武魂销汉使前　　　蘇武魂銷漢使前
古祠高树两茫然　　　古祠高樹兩茫然
云边雁断胡天月　　　雲邊雁斷胡天月
陇上羊归塞草烟　　　隴上羊歸塞草煙
回日楼台非甲帐　　　迴日樓臺非甲帳
去时冠剑是丁年　　　去時冠劍是丁年
茂陵不见封侯印　　　茂陵不見封侯印
空向秋波哭逝川　　　空向秋波哭逝川

The Temple of Su Wu

Su Wu had to be very emotional
when he saw the Han envoy.
Gazing at the ancient temple and the tall tree,
I was at a loss for what to feel.
Not a single wild goose appeared
near the clouds in the Tartar's sky.
A flock of sheep on the mound
returned amid frontier grass and mist.
He left his country as a youth
with cap and sword.
He returned home without
ceremonial canopy on the terrace.
No longer could Emperor Wudi at Maoling
bestow upon him the honor of nobility.
Looking at the stream's autumn waves,
he cried over the water of no return.

温庭筠　苏武庙

蘇△武△[1] sū wǔ Su Wu	魂○銷○ hún xiāo got emotional	漢△使△前● hàn shǐ qián in front of Han envoy
古△祠○ gǔ cí ancient shrine	高○樹△ gāo shù tall tree	兩△茫○然● liǎng máng rán both at a loss
雲○邊○ yún biān around the clouds	雁△斷△ yàn duàn wild goose disappeared	胡○天○月△ hú tiān yuè Tartar's sky and moon
隴△上△ lǒng shàng above the mound	羊○歸○ yáng guī sheep returned	塞△草△煙● sài cǎo yān frontier's grass and mists
迴○日△ huí rì returning day	樓○臺○ lóu tái pavilion and terrace	非○甲△帳△[2] fēi jiǎ zhàng saw no top canopy
去△時○ qù shí parting time	冠○劍△ guān jiàn hat and sword	是△丁○年● shì dīng nián was in his youth
茂△陵○[3] mào líng Moaling	不△見△ bù jiàn didn't see	封△侯○印△ fēng hóu yìn seal of nobility
空○向△ kōng xiàng facing in vain	秋○波○ qiū bō autumn waves	哭△逝△川● kū shì chuān cried over stream of no return

[1] Su Wu (140-60 B.C.), an emissary, was held in captivity by the Huns for nineteen years. When he was released and returned to the capital, the emperor who sent him there already died.
[2] A canopy used by Emperor Wudi of Han for ceremonial purpose.
[3] Emperor Wudi's imperial tomb, in modern Shanxi Province.

Xue Feng 薛逢

宫词

十二楼中尽晓妆　　　十二樓中盡曉妝
望仙楼上望君王　　　望仙樓上望君王
锁衔金兽连环冷　　　鎖衔金獸連環冷
水滴铜龙画漏长　　　水滴銅龍畫漏長
云鬟罢梳还对镜　　　雲鬟罷梳還對鏡
罗衣欲换更添香　　　羅衣欲換更添香
遥窥正殿廉开处　　　遙窺正殿廉開處
袍裤官人扫御床　　　袍褲官人掃御床

The Imperial Concubines

The concubines in the Twelve Pavilions
were all decked out in the early morning.
On the Immortal-Watching Tower,
they hoped for the emperor's arrival.
The gold animal knockers
with interlocked rings remained cold.
Water dripping down to the bronze dragon,
the day seemed so long.
Having combed hair to form topknots
they looked at the mirror once more.
To the thin silk raiment on the body
they added a few drops of perfume.
When the curtain was lifted,
they peeped at his majesty's chamber.
Inside, the court attendants
were making the emperor's bed.

薛逢　宮詞

十△二△樓○[1]
shí èr lóu
the Twelve Chambers

中○
zhōng
in

盡△曉△妝●
jìn xiǎo zhuāng
all in morning dress

望△仙○樓○[2]
wàng xiān lóu
Immortal-Watching Tower

上△
shàng
on

望△君○王●
wàng jūn wáng
hoped for the emperor's arrival

鎖△衘○
suǒ xián
lock holding

金○獸△
jīn shòu
golden beast

連○環○冷△
lián wán lěng
interlocked rings were cold

水△滴△
shuǐ dī
water dripping

銅○龍○
tóng lóng
copper dragon

晝△漏△長●
zhòu lòu cháng
water-clock time was long

雲○鬢△
yún jì
hair tied in a knot

罷△梳○
bà shū
finished combing

還○對△鏡△
huán duì jìng
still faced the mirror

羅○衣○
luó yī
garment of thin silk

欲△換△
yù huàn
wanted to change

更△添○香●
gèng tiān xiāng
even added more fragrance

遙○窺○
yáo kuī
peeping from a distance

正△殿△
zhèng diàn
main palace

廉○開○處△
lián kāi chù
where curtain lifted

袍○褲△
páo kù
robe trousers

官○人○
guān rén
court attendants

掃△御△床●
sǎo yù chuáng
were making the emperor's bed

[1] The Twelve Pavilions were the private quarters of the court ladies in the palace.
[2] Immortal-Watching Tower was built by Emperor Wuzhong in the Tang dynasty.

249

Yuan Zhen 元禛

遣悲怀 (三首)

谢公最小偏怜女	謝公最小偏憐女
自嫁黔娄百事乖	自嫁黔婁百事乖
顾我无衣搜荩箧	顧我無衣搜藎篋
泥他沽酒拔金钗	泥他沽酒拔金釵
野蔬充膳甘长藿	野蔬充膳甘長藿
落叶添薪仰古槐	落葉添薪仰古槐
今日俸钱过十万	今日俸錢過十萬
与君营奠复营斋	與君營奠復營齋

Elegizing My Wife: The First Poem

Of all his children, he loved
the youngest daughter the most.
Ever since you married this poor scholar,
nothing went well.
For my clothes, you ransacked
the entire wicker suitcase.
For my wine, you pulled out
your gold hairpin.
For our meal, you ate willingly
wild herbs and bean leaves.
For firewood, you waited the leaves
of the old locust tree to fall.
Now they pay me more than
a hundred thousand coins.
All I bring to you are
still vegetarian's sacrifices.

元禛　遣悲懷 （三首）

謝△公○¹
xiè gōng
Mr. Xie's

最△小△
zuì xiǎo
youngest

偏○憐○女△
piān lián nǚ
and most beloved daughter

自△嫁△
jì jià
since married to

黔○婁○²
qián lóu
this poor man

百△事△乖●
bǎi shì guāi
everything went wrong

顧△我△
gù wǒ
knowing me

無○衣○
wú yī
without clothes

搜○藎△篋△³
sōu jìn qiè
ransacked a wicker suitcase

泥○他○
ní tā
begging her

沽○酒△
gū jiǔ
to buy wine

拔△金○釵●
bá jīn chāi
pulled out a gold hairpin

野△蔬○
yě shū
wild vegetables

充○膳△
chōng shàn
as meal

甘○長○藿△⁴
gān cháng huò
willingly ate bean leaves

落△葉△
luò yè
falling leaves

添○薪○
tiān xīn
used as fuel

仰△古△槐●
yǎng gǔ huái
relied on old locust tree

今○日△
jīn rì
today

俸△錢○
fèng qián
government salary

過○十△萬△
guō shí wàn
exceeds a hundred thousand

與△君○
yǔ jūn
to offer you

營○奠△
yīng diàn
as sacrifices

復△營○齋●
fù yīng zhāi
vegetarian meal again

[1] A reference to Xie An, the prime minister of the East Jin Dynasty. Here the poet likens his father-in-law to Xie, who also loved his youngest daughter the most.
[2] Qian Lou was a poor but famous scholar during the period of the Warring States.
[3] A small chest that was made from tall weeds and grasses.
[4] A coarse food consisting of long leaves of legumes.

251

Yuan Zhen

元稹

遣悲怀 (其二)

昔日戏言身后意　　昔日戲言身後意
今朝都到眼前来　　今朝都到眼前來
衣裳已施行看尽　　衣裳已施行看盡
针线犹存未忍开　　針線猶存未忍開
尚想旧情怜婢仆　　尚想舊情憐婢僕
也曾因梦送钱财　　也曾因夢送錢財
诚知此恨人人有　　誠知此恨人人有
贫贱夫妻百事哀　　貧賤夫妻百事哀

Elegizing My Wife: The Second Poem

We once joked about what
to do after one of us died.
Today, all these have come
before my own eyes.
Your clothes have been donated
to others, with only a few left.
But your needle case I still can't bear
to open and give away.
I am kind to your maids
as you were kind to them.
Prompted by you in a dream,
I gave them my monetary gifts.
Parting at death is a sadness
felt by everyone.
To a humble and destitute couple,
each hurt is of greater pain.

元禎　遣悲懷（其二）

昔○日△
xī rì
in the past

今○朝○
jīn zhāo
today

衣○裳○¹
yī cháng
clothes

針○線△
zhēn xiàn
needle case

尚△想△
shàng xiǎng
thinking about

也△曾○
yě zēng
to have also

誠○知○
chéng zhī
truly know

貧○賤△
pín jiàn
poor and humble

戲○言○
xì yán
joked about

都○到△
dōu dào
all have fulfilled

已△施△
yǐ shī
already given away

猶○存○
yóu cún
is still kept

舊△情○
jiù qíng
old affection

因○夢△
yīn mèng
after a dream

此△恨△
cǐ hèn
this regret

夫○妻○
fū qī
couple

身○後△意△
shēn hòu yì
what to do after death

眼△前○來●
yǎn qián lái
in front of the eyes

行○看○盡△
xíng kān jìn
only a few things left

未△忍△開●
wèi rěn kāi
can't bear to open

憐○婢△僕△
lián bì pú
be kind toward servants

送△錢○財●²
sòng qián cái
given away money

人○人○有△
rén rén yǒu
everyone must have

百△事△哀●
bǎi shì āi
one hundred miserable things

---

¹ To give away all clothes to others as the poet's wife had wished.
² According to some scholars, the money here refers to paper money to be burnt for the deceased. However, it is more consistent with the spirit of the poem that it was the real money to be given to others who were in need.

Yuan Zhen 元稹

遣悲怀 (其三)

闲坐悲君亦自悲	閑坐悲君亦自悲
百年多是几多时	百年多是幾多時
邓攸无子寻知命	鄧攸無子尋知命
潘岳悼亡犹费词	潘岳悼亡猶費詞
同穴窅冥何所望	同穴窅冥何所望
他生缘会更无期	他生緣會更無期
惟将终夜长开眼	惟將終夜長開眼
报答平生未展眉	報答平生未展眉

Elegizing My Wife: The Third Poem

Sitting idle, I feel sad for you
and for myself.
A lifetime of one hundred years
is felt like a brief time.
Deng You accepted his fate
for not having a son.
Pan Yue wrote poems
to mourn his wife in vain.
For a same-grave burial—
an idea so vague to ponder.
For a reunion in next life—
a wish that may never be fulfilled.
Tonight I will keep my eyes
opened till dawn
to repay you for a lifetime
of knitting your eyebrows.

元禎　遣悲懷(其三)

閑○坐△	悲○君○	亦△自△悲●
xián zuò	bēi jūn	yì zì bēi
sitting idle	feeling sad for you	and for myself
百△年○	多○是△	幾△多○時●
bǎi nián	duō shì	jǐ duō shí
one hundred years	often to feel like	a brief time
鄧△攸○[1]	無○子△	尋○知○命△
dèng yōu	wú zǐ	xún zhī mìng
Deng You	without a son	knew his fate at once
潘○岳△[2]	悼△亡○	猶○費△詞●
pān yuè	dào wáng	yóu fèi cí
Pan Yue	mourning the death	words not helpful
同○穴△	窅△冥○	何○所△望△
tóng xué	yǎo míng	hé suǒ wàng
sharing one grave	far and deep	is with little hope
他○生○	緣○會△	更△無○期●
tā shēng	yuán huì	gèng wú qī
next life	to meet and marry	no end in sight
惟○將○	終○夜△	長○開○眼△
wéi jiāng	zhōng yè	cháng kāi yǎn
can only let	the whole night	with eyes opened
報△答△	平○生○	未△展△眉●
bào dá	píng shēng	wèi zhǎn mé
to repay	a life time	of knitted brows

[1] Deng You of the West Jin Dynasty sacrificed his son in order to save his nephew, his brother's only son, on the assumption that his wife would give birth to another son. Unfortunately, his wish had never fulfilled.

[2] Pan Yue, a poet in the Western Jin Dynasty, wrote three poems to mourn his deceased wife.

Zu Yong 祖咏

望蓟门

燕台一去客心惊	燕臺一去客心驚
萧鼓喧喧汉将营	蕭鼓喧喧漢將營
万里寒光生积雪	萬里寒光生積雪
三边曙色动危旌	三邊曙色動危旌
沙场烽火侵胡月	沙場烽火侵胡月
海畔云山拥蓟城	海畔雲山擁薊城
少小虽非投笔吏	少小雖非投筆吏
论功还欲请长缨	論功還欲請長纓

Looking at Ji Gate*

The scene from the Golden Terrace
stirs my heart.
Thunderous sounds of pipe and drum
fill the Han general's camp.
Accumulated snow chills the light
mile upon mile;
tall banners from all sides
flutter at dawn.
Beacon fires in the battlefield
overshadow the Hu moonlight.
Cloudy mountains embrace
Ji Gate at the seaside.
Though, when young, I did not
give up my pen for the army,
to fulfill my duty, I yearn to request a long rope
to tie a captive's hands.

祖詠　望薊門

燕○臺○[1] yān táo Yan terrace	一△去△ yī qù once there	客△心○驚● kè xīn jīng visitor was terrified
蕭○鼓△ xiāo gǔ flute and drum	喧○喧○ xuān xuān was noisy	漢△將△營●[2] hàn jiàng yíng Han general's camp
萬△里△ wàn lǐ ten thousand *li*	寒○光○ hán guāng cold light	生○積△雪△ shēng jì xuě shone on accumulated snow
三○邊○ sān biàn three sides	曙△色△ shù sè color at daybreak	動△危○旌● dòng wéi jíng moved lofty banner
沙○場○ shā cháng battlefield	烽○火△ fēng huǒ beacon fires	侵○胡○月△[3] qīn hú yuè invaded Tartar's moon
海△畔△ hǎi pàn sea bank	雲○山○ yún shān cloudy mountain	擁△薊△城● yǒng jì chéng embraced Ji City
少△小△ shào xiǎo very young	雖○非 suī fēi although not	投○筆△吏△[4] tóu bǐ lì pen-throwing officer
論△功○ lùng gōng achieving distinction	還○欲△ hái yù still wish	請△長○纓●[5] qǐng cháng yīng to request long tassel

* Ji Gate was located in what is now northern Beijing.
[1] Yan Terrace, also called Goldern Terrace.
[2] The camp of the Tang soldiers.
[3] Refers to the non-Han nationalities living in the North.
[4] Ban Chao of the Han Dynasty threw away his pen and joined the army voluntarily to defend his country.
[5] .A long tassel, a metaphor for a military assignment, was used to tie the hands of a captive.

PART 4

Five-Character Truncated Verses

五言绝句

Bai Juyi   白居易

问刘十九

绿蚁新醅酒　　　綠螘新醅酒
红泥小火炉　　　紅泥小火爐
晚来天欲雪　　　晚來天欲雪
能饮一杯无　　　能飲一杯無

An Invitation to Liu Shijiu*

A freshly-brewed wine,
unstrained with green froths,
and a little red-clay
stove to keep warm.
After nightfall,
I expect it will snow.
Can you come over for a cup,
yes or no?

白居易　問劉十九

綠△螘△ lǜ yǐ green froths	新○醅○酒△ xīn pēi jiǔ newly unstrained wine
紅○泥○ hōng ní red mud	小△火△爐● xiǎo huǒ lú little stove with fire
晚○來○ wǎn lái after nightfall	天○欲△雪△ tiān yù xuě it may snow
能○飲△ néng yǐn can you drink	一△杯○無● yī bēi wú a cup or what?

* Bai Juyi met Liu Shijiu after he was banished to Jiangzhou.

○ = *ping* (level) tone
△ = *ze* (deflected) tone
● = rhyme (*ping* tone)
▲ = rhyme (*ze* tone)

Du Fu   杜甫

八阵图

功盖三分国   功蓋三分國
名成八阵图   名成八陣圖
江流石不转   江流石不轉
遗恨失东吴   遺恨失東吳

The Eight-Battle Formations

His meritorious services surpassed
all in the three kingdoms.
His fame started from his
eight-battle formations.
In the flowing river, the stones
he laid remain unchanged.
It was an eternal regret
that his plan to annex Wu had failed.

杜甫　八陣圖

功○蓋△ gōng gài merit surpasses	三○分○國△ sān fēn guó three divided nations
名○成○ míng chéng fame established	八△陣△圖●[1] bā zhèn tú the eight-battle formations
江○流○ jiāng liú river flows	石△不△轉△ shí bù zhuǎn stones not shifted
遺○恨△ yí hèn eternal regret	失△東○吳●[2] shī dōng wú lost the Wu country

[1] A military tactic developed by Zhuge Liang, the prime minister of the Kingdom of Shu during the period of the Three Kingdoms.
[2] Liu Bei, the ruler of Shu, rejected Zhuge Liang's advice to attack Wei. Instead, he chose to attack Wu and was defeated.

Li Bai

李白

怨情

美人卷珠帘	美人捲珠簾
深坐蹙娥眉	深坐蹙娥眉
但见泪痕湿	但見淚痕溼
不知心恨谁	不知心恨誰

Repining

A pretty woman
rolls up the beaded blind.
Knitting her beautiful eyebrows,
she sits for a long while.
One can only see
her wet traces of tears
but cannot tell against whom
she in her heart repines.

李白　怨情

美△人○
měi rén
pretty woman

捲△珠○簾○
juǎn zhū lián
roll up the beaded blind

深○坐△
shēn zuò
sit for long time

蹙△娥○眉●
cù é méi
knitting the beautiful brows

但△見△
dàn jiàn
only see

淚△痕○溼△
lèi hén shī
wet traces of tears

不△知○
bù zhī
can't tell

心○恨△誰●
xīn hèn shuí
against whom she repines

Li Duan

李端

听筝

<table>
<tr><td>鸣筝金粟柱</td><td>鳴箏金粟柱</td></tr>
<tr><td>素手玉房前</td><td>素手玉房前</td></tr>
<tr><td>欲得周郎顾</td><td>欲得周郎顧</td></tr>
<tr><td>时时误拂弦</td><td>時時誤拂絃</td></tr>
</table>

Listening to the Music of Zheng

Playing the zheng
with gold-millet pegs,
She moves her fair hands
in front of the jade-framed stand.
Hoping that Master Zhou
will turn around and look,
she often flicks
the strings with a false note.

李端　聽箏

鳴○箏○[1]
míng zhēng
sound of zheng

金○粟△柱△
jīn sù zhù
gold-millet post

素△手△
sù shǒu
fair hands

玉△房○前●
yù fáng qián
in front of jade-framed stand

欲△得△
yù dé
wanting to obtain

周○郎○顧△[2]
zhōu láng gù
Zhou's turning round and look

時○時○
shí shí
often

誤△拂△絃●
wù fú xián
flicks the string incorrectly

[1] An ancient Chinese plucked stringed instrument that is similar to the zither.
[2] Master Zhou refers to Zhou Yu, the outstanding general of the state of Wu in the Epoch of the Three Kingdoms. It was said that Zhou, who was also gifted in music, would turn back and look at the performer whenever he heard a wrong note.

267

Li Pin　　　　　　　李频

渡汉江

岭外音书绝　　　嶺外音書絕
经冬复历春　　　經冬復歷春
近乡情更怯　　　近鄉情更怯
不敢问来人　　　不敢問來人

On Crossing the River Han

No news from
outside the mountain range.
Gone is winter;
spring is again here.
The closer to home
the more I feel nervous.
I dare not ask anyone
from my hometown.

李頻　渡漢江

嶺△外△[1]
lǐng wài
outside the ridge

音○書○絕△
yīng shū jué
news is cut off

經○冬○
jīng dōng
through winter

復△歷△春●
fù lì chūn
it is spring again

近△鄉○
jìn xiāng
closer to home village

情○更△怯△
qíng gèng qiē
feel more nervous

不△敢△
bù gǎn
dare not

問△來○人●
wèn lái rén
ask people from the village

[1] Refers to present-day Guangdong Province.

269

Li Shangyin   李商隐

登乐游原

向晚意不适	向晚意不適
驱车登古原	驅車登古原
夕阳无限好	夕陽無限好
只是近黄昏	只是近黃昏

Climbing Happy-Roaming Highland

Toward the evening,
I have some unpleasant thoughts.
I drive a carriage
and come up to this ancient highland.
The setting sun is
immensely beautiful,
only it will soon
be dusk.

李商隱　登樂游原

向△晚△
xiàng wǎn
toward the evening

意△不△適△
yǐ bù shì
some unpleasant thoughts

驅○車○
qū jū
drive a carriage

登○古△原●[1]
dēng gǔ yuán
ascend the ancient highland

夕△陽○
xī yáng
setting sun

無○限△好△
wú xiàn hǎo
immensely beautiful

只△是△
zhǐ shì
but then

近△黃○昏●
jìn huáng hūn
near dusk

[1] Refers to Happy-Roaming Highland (樂遊原), which was situated to the south of the capital Chang'an (present-day Xian).

Liu Changqing   刘长卿

送灵澈

苍苍竹林寺　　　蒼蒼竹林寺
杳杳钟声晚　　　杳杳鐘聲晚
荷笠带斜阳　　　荷笠帶斜陽
青山独归远　　　青山獨歸遠

Farewell to the Monk Lingche

The Bamboo Grove Temple is
deep in the woods.
From afar the sound
of the evening bell drifts in the air.
With beams of the setting sun
lingering on your lotus-leaf hat,
you are going back alone
to the distant blue mountain.

劉長卿　送靈澈

蒼○蒼○
cāng cāng
deep green

杳△杳△
yǎo yǎo
out of sight

荷△笠△
hè lì
lotus-leaf hat

青○山○
qīng shān
blue mountain

竹△林△寺△[1]
zhú lín sì
Bamboo Grove Temple

鐘○聲○晚▲
zhōng shēng wǎn
sound of evening bell

帶△斜○陽○
dài xié yáng
with slanting beams

獨△歸○遠▲
dú guī yuǎn
returning alone far away

[1] Bamboo Grove Temple was in what is now Zhenjiang, Jiangsu Province.

Liu Changqing　刘长卿

弹琴

冷冷七弦上　冷冷七弦上
静听松风寒　静聽松風寒
古调虽自爱　古調雖自愛
今人多不弹　今人多不彈

Lute Playing

Clear and crisp, it is from
the seven-stringed lute.
I listen quietly to
"Wind Through the Pines."
Old tunes are
what I love the most,
but very few
want to play them these days.

劉長卿　彈琴

冷△冷△　　　　　七△絃○上△[1]
léng léng　　　　qī xián shàng
clear and crisp　　above the seven-stringed

靜△聽○　　　　　松○風○寒●
jìng tīng　　　　sōng fēng hán
listen quietly to　"Wind through the Pines"

古△調△　　　　　雖○自△愛△
gǔ diào　　　　　suī zì ài
old tune　　　　　though I love

今○人○　　　　　多○不△彈●
jīng rén　　　　　duō bù tán
people now　　　most do not play

[1] Seven-stringed: an ancient Chinese musical instrument that resembles a lute.

275

Liu Changqing　　　　　刘长卿

送上人

孤云将野鹤　　　　孤雲將野鶴
岂向人间住　　　　豈向人間住
莫买沃洲山　　　　莫買沃洲山
时人已知处　　　　時人已知處

Seeing a Monk Off

A lone cloud
goes away with a wild crane.
How could you live
in a human world?
Don't settle on
the Wozhou Mountain:
Too familiar a place
for people these days.

劉長卿　送上人

孤○雲○　　　將○野△鶴▲
gū yún　　　jiāng yě hè
lone cloud　　and a wild crane

豈△向△　　　人○間○住▲
qǐ xiàng　　　rén jiān zhù
how could you　live in man's world

莫△買△　　　沃△洲○山○[1]
mò mǎi　　　wò zhōu shān
don't buy　　Wozhou Mountain

時○人○　　　已△知○處▲
shí rén　　　yǐ zhī chù
contemporaries　know already its location

[1] Wozhou Mountain: in what is now Xinchang County, Zhejiang Province.

277

Meng Haoran   孟浩然

宿建德江

移舟泊烟渚   移舟泊煙渚
日暮客愁新   日暮客愁新
野旷天低树   野曠天低樹
江清月近人   江清月近人

Mooring on the River at Jiande[*]

I steer and moor
my boat by a misty islet.
At dusk,
my anxiety sets in anew.
In a field that is wide open,
the sky is seen lower than trees;
on a river that is clear,
the moon appears close to me.

孟浩然　宿建德江

移○舟○
yí zhōu
steering the boat

泊△煙○渚△
bó yán zhǔ
moor at misty islet

日△暮△
rì mù
sun setting

客△愁○新●
kè chóu xīn
traveler's anxiety anew

野△曠△
yě kuàng
field: wide open

天○低○樹△
tiān dī shù
sky seen lower than trees

江○清○
jiāng qīng
river: clear

月△近△人●
yuè jìn rén
moon appears close to person

* Jiande, in Zhejiang Province, near Zhejiang River.

279

Meng Haoran

孟浩然

春晓

春眠不觉晓	春眠不覺曉
处处闻啼鸟	處處聞啼鳥
夜来风雨声	夜來風雨聲
花落知多少	花落知多少

A Spring Morning

Still in sound sleep
is this spring dawn
till birds everywhere
sing their song.
Last night, I heard the
sound of wind and rain.
I wonder how many
flowers have fallen?

孟浩然　春曉

春○眠○
chūn mián
spring sleep

不△覺△曉▲
bù jué xiǎo
unaware of dawn

處△處△
chù chù
everywhere

聞○啼○鳥▲
wén tí niǎo
hear birds chirping

夜△來○
yè lái
during the night

風○雨△聲○
fēng yǔ shēng
sound of wind and rain

花○落△
huā luò
flowers falling

知○多○少▲
zhī duō shǎo
know how many

Pei Di

裴迪

送崔九

归山深浅去　　　　歸山深淺去
须尽丘壑美　　　　須盡丘壑美
莫学武陵人　　　　莫學武陵人
暂游桃源里　　　　暫遊桃源裡

Farewell to Cui Jiu

Wherever you retire
in the mountain: deep or near,
fully enjoy the beauty
of hills and ravines.
Don't be like the
fisherman from Wuling,
who stayed only briefly
in the Peach Flower Spring.

裴迪　送崔九

歸○山○ guī shān retiring to mountain	深○淺△去△ shēn qiǎn qù be it deep or shallow
須○盡△ xū jìn must enjoy fully	丘○壑△美▲ qiū hè měi beauty of hills and ravines
莫△學△ mò xué don't imitate	武△陵○人○[1] wú líng rén Wuling fisherman
暫△遊○ zàn yóu tour briefly	桃○源○裡▲ táo yuán lǐ in the Peach Flower Spring

[1] Tao Qian, one of China's great poets, describes in his "Peach Flower Spring" that a fisherman from Wuling (now Hunan Province) unknowingly entered the human paradise but did not stay long.

Wang Wei　　　　　　　　王维

鹿柴

空山不见人	空山不見人
但闻人语响	但聞人語響
返景入深林	返景入深林
复照青苔上	復照青苔上

The Deer Enclosure

In the empty mountain,
no one is seen.
Yet echoes of human voices
can be heard.
The afternoon ray
penetrates the deep wood, and
it sheds light on
the green moss.

王維　鹿柴

空○山○[1]
kōng shān
empty mountain

不△見△人○
bù jiàn rén
no one is seen

但△聞○
dàn wén
but hear

人○語△響▲
rén yǔ xiǎng
human voice echoing

返△景△[2]
fǎn jǐng
returning light

入△深○林○
rù shēn lín
enters deep wood

復△照△
fù zhào
shines also

青○苔○上▲
qīng tái shàng
on the green moss

[1] The word *empty* here implies a sense of serenity and tranquility as in Buddhism.
[2] The time of the day when the sun shines from the west.

Wang Wei 王维

竹里馆

独坐幽篁里　　　獨坐幽篁裡
弹琴复长啸　　　彈琴復長嘯
深林人不知　　　深林人不知
明月来相照　　　明月來相照

In a Retreat Among the Bamboos*

Sitting alone among
the dim bamboos,
I play my lute and
whistle long notes.
No one knows I am
deep in the woods.
Only the bright moon
shines upon me.

王維　竹里館

獨△坐△
dú zuò
sitting alone

彈○琴○
tán qín
play lute

深○林○
shēn lín
deep wood

明○月△
míng yuè
bright moon

幽○篁○裡△
yōu huáng lǐ
in a dim bamboo grove

復△長○嘯▲
fù cháng xiào
and whistle freely

人○不△知○
rén bù zhī
no one knows

來○相○照▲
lái xiāng zhào
comes to shine

[1] One of the scenic spots near the poet's Wangchuan retreat in what is now Lantian County, Shanxi Province.

Wang Wei 王维

送别

山中相送罢　　山中相送罷
日暮掩柴扉　　日暮掩柴扉
春草明年绿　　春草明年綠
王孙归不归　　王孫歸不歸

Seeing a Friend Off

In the mountain,
I bade you farewell.
I closed my wicket gate
upon return at dusk.
Grass will turn green
again next spring.
Will you be back by then,
my dear friend?

王維　送別

山○中○ shān zhōng in the mountain	相○送△罷△ xiāng sòng bà having said good-bye
日△暮△ rì mù at dusk	掩△柴○扉● yǎn chái fēi shut the wicket gate
春○草△ chūn cǎo spring grass	明○年○綠△ míng nián lǜ green next year
王○孫○[1] wáng sūn my friend	歸○不△歸● guī bù guī will you return

[1] Literally, descendents of the nobility. Here it refers to friends in general.

Wang Wei

王维

相思

红豆生南国	紅豆生南國
春来发几枝	春來發幾枝
愿君多采撷	願君多采擷
此物最相思	此物最相思

Missing Each Other

Red berries
grow in the South.
When spring arrives,
the tree branches off.
Gather as many as
you can,
for this thing can best
convey our yearning thoughts.

王維　相思

紅○豆△　　　　　生○南○國△
hóng dòu　　　shēng nán guó
red berries　　grow in the South

春○來○　　　　　發△幾△枝●
chūn lái　　　　fā jǐ zhī
spring arrives　new branches come out

願△君○　　　　　多○采△擷△
yuàn jūn　　　　duō cǎi xié
wishing you　　to gather more

此△物△　　　　　最△相○思●
cǐ wù　　　　　zuì xiāng sī
this thing　　best conveys yearning thoughts

291

Wang Wei

王维

杂诗

君自故乡来	君自故鄉來
应知故乡事	應知故鄉事
来日绮窗前	來日綺窗前
寒梅著花未	寒梅著花未

Random Thoughts

You came
from my hometown.
You must know
what had happened there.
On the day you left,
did the winter plum
by the fair window
begin to blossom?

王維　雜詩

君○自△　　　　故△鄉○來○
jūn zì　　　　　gù xiāng lái
you are from　　my hometown

應○知○　　　　故△鄉○事▲
yīng zhī　　　　gù xiāng shì
should know　　affairs in my hometown

來○日△　　　　綺△窗○前○
lái rì　　　　　qǐ chuāng qián
day you left　　by the fair window

寒○梅○　　　　著△花○未▲
hán méi　　　　zhuó huā wèi
cold plum tree　begin to blossom?

Wang Zhihuan   王之涣

登鹳雀楼

白日依山尽　　　　白日依山盡
黄河入水流　　　　黄河入水流
欲穷千里目　　　　欲窮千里目
更上一层楼　　　　更上一層樓

Climbing the Stork Tower*

The white sun sinks
behind the hills.
The Yellow River rushes
forward to the sea.
To get a view
of three hundred miles,
go up the tower
one more story of height.

王之渙　登鸛雀樓

白△日△
bái rì
white sun

依○山○盡△
yī shān jìn
descending behind mountain

黃○河○
huáng hé
Yellow River

入△水△流●
rù shuǐ liú
flowing toward sea

欲△窮○
yù qióng
wanting to exhaust

千○里△目△
qiān lǐ mù
a thousand-*li* view

更△上△
gèng shàng
climb still

一△層○樓●
yī céng lóu
one more story of the tower

* The Stork Tower, which overlooked the Yellow River, was originally built in what is now Yongji County, Shanxi Province. It was later destroyed by a flood.

Yuan Zhen 元稹

行宫

寥落古行宫　　　　寥落古行宫
宫花寂寞红　　　　宫花寂寞紅
白头宫女在　　　　白頭宫女在
闲坐说玄宗　　　　閒坐說玄宗

The Imperial Abode away from the Capital

So deserted and quiet,
the former traveling abode!
Still blooming in red
are the imperial flowers.
Court ladies,
with white hair now,
sit idly and talk
about Emperor Xuanzong.

元禎　行宮

寥○落△
liáo luò
desolate

古△行○宮●[1]
gǔ xíng gōng
old imperial abode for the traveling emperor

宮○花○
gōng huā
court flowers

寂△寞△紅●
jì mò hóng
blooming in red quietly

白△頭○
bái tóu
white head

宮○女△在△
gōng nǚ zài
court ladies remain

閒○坐△
xián zuò
sitting idly

說△玄○宗●[2]
shuō xuán zōng
talking about Emperor Xuanzong

[1] It was the abode of Emperor Xuanzong while he was on a tour in Luoyang.
[2] Emperor Xuanzong (712—755) was known for his preoccupation with his concubine Yang Gui Fei.

Zhang Hu 张祜

何满子

故国三千里　　　　故國三千里
深宫二十年　　　　深宮二十年
一声何满子　　　　一聲何滿子
双泪落君前　　　　雙淚落君前

He Man Zi

My homeland is
one thousand miles away.
For twenty years
I have lived in the forbidden palace.
Suddenly I hear the tune
of "He Man Zi."
Two drops of tears
fall in front of you.

張祐　何滿子

故△國△　　　　三○千○里△
gù guó　　　　sān qiān lǐ
homeland　　　three thousand *li*

深○宮○　　　　二△十△年●
shēn gōng　　　èr shí nián
forbidden palace　twenty years

一△聲○　　　　何○滿△子△[1]
yī shēng　　　hé mǎn zǐ
a tune of　　　"He Man Zi"

雙○淚△　　　　落△君○前●
shuāng lèi　　luò jūn qián
two drops of tear　fall in front of you

[1] The title of a song that was presumably composed by a prisoner named
He Man Zi before he was put to death.

299

Zu Yong   祖咏

终南望余雪

终南阴岭秀	終南陰嶺秀
积雪浮云端	積雪浮雲端
林表明霁色	林表明霽色
城中增暮寒	城中增暮寒

A Snow Scene at Mt. Zhongnan

What a beautiful scene is
Mt. Zhongnan's northern slope!
Its accumulated snow rises
afloat in the clouds.
Beyond the woods,
the sky is bright after the snow.
Inside the city,
it feels colder in the evening.

祖詠　終南望餘雪

終○南○[1]
zhōng nán
Mt. Zhongnan

陰○嶺△秀△
yīn lǐng xiù
north ridge beautiful

積△雪△
jí xuě
accumulated snow

浮○雲○端●
fú yún duān
afloat in the clouds

林○表△
lín biǎo
beyond forest

明○霽△色△
míng jì sé
sky after snow is clear

城○中○
chéng zhōng
in the city

增○暮△寒●
zēng mù hán
add more evening chill

[1] Mt. Zhongnan runs across several provinces, including Shanxi, Hunan, and Gansu.

301

PART 5

Seven-Character Truncated Verses

七言绝句

Bai Juyi 白居易

后宫词

泪湿罗巾梦不成　　淚濕羅巾夢不成
夜深前殿按歌声　　夜深前殿按歌聲
红颜未老恩先断　　紅顏未老恩先斷
斜倚薰笼坐到明　　斜倚薰籠坐到明

The Song of a Concubine

A dream is no longer possible;
tears wet her gauzy kerchief.
From the front palace, the beat
of music is loud and the night is deep.
A young beauty is out of favor
before she gets old.
Leaning against the fragrant basket,
she sits until daybreak.

白居易　後宮詞

淚△濕△ lèi shī tears moisten	羅○巾○ luó jīn thin handkerchief	夢△不△成● mèng bù chéng dream fails
夜△深○ yè shēn night is deep	前○殿△ qián diàn front palace	按△歌○聲● àn gē shēng singing in beat
紅○顏○ hóng yán a young beauty	未△老△ wèi lǎo not yet old	恩○先○斷△ ēn xiān duàn out of favor
斜○倚△ xié yǐ leaning on obliquely	薰○籠○ xūn lóng fragrant basket	坐△到△明● zuò dào míng sits until dawn

Cen Shen 岑参

逢入京使

故园东望路漫漫　　故園東望路漫漫
双袖龙钟泪不干　　雙袖龍鐘淚不乾
马上相逢无纸笔　　馬上相逢無紙筆
凭君传语报平安　　憑君傳語報平安

Meeting a Messenger on His Way to the Capital

Looking east to my hometown,
I see the road endlessly long.
Tears keep falling;
my sleeves are wet.
Meeting you on horseback
without paper and pen,
please tell my folks
I am safe and sound!

岑參　逢入京使

故△園○
gù yuán
my hometown

東○望△
dōng wàng
looking east to

路△漫○漫●
lù màn màn
road is very long

雙○袖△
shuāng xiù
both sleeves

龍○鐘○
lóng zhōng
be moistened

淚△不△乾●
lèi bù gān
tears keep falling

馬△上△
mǎi shàng
on horseback

相○逢○
xiāng féng
meeting each other

無○紙△筆△
wú zhǐ bǐ
without paper and pen

憑○君○
píng jūn
relying on you

傳○語△
chuán yǔ
to pass a word

報△平○安●
bào píng ān
telling I am safe and sound

307

Chen Tao　　　　　　　陈陶

陇西行

誓扫匈奴不顾身	誓掃匈奴不顧身
五千貂锦丧胡尘	五千貂錦喪胡塵
可怜无定河边骨	可憐無定河邊骨
犹是深闺梦里人	猶是深閨夢裡人

A Trip to Longxi

They swore to crush the Xiongnu
without regard to their own lives.
Five thousand of them, in marten coat,
ended their lives in the northern dust.
Have a pity on the bones
by the side of Wuding River,
for they are still alive
in the dreams of their wives

陳陶　隴西行

誓△掃△
shì sǎo
swore to sweep

匈○奴○[1]
xiōng nú
Xiongnu

不△顧△身●
bù gù shēn
with no regard for own life

五△千○
wǔ qiān
five thousand

貂○錦△
diāo jǐn
in marten coats

喪△胡○塵●
sàng hú chén
died in northern dust

可△憐○
kě lián
have a pity on

無○定△河○[2]
wú dìng hé
Wunding River

邊○骨△
biān gǔ
bones by riverside

猶○是△
yóu shì
still are

深○閨○
shēn guī
boudoir

夢△裡△人●
mèng lǐ rén
persons in the dream

[1] Xiongnu, an ancient nationality in Northern China.
[2] Wuding River runs from Inner Mongolia to the Yellow River.

Du Fu   杜甫

江南逢李龟年

歧王宅里寻常见　　　歧王宅裡尋常見
崔九堂前几度闻　　　崔九堂前幾度聞
正是江南好风景　　　正是江南好風景
落花时节又逢君　　　落花時節又逢君

Meeting Li Guinian* in Jiangnan

I often saw you in
Prince Qi's residence.
Occasionally, in the hall of Cui Jiu,
I watched your performance.
What beautiful scenery
right now in Jiangnan!
At the time of petals falling,
I run into you once again.

杜甫　江南逢李龜年

岐○王○[1]	宅△裡△	尋○常○見△
qí wáng	zhái lǐ	xún cháng jiàn
Prince Qi	palace residence	saw you often

崔○九△[2]	堂○前○	幾△度△聞●
chī jiǔ	táng qián	jǐ dù wén
Cui Jiu	front hall	listened to you several times

正△是△	江○南○	好△風○景△
zhèng shì	jiāng nán	hǎo fēng jǐng
just in time	south of river	beautiful scenery

落△花○	時○節△	又△逢○君●
luò huā	shí jié	yòu féng jūn
petals falling	season	meet you again

* Li Guinian, a well-known singer of the time.
[1] Prince Qi was the fourth son of Emperor Ruizhong.
[2] Cui Jiu, a courtier.

Du Mu 杜牧

将赴吴兴登乐游原

清时有味是无能　　　清時有味是無能
闲爱孤云静爱僧　　　閒愛孤雲靜愛僧
欲把一麾江海去　　　欲把一麾江海去
乐游原上望昭陵　　　樂遊原上望昭陵

Climbing onto Leyou Height Before Departing for Wuxing*

In peaceful times, I have the desire
but not the talent.
I like to be as idle as a lonely cloud,
and as quiet as a monk.
Before leaving for river and sea
to assume my new post,
I want to go up Leyou Height
and look at the bright tomb.

杜牧　將赴吳興登樂游原

清○時○ qīng shí peaceful times	有△味△ yǒu wèi show interest	是△無○能● shì wú néng but without talent
閒○愛△ xián ài love leisure in a	孤○雲○ gū yún lone cloud	靜△愛△僧● jìng ài sēng love quietness in a monk
欲△把△ yù bǎ about to	一△麾○ ¹ yī huī hold a banner	江○海△去△ jiāng hǎi qù bound for river and sea
樂△遊○原○ lè yóu yuán Leyou Height	上△ shàng go up	望△昭○陵● ² wàng zhāo líng looking at the bright tomb

*　Wuxing, present-day Wunxing County, Zhejiang Province, where the poet was to become a district magistrate.
[1] In ancient China, it was a common practice to carry a banner when an official was out on a tour.
[2] Zhao Ling was the tomb of Emperor Taizhong of the Tang Dynasty.

Du Mu   杜牧

赤壁

折戟沉沙铁未销　　折戟沉沙鐵未銷
自将磨洗认前朝　　自將磨洗認前朝
东风不与周郎便　　東風不與周郎便
铜雀春深锁二乔　　銅雀春深鎖二喬

Red Cliff

Buried in the sand, the twisted lance
has not been dissolved.
After rubbing and washing it,
I recognized it to be of an ancient dynasty.
If the east wind did not blow
Zhou Yu's way,
the two Qiao sisters would have been
locked in Bronze Bird for the entire spring.

杜牧　赤壁

折△戟△
zhé jǐ
twisted lance

沉○沙○
chén shā
sunk to the sand

鐵△未△銷●
tiě wèi xiāo
iron not yet melt

自△將○
zī jiāng
I have it

磨○洗△
mó xǐ
polished and washed

認△前○朝●
rén qián cháo
knew it to be ancient artifact

東○風○¹
dōng fēng
(if) east wind

不△與△
bù yǔ
didn't give

周○郎○便△²
zhōu láng biàn
Zhou Yu opportunity

銅○雀△³
tóng què
Bronze Bird

春○深○
chūn shēn
deep in spring

鎖△二△喬●⁴
suǒ èr qiáo
locked the two Qiaos

---

[1] Aided by the east wind, Zhou Yu defeated the Wu's army by setting the enemy's warships on fire in the battle fought at the Red Cliff during the Epoch of the Three Kingdoms.

[2] Master Zhou refers to Zhou Yu, the general of the State of Wu.

[3] Bronze Bird, a terrace, built by Cao Cao, who was defeated by Zhou Yu in the battle of Red Cliff.

[4] The two daughters of Qiao Xian. The younger one was married to Zhou Yu.

Du Mu 杜牧

泊秦淮

烟笼寒水月笼沙　　煙籠寒水月籠沙
夜泊秦淮近酒家　　夜泊秦淮近酒家
商女不知亡国恨　　商女不知亡國恨
隔江犹唱后庭花　　隔江猶唱後庭花

Mooring on the Qinhuai River

Mist veils the cold water;
moonlight shrouds the sand.
I moor on the Qinhuai,
near a tavern for the night.
Song girls don't know the sorrow
of a conquered nation—
they still sing, across the river,
the "Courtyard Flowers."

杜牧　泊秦淮

煙○籠○
yān lóng
mist shrouds

寒○水△
hán shuǐ
cold water

月△籠○沙●
yuè lóng shā
moonlight shrouds the sand

夜△泊△
yè bó
mooring at night

秦○淮○[1]
qín huái
on Qinhuai

近△酒△家●
jìn jiǔ jiā
near a wine-shop

商○女△
shāng nǚ
singing girls

不△知○
bù zhī
do not know

亡○國△恨△
wáng guó hèn
sorrow of a conquered nation

隔△江○
gé jiāng
across the river

猶○唱△
yóu chàng
still sing

後△庭○花●[2]
hòu tíng huā
Courtyard Flowers

[1] Qinhuai or Qinghuai River runs through what is now Nanjing City.
[2] "Courtyard Flowers" was a song composed by Chen Shu Bao, the last monarch of the Chen Dynasty.

Du Mu 杜牧

寄扬州韩绰判官

青山隐隐水迢迢　　青山隱隱水迢迢
秋尽江南草未凋　　秋盡江南草未凋
二十四桥明月夜　　二十四橋明月夜
玉人何处教吹箫　　玉人何處教吹簫

For Han Chuo, Assistant Magistrate of Yangzhou

Bluish mountains half-hidden;
the river is endlessly long.
South of the river, autumn is over,
but grass has not yet faded.
The bright moon shines on
the Twenty-Four Bridge tonight.
Are you there to teach the beauties
how to play the flute?

杜牧　寄揚州韓綽判官

青○山○
qīng shān
bluish mountain

隱△隱△
yǐn yǐn
half hidden

水△迢○迢●
shuǐ tiáo tiáo
water far away

秋○盡△
qiū jìn
autumn is over

江○南○
jiāng nán
south of the river

草△未△凋●
cǎo wèi diāo
grass not yet withered

二△十△四△¹
èr shí sì
Twenty-Four

橋○
qiáo
Bridge

明○月△夜△
míng yuè yè
bright-moon night

玉△人○
yù rén
beautiful woman

何○處△
hé chù
where

教△吹○簫●
jiào chuī xiāo
teach to play the flute

¹ The Twenty-Four Bridge was in what is now Jiangdu County, Jiangsu Province. It was believed that at one time, there were twenty four beauties playing the flute there.

Du Mu 杜牧

遣怀

落魄江湖戴酒行　　　　落魄江湖戴酒行
楚腰纤细掌中轻　　　　楚腰纖細掌中輕
十年一觉扬州梦　　　　十年一覺揚州夢
赢得青楼薄幸名　　　　赢得青樓薄倖名

A Confession

Down on my luck, I often rowed around
rivers and lakes with my wine.
I spent time with Southern girls
whose waists were slender and fine.
Awakened after ten years of
dreaming in Yangzhou,
all I have earned among green mansions
is the name of a heartless lover.

杜牧　遣懷

落△魄△ luò pò down on my luck	江○湖○ jiāng hú rivers and lakes	戴△酒△行● dài jiǔ xīng walking with wine
楚△腰○ chǔ yāo Southern girls' waist	纖○細△ xiān xì slender	掌△中○輕●[1] chǎng zhōng qīng light enough to be held in palm
十△年○ shí nián ten years	一△覺△ yī jué waking up from sleep	揚○州○夢△ yáng zhōu mèng Yangzhou dream
贏○得△ yíng dé have gained	青○樓○[2] qīng lóu green mansions	薄△倖△名● bó xìng míng reputation as a heartless person

[1] Zhao Feiyan, a favorite concubine of Emperor Cheng, was said to be so light that she could dance in a palm.
[2] Green mansions: brothels

Du Mu 杜牧

秋夕

银烛秋光冷画屏	銀燭秋光冷畫屏
轻罗小扇扑流萤	輕羅小扇撲流螢
天阶夜色凉如水	天階夜色涼如水
坐看牵牛织女星	坐看牽牛織女星

An Autumn Night

The painted screen is chilled
in silvery candle and autumn light.
With a little silken fan, she tries
to flap away the fireflies.
The moonlight in the sky
is as cool as water.
She sits and watches the stars of
the Cowherd and Weaving Maid.

杜牧　秋夕

銀○燭△ yín zhú silver candles	秋○光○ qiū quāng autumn light	冷△畫△屏● lěng huà píng chill the painted screen
輕○羅○ qīng luó thin silken	小△扇△ xiǎo shàn little fan	撲△流○螢● pū liú yíng pat at fireflies
天○階○ tiān jiē the sky	夜△色△ yè sè dim light of night	涼○如○水△ liáng rú shuǐ cold as water
坐△看△ zuò kàn sitting down and look	牽○牛○ qiān niú the star Altair	織△女△星●[1] zhī nǚ xīng star Weaving-Damsel

[1] According to the Chinese folklore, the Cowherd and the Weaving Maid meet once a year on the seventh day of the seventh month, over a bridge across the Milky Way.

Du Mu

杜牧

赠别 (一)

娉娉袅袅十三余　　娉娉嬝嬝十三餘
豆蔻梢头二月初　　豆蔻梢頭二月初
春风十里扬州路　　春風十里揚州路
卷上珠帘总不如　　卷上珠簾總不如

Parting (1)

Not quite fourteen, she is
gracefully slender,
like a nutmeg bud on a twig
in early March.
On the three-mile Yangzhou Road
caressed by the vernal wind,
who can compare with her
when all roll up their bead screens?

杜牧　贈別 (一)

娉○娉○	嫋△嫋△	十△三○餘●
pīng pīng	niǎo niǎo	shí sān yú
gracefully	slender and delicate	a little over thirteen

豆△蔻△[1]	梢○頭○	二△月△初●
dòu kòu	shāo tóu	èr yuè chū
a nutmeg bud	on a twig	early second lunar month

春○風○	十△里△	揚○州○路△
chūn fēng	shí lǐ	yáng zhōu lù
spring breeze	ten *li*	Yangzhou Road

卷△上△	珠○簾○	總△不△如●
juǎn shàng	zhū lián	zǒng bù rú
roll up	bead curtains	none as good as

[1] A nutmeg bud is often used by the Chinese to indicate the teenage years of a girl.

Du Mu 杜牧

赠别 (二)

多情却似总无情　　多情卻似總無情
唯觉樽前笑不成　　唯覺樽前笑不成
蜡烛有心还惜别　　蠟燭有心還惜別
替人垂泪到天明　　替人垂淚到天明

Parting (2)

Full of love, but
appearing not in love.
It is so hard to laugh
in front of the wine cups!
A wax candle that has a heart
feels sad to witness the parting.
Its tears keep falling down
for others until dawn.

杜牧　贈別 (二)

多○情○
duō qíng
full of love

卻△似△
què sì
yet look like

總△無○情●
zǒng wú qíng
without affection

唯○覺△
wéi jué
just feel

樽○前○
zūn qián
before wine cups

笑△不△成●
xiǎo bù chéng
unable to smile

蠟△燭△
là zhú
wax candles

有△心○[1]
yǒu xīn
to have wicks

還○惜△別△
hái xī bié
feel sad to witness the parting

替△人○
tì rén
for others

垂○淚△[2]
chuí lèi
shedding tears

到△天○明●
dào tiān míng
until dawn

---

[1] The character for the wick of a candle in Chinese is written and pronounced the same as the character for human heart.
[2] The melted wax of the candle is compared to tears.

Du Mu   杜牧

金谷园

繁华事散逐香尘   繁華事散逐香塵
流水无情草自春   流水無情草自春
日暮东风怨啼鸟   日暮東風怨啼鳥
落花犹似坠楼人   落花猶似墜樓人

Golden Valley Garden*

Extravagant things are gone
with the fragrant dust.
Unfeeling water keeps flowing;
grass turns green in spring.
At sundown in the east wind,
birds cry sorrowfully.
Fallen petals still remind me of her
jumping down from a high tower.

328

杜牧　金谷園

繁○華○
fán huá
extravagant things

事△散△
shì sàn
breaking up

逐△香○塵●
zhú xiāng chén
follow fragrant dust

流○水△
liú shuǐ
flowing water

無○情○
wú qíng
apathetic

草△自△春●
cǎo zì chūn
green grass returns itself

日△暮△
rì mù
at dusk

東○風○
dōng fēng
east wind

怨△啼○鳥△
yuàn tí niǎo
birds cry sorrowfully

落△花○
luò huā
falling petals

猶○似△
yóu sì
still look like

墜△樓○人●[1]
zhuì lóu rén
one who jumped from tower

* Golden Valley Garden, a gorgeous villa built by Shi Chong of the Jin Dynasty, was in what is now Luoyang, Henan Province.
[1] Lu Zhu (Green Pearl), Shi Chong's favorite concubine, killed herself by jumping down from a high tower to show her faithfulness to him.

Gu Kuang

顾况

宫词

玉楼天半起笙歌
风送宫嫔笑语和
月殿影开闻夜漏
水晶帘卷近秋河

玉樓天半起笙歌
風送宮嬪笑語和
月殿影開聞夜漏
水晶簾捲近秋河

A Palace Verse

From the jade tower high above,
music and song drift down.
Wind carries far
the court ladies' laughing sound.
Clouds dissipating, the moon is clear;
the drips of the water clock can be heard.
Rolling up the crystal screen, I see
the autumn Milky Way draws near.

顧況　宮詞

玉△樓○
yù lóu
a jade tower

風○送△
fēng sòng
wind escorts

月△殿△
yuè diàn
palace on moon

水△晶○
shuǐ jīng
crystal

天○半△
tiān bàn
to the skies

宮○嬪○
gōng pín
court ladies

影△開○
yǐng kāi
clouds dissipating

簾○捲△
lián juǎn
screen rolled up

起△笙○歌●
qǐ shēng gē
send out music and songs

笑△語△和●
xiào yǔ hé
blending with laughing talks

聞○夜△漏△
wén yè lòu
hear water clock at night

近△秋○河●[1]
jìn qiū hé
near autumn's Silver River

---

[1] According to Chinese folklore, the Cowherd and the Weaving Maid meet once a year on the seventh day of the seventh lunar month over a bridge (formed by magpies) across the Milky Way (Silver River).

331

Han Hong 韩翃

寒食

春城无处不飞花　　春城無處不飛花
寒食东风御柳斜　　寒食東風御柳斜
日暮汉宫传蜡烛　　日暮漢宮傳蠟燭
轻烟散入五侯家　　輕煙散入五侯家

Cold Food Day

Petals fly all over the city
in springtime.
On Cold Food Day, an east wind
tilts the imperial willows to one side.
In the Han Palace after sunset,
wax candles are handed down.
Light smoke drifts into
the mansions of five noblemen.

韓翃　寒食

春○城○　　　　無○處△　　　　不△飛○花●
chūn chéng　　wú chù　　　　bù fēi huā
city in springtime　not one place　without flying petals

寒○食△[1]　　　東○風○　　　　御△柳△斜●
hán shí　　　　dōng fēng　　yù liǔ xié
Cold Food Day　east wind　　bends palace willows

日△暮△　　　　漢△宮○　　　　傳○蠟△燭△
rì mù　　　　　hàn gōng　　chuán là zhú
at dusk　　　　Han Palace　distributes candles

輕○煙○　　　　散△入△　　　　五△侯○家●[2]
qīng yān　　　sàn rù　　　　wǔ hóu jiā
light smoke　　drifts into　　mansions of five
　　　　　　　　　　　　　　　noblemen

[1] Cold Food Day, the 105th to 107th day after the winter solstice, during
which fire was forbidden and food was to be eaten cold.
[2] The five noblemen allude to the creation of five feudal lords by Emperor
Cheng of the Han Dynasty on one single day.

Han Wo 韩偓

已凉

碧阑干外绣帘垂　　碧闌干外繡簾垂
猩色屏风画折枝　　猩色屏風畫折枝
八尺龙须方锦褥　　八尺龍鬚方錦褥
已凉天气未寒时　　已涼天氣未寒時

Cooler Weather

An embroidered curtain hangs down
behind the jade green railings.
Flowery branches are painted
on the scarlet screen.
A brocaded guilt is spread
on the eight-foot dragon-bearded mat.
The weather is cool now,
but it is not yet cold.

韓偓　已涼

碧△闌○干○	外△	繡△簾○垂●
bì lán gān	wài	xiù lián chuí
jade green railings	outside	embroidered curtain hanging
猩○色△	屏○風○	畫△折△枝●
xīng sè	píng fēng	huà zhé zhī
scarlet color	screen	painted with cut branches
八△尺△[1]	龍○鬚○[2]	方○錦△褥△
bā chǐ	lóng xū	fāng jǐn rù
eight *chi*	dragon-beard mat	and brocaded quilt
已△涼○	天○氣△	未△寒○時●
yǐ liáng	tiān qì	wèi hán shí
already cool	weather	not yet cold

[1] Chi, a unit in Chinese linear measurement, equivalent to one-third of a meter.
[2] A mat that was woven with the kind of grass called dragon beard.

335

He Zhizhang 贺之章

回乡偶书

少小离家老大回　　少小離家老大回
乡音未改鬓毛衰　　郷音未改鬢毛衰
儿童相见不相识　　兒童相見不相識
笑问客从何处来　　笑問客從何處來

Coming Home

A youngster when I left;
an old man when I return.
Unchanged is my local accent
but thinner my hair has become.
Children who greet me
do not know who I am.
They ask with a smile,
"Where do you come from?"

賀之章　回鄉偶書

少△小△ shào xiǎo very young	離○家○ lí jiā left home	老△大△回● lǎo dà huí very old returning
鄉○音○ xiāng yīn native accent	未△改△ wèi gǎi unchanged	鬢△毛○衰● bìn máo shuāi hair on temples receding
兒○童○ ér tóng children	相○見△ xiāng jiàn see me	不△相○識△ bù xiāng shí do not know me
笑△問△ xiào wèn ask smilingly	客△從○ kè cóng visitor comes	何○處△來● hé chù lái from where?

Li Bai

李白

送孟浩然之广陵

故人西辞黄鹤楼　　故人西辭黃鶴樓
烟花三月下扬州　　煙花三月下揚州
孤帆远影碧空尽　　孤帆遠影碧空盡
惟见长江天际流　　惟見長江天際流

Seeing Meng Haoran Off to Guangling

My old friend bid farewell to the West
at the Yellow Crane Tower.
He is going downstream to Yangzhou
on this April day of misty flowers.
The distant image of his lonely sail
vanishes under the emerald sky.
All I see now is the Long River
flowing to the end of the horizon.

李白　送孟浩然之廣陵

故△人○　　西○辭○　　黃○鶴△樓●[1]
gù rén　　xī cí　　huáng hè lóu
old friend　farewell to the West　Yellow Crane Tower

煙○花○　　三○月△　　下△揚○州●[2]
yān huā　　sān yuè　　xià yáng zhōu
misty flowers　third lunar month　downstream to Yangzhou

孤○帆○　　遠△影△　　碧△空○盡△
gū fān　　yuǎn yǐng　　bì kōng jìn
lonely sail　distant image　emerald sky to the limit

惟○見△　　長○江○　　天○際△流●
wéi jiàn　　cháng jiāng　　tiān jì liú
only see　Yangtze River　flowing to the horizon

[1] Yellow Crane Tower is in Hubei Province.
[2] Yangzhou (Guangling) is in Jiangsu Province.

339

Li Bai   李白

下江陵

朝辞白帝彩云间   朝辭白帝彩雲間
千里江陵一日还   千里江陵一日還
两岸猿声啼不住   兩岸猿聲啼不住
轻舟已过万重山   輕舟已過萬重山

A Voyage to Jiangling

I left Baidi early in the morning
amid rosy clouds.
A journey of one thousand *li*,
we made it to Jinagling in one day.
While the gibbons on both shores
were howling without pause,
our skiff had left
endless mountains behind.

李白　下江陵

朝○辭○ zhāo cí leaving at dawn	白△帝△[1] bái dì Baidi	彩△雲○間● cǎi yún jiān amid rosy clouds
千○里△ qiān lǐ one thousand *li*	江○陵○[2] jiāng líng Jiangling	一△日△還● yī rì huán arrived in one day
兩△岸△ liǎng àn both shores	猿○聲○ yuán shēng sound of gibbons	啼○不△住△ tí bù zhù howling repeatedly
輕○舟○ qīng zhōu light boat	已△過△ yǐ guò already passed	萬△重○山● wàn cóng shān endless mountain ranges

[1] Baidi (White Emperor Town), situated high on the hill of Baidi, is in Fengjie County, Sichuan Province.
[2] Jiangling was in present-day Jiangling County, Hubei Province.

Li Bai 李白

清平调 (一)

云想衣裳花想容　　　雲想衣裳花想容
春风拂槛露华浓　　　春風拂檻露華濃
若非群玉山头见　　　若非群玉山頭見
会向瑶台月下逢　　　會向瑤臺月下逢

Song of Purity and Peace *(1)

Clouds remind me of her dress,
flowers her face.
Spring breeze brushes the balustrade;
dewdrops are thick.
If you don't see her on the
Mountain of Jades,
you will meet her in the moonlight
on a terrace of the fairyland.

李白　清平調 (一)

雲○想△
yún xiǎng
clouds: think of

衣○裳○
yī cháng
dress

花○想△容●
huā xiǎng róng
flowers: think of face

春○風○
chūn fēng
spring wind

拂△檻△
fú jiàn
strokes balustrade

露△華○濃●
lù huā nóng
dew is thick

若△非○
ruò fēi
if not

群○玉△山○頭○[1]
qún yù shān tóu
on the Mountain of Jades

見△
jiān
to be seen

會△向△
huì xiàng
may well face

瑤○臺○[2]
yáo tái
Jade Terrace

月△下△逢●
yuè xià fēng
meet under the moon

---

* Qing and ping tunes are two of the three tunes used in poems written for music. These three poems were written to describe the beauty of Yang Gui Fei, the favorite concubine of Xuanzhong of the Tang Dynasty.
[1] According to the Chinese legend, Mountain of Jades was the fairyland where Xi Wang Mu (Queen Mother from the West) resided.
[2] A jade terrace in a fairyland.

343

Li Bai 李白

清平调 (二)

一枝红艳露凝香　　一枝紅艷露凝香
云雨巫山枉断肠　　雲雨巫山枉斷腸
借问汉宫谁得似　　借問漢宮誰得似
可怜飞燕倚新妆　　可憐飛燕倚新粧

Song of Purity and Peace (2)

She is a red peony
made more fragrant with dew.
His romantic encounter with the goddess of
Wu Mountain was but a dream after all.
May I ask who in the Han Palace
was as beautiful as she?
Not even the lovable Zhao Feiyan—
without her best makeup.

李白　清平調 (二)

一△枝○
yī zhī
a twig

紅○艷△
hóng yàn
red peony

露△凝○香●
lù níng xiāng
more fragrant with dew

雲○雨△
yún yǔ
love affairs

巫○山○[1]
wū shān
Wu Mountain

枉△斷△腸●
wǎng duàn cháng
heartbroken in vain

借△問△
jiè wèn
may I ask

漢△宮○
hàn gōng
Han Palace

誰○得△似△
shuí dé sì
who could compare

可△憐○
kě lián
lovable

飛○燕△[2]
fēi yàn
Feiyan

倚△新○粧●
yǐ xīn zhuāng
dressed in her best

[1] The king of Chu dreamt that he had a romantic encounter with the goddess of Wu Mountain.
[2] Zhao Feiyan (Flying Swallow), delicate and attractive, was the favorite concubine of Emperor Chengdi of the Han Dynasty.

Li Bai 李白

清平调 (三)

名花倾国两相欢　　名花傾國兩相歡
常得君王带笑看　　常得君王帶笑看
解释春风无限恨　　解釋春風無限恨
沉香亭北倚阑干　　沉香亭北倚闌干

Song of Purity and Peace (3)

Famous flowers and an exceptional beauty,
they are there to complement each other.
No wonder the supreme ruler
often gazes on them with laughter.
To explain why the spring wind
is so envious of them,
just look at how they lean against the
balustrade, north of the Aloeswood Pavilion.

李白　清平調 (三)

名○花○
míng huā
famous flowers

傾○國△
qīng guó
exceptional beauty

兩△相○歡●
liǎng xiāng huān
happy for each other

常○得△
cháng dé
often get

君○王○
jūn wáng
supreme ruler

帶△笑△看●
dài xiào kān
to look with smile

解△釋△
jiě shì
to explain why

春○風○
chūn fēng
spring wind

無○限△恨△
wú xiàn hèn
immensely envious

沉○香○亭○[1]
chén xiāng tíng
Aloeswood Pavilion

北△
běi
north

倚△闌○干●
yǐ lán gān
to lean against
balustrade

[1] The Chenxiang Pavilion, built with aloeswood, was in the Chang'an Palace where Emperor Xuangzong and Lady Yang Guifei of the Tang Dynasty spent time together.

Li Shangyin 李商隐

夜雨寄北

君问归期未有期　　君問歸期未有期
巴山夜雨涨秋池　　巴山夜雨漲秋池
何当共剪西窗烛　　何當共剪西窗燭
却话巴山夜雨时　　卻話巴山夜雨時

Written to My Wife in the North on a Rainy Night

You asked about my date of return,
but I don't really have one.
Here in Ba Hill, a night rain
brings the autumn pool to brim.
When can we, by the west window,
together trim the lamp wicks
and talk about how I felt
during Ba Hill's night rain?

李商隱　夜雨寄北

君○問△ jūn wèn you asked	歸○期○ guī qī date of return	未△有△期● wèi yǒu qī not yet set a date
巴○山○[1] bā shān Ba Hill	夜△雨△ yè yǔ night rain	漲△秋○池● zhǎng qiū chí to brim autumn pool
何○當○ hé dāng when	共△翦△ gòng jiǎn together trim	西○窗○燭△ xī chuāng zhú wicks by west window
卻△話△ què huà recount	巴○山○ bā shān Ba Hill	夜△雨△時● yè yǔ shí at the time of raining

[1] Hills in Sichuan.

Li Shangyin　　　　　李商隐

寄令狐中

嵩云秦树久离居　　　嵩雲秦樹久離居
双鲤迢迢一纸书　　　雙鯉迢迢一紙書
休问梁园旧宾客　　　休問梁園舊賓客
茂陵秋雨病相如　　　茂陵秋雨病相如

A Note to Official Ling Hu

We have long been separated in distance, like
Mt. Song's clouds and Qin's trees.
So far apart are we that we
need the service of two carps.
Ask no more about the former guest
in the garden of Prince Liang.
I am just like the ailing Xiangru,
who had to cope with Maoling's autumn rain.

李商隱　寄令狐中

嵩○雲○
sōng yún
clouds of Mt. Song

秦○樹△
qín shù
trees of Qin

久△離○居●
jiǔ lí jū
long separation

雙○鯉△[1]
shuāng lǐ
two carps

迢○迢○
tiáo tiáo
far away

一△紙△書●
yī zhǐ shū
one sheet of letter

休○問△
xiū wèn
don't ask

梁○園○[2]
liáng yuán
Liang Garden

舊△賓○客△
jiù bīn kè
former guests

茂△陵○[3]
mào lín
at Maoling

秋○雨△
qiu yǔ
autumn rain

病△相○如●
bìng xiāng rú
as sick as Xiangru

[1] Carp is a symbol of messenger that carries a letter or note.
[2] Liang Garden: the garden of a prince in the Han Dynasty, where talented individuals were invited to stay in residence.
[3] Maoling, in present-day Shanxi Province, was a place where Sima Xiangru once lived, supposedly to take care of his health.

Li Shangyin 李商隐

为有

为有云屏无限娇　　為有雲屏無限嬌
凤城寒尽怕春宵　　鳳城寒盡怕春宵
无端嫁得金龟婿　　無端嫁得金龜婿
辜负香衾事早朝　　辜負香衾事早朝

Spring Nights

She is so lovely
behind the mica screen.
Winter is over in the capital,
but she fears the nights of spring.
Unexpectedly she married a husband
who wears a golden tortoise robe.
But he has to let the scented quilt down
to be at the court in the early morning.

李商隱　為有

為○有△	雲○屏○	無○限△嬌●
wéi yǒu	yún píng	wú xiàn jiāo
also to have	mica screen	immensely lovely

鳳△城○	寒○盡△	怕△春○宵●
fèng chéng	hán jìn	pà chūn xiāo
capital city	winter is over	afraid of spring nights

無○端○	嫁△得△	金○龜○婿△[1]
wú duān	jià dé	jīn guī xù
for no reason	married to	golden-tortoise husband

辜○負△	香○衾○	事△早△朝●
gū fù	xiāng qīn	shì zǎo cháo
let down	scented quilt	to attend morning court

[1] One who wears a court robe that is embroidered with golden tortoise—a symbol of the rich and powerful.

Li Shangyin

李商隐

隋宫

乘兴南游不戒严
九重谁省谏书函
春风举国裁宫锦
半作障泥半作帆

乘興南遊不戒嚴
九重誰省諫書函
春風舉國裁宮錦
半作障泥半作帆

The Sui Palace

When in the mood, he left for the South
without a curfew.
In the entire palace, none dared
to submit petitions to counter his will.
The whole nation was busy cutting
brocade into pieces in spring wind.
Half were for the mudguards,
and half were used as sail-shields.

李商隱　隋宮

乘○興△	南○遊○[1]	不△戒△嚴●
chéng xìng	nán yóu	bù jiè yán
in joyful mood	toured to the South	without a curfew
九△重○	誰○省△	諫△書○函●
jiǔ chóng	shuí xǐng	jiàn shū hán
nine-section palace	who avoided	written admonition
春○風○	舉△國△	裁○宮○錦△
chūn fēng	jǔ guó	cái gōng jǐn
spring wind	whole nation	cutting out brocades
半△作△	障○泥○	半△作△帆●
bàn zuó	zhàng ní	bàn zuó fān
half for	horse mudguards	half for sails

[1] Emperor Yangdi of Sui Dynasty, known for his extravagant and ruthless style, made frequent trips to the South for personal pleasures. Two of his officials were put to death for admonishing him not to exhaust the nation's resources.

Li Shangyin   李商隐

瑶池

瑶池阿母绮窗开	瑤池阿母綺窗開
黄竹歌声动地哀	黃竹歌聲動地哀
八骏日行三万里	八駿日行三萬里
穆王何事不重来	穆王何事不重來

Jade Pool

In Jade Pool, the Grand Old Lady
opened her elegant window.
There came the song of "Yellow Bamboos"
that filled the earth with sadness.
His eight fine horses could gallop
thirty thousand *li* in a single day.
Why then did he fail to return
as he had promised?

李商隱　瑤池

瑤○池○ yáo chí Jade Pool	阿△母△[1] ā mǔ Grand Old Lady	綺△窗○開● qǐ chuāng kāi opened beautiful window
黃○竹△[2] huáng zhú Yellow Bamboo	歌○聲○ gē shēng notes of the song	動△地△哀● dòng dì āi earth-moving sadness
八△駿△ bā jùn eight fine horses	日△行○ rì xíng galloped daily	三○萬△里△ sān wàn lǐ thirty thousand *li*
穆△王○[3] mù wáng King Mu	何○事△ hé shì for what reason	不△重○來● bù cóng lái did not come back

[1] Xi Wang Mu (The Queen Mother of the West), a goddess, was said to live in a fairyland called Yao Chi (Jade Pool).

[2] "Yellow Bamboo" was a song composed by King Mu in a place called Huang Zhu (Yellow Bamboo).

[3] According to the Chinese legend, King Mu met Xi Wang Mu at Yao Chi. Although the king promised to come back in three years, on the assumption that he would become an immortal after he had eaten the magical peach, he died before he could keep his promise.

Li Shangyin   李商隐

嫦娥

云母屏风烛影深	雲母屏風燭影深
长河渐落晓星沉	長河漸落曉星沉
嫦娥应悔偷灵药	嫦娥應悔偷靈藥
碧海青天夜夜心	碧海青天夜夜心

The Goddess of the Moon

The candle light casts a deep shadow
on the mica screen.
As the Milky Way is ebbing down,
the morning stars are ready to sink.
Chang'e must have some regret
for having stolen the elixir of life,
for night after night, she faces alone
the blue sky and the emerald sea.

李商隱　嫦娥

雲○母△	屏○風○	燭△影△深●
yún mǔ	píng fēng	zhú yǐng shēn
mica	screen	deep shadow of candles

長○河○	漸△落△	曉△星○沉●
cháng hé	jiàn luò	xiǎo xīng chén
Milky Way	gradually goes down	morning stars sinking

嫦○娥○[1]	應○悔△	偷○靈○藥△
cháng é	yīng huǐ	tōu líng yào
Chang'e	surely regret	stealing an elixir of life

碧△海△	青○天○	夜△夜△心●
bì hǎi	qīng tiān	yè yè xīn
emerald sea	blue sky	lonely night after night

[1] According to Chinese legend, Chang'e, who stole and ate her husband's pill of immortality, ascended to the moon to become the Goddess of the Moon.

Li Shangyin 李商隐

贾生

宣室求贤访逐臣　　宣室求賢訪逐臣
贾生才调更无伦　　賈生才調更無倫
可怜夜半虚前席　　可憐夜半虚前席
不问苍生问鬼神　　不問蒼生問鬼神

Jia Yi, the Scholar

Looking for talent, the emperor
granted an audience to the banished officials.
Among them Jia Yi's talent and style
are without equal.
What a pity—the emperor eagerly
listened to him until midnight,
asking not about the common people,
but about ghosts and gods.

李商隱　賈生

宣○室△	求○賢○	訪△逐△臣●
xuān shì	qiú xián	fǎng zhú chén
the emperor	looking for talent	visited banished officials
賈○生○[1]	才○調△	更△無○倫●
jiǎ shēng	cái diào	gèng wú lún
Jia Yi	talent and style	without equal
可△憐○	夜△半△	虛○前○席△
kě lián	yè bàn	xú qián xí
what a pity	at midnight	listen attentively
不△問△	蒼○生○	問△鬼△神●
bù wèn	cāng shēng	wèn guǐ shén
asked not about	common people	but ghosts and gods

[1] Jia Yi, a famous statesman during the time of Han Wendi (Emperor Wen of Han), was banished for his political philosophy. He died at the age of thirty two.

Liu Zhongyong 柳中庸

征人怨

岁岁金河复玉关　　　　歲歲金河復玉關
朝朝马策与刀环　　　　朝朝馬策與刀環
三春白雪归青冢　　　　三春白雪歸青塚
万里黄河绕黑山　　　　萬里黃河繞黑山

A Soldier's Complaint

Year after year, I would be at Golden River
if not at Jade-Gate Pass.
Day in and day out, I either grasp a horse whip
or hold the hilt of a sword.
White snow of spring once again
covers the green tomb.
The ten-thousand-*li* Yellow River
coils through Black Mountain as ever.

柳中庸　征人怨

歲△歲△ suì suì year after year	金○河○[1] jīn hé Golden River	復△玉△關●[2] fù yù guān and Jade-Gate Pass
朝○朝○ zhāo zhāo day after day	馬△策△ mǎ cè a horsewhip	與△刀○環● yǔ dāo huán and hilted sword
三○春○ sān chūn three springs	白△雪△ bái xiě white snow	歸○青○塚△[3] guī qīng zhǒng return to green tomb
萬△里△ wàn lǐ ten thousand li	黃○河○ huáng hé Yellow River	繞△黑△山●[4] rào hēi shān circles around Black Mountain

[1] Golden River, also called Black River, was so named because the soil below the water was of a gold color.
[2] Yumen Pass, a gate on the Great Wall in Gansu Province.
[3] Green tomb, where Wang Zhaojun, a court lady during the Han Dynasty, was buried.
[4] Black Mountain is in Liaoning Province.

363

Liu Fangping   刘方平

月夜

更深月色半人家　　　　　更深月色半人家
北斗阑干南斗斜　　　　　北斗闌干南斗斜
今夜偏知春气暖　　　　　今夜偏知春氣暖
虫声新透绿窗纱　　　　　蟲聲新透綠窗紗

Moonlit Night

Moonlight bathes half of the house
as the night deepens.
The Big Dipper hangs horizontally;
the southern stars slope down.
On this very night, I find out
the spring air is warm.
The sound of insects begins to
penetrate my green window gauze.

劉方平　月夜

更○深○ gēng shēn night is so deep	月△色△ yuè sè moonlight	半△人○家● bàn rén jiā half of the house
北△斗△ běi dǒu the Big Dipper	闌○干○ lán gān hangs horizontally	南○斗△斜● nán dǒu xié southern stars tilt
今○夜△ jīn yè tonight	偏○知○ piān zhī become aware of	春○氣△暖△ chūn qì nuǎn spring air is warm
蟲○聲○ chōng shēng sound of insects	新○透△ xīn tòu just passes through	綠△窗○紗● lǜ chuāng shā green window gauze

Liu Fangping   刘方平

春怨

纱窗日落渐黄昏　　　紗窗日落漸黃昏
金屋无人见泪痕　　　金屋無人見淚痕
寂寞空庭春欲晚　　　寂寞空庭春欲晚
梨花满地不开门　　　梨花滿地不開門

Repining in Spring

Outside the window screen,
the sun is about to set.
In this magnificent house,
no one sees the trace of tears.
Spring is in a hurry,
but the courtyard is quiet and lonely.
The door remains closed;
the ground is covered with pear petals.

劉方平　春怨

紗○窗○	日△落△	漸△黃○昏●
shā chuāng	rì luò	jiàn huáng hūn
window screen	sunset	near dusk

金○屋△	無○人○	見△淚△痕●
jīn wū	wú rén	jiàn lèi hén
golden house	nobody	see trace of tears

寂△寞△	空○庭○	春○欲△晚△
jì mò	kōng tíng	chūn yù wǎn
lonely	empty courtyard	spring in a hurry

梨○花○	滿△地△	不△開○門●
lí huā	mǎn dì	bù kāi mén
pear petals	all over the ground	door is closed

367

Liu Yuxi

刘禹锡

乌衣巷

朱雀桥边野草花　　　朱雀橋邊野草花
乌衣巷口夕阳斜　　　烏衣巷口夕陽斜
旧时王谢堂前燕　　　舊時王謝堂前燕
飞入寻常百姓家　　　飛入尋常百姓家

Black Gown Lane

Wild grasses and flowers grow
by the Red Bird Bridge.
The setting sun shines obliquely
upon the entrance of Black Gown Lane.
Swallows that used to perch on the
front mansions of the Wang and Xie
now fly into the
houses of ordinary people.

劉禹錫　烏衣巷

朱○雀△橋○[1]
zhū què qiáo
Red Bird Bridge

邊○
biān
at the side of

野△草△花●
yě cǎo huā
wild grasses and flowers

烏○衣○巷△[2]
wū yī xiàng
Black Gown Lane

口△
kǒu
entrance

夕△陽○斜●
xī yáng xié
setting sun is oblique

舊△時○
jiù shí
In the past

王○謝△[3]
wáng xiè
the Wangs and Xies

堂○前○燕△
táng qián yàn
swallows at front hall

飛○入△
fēi rù
fly into

尋○常○
xún cháng
ordinary

百△姓△家●
bǎi xìng jiā
houses of common people

[1] Red Bird Bridge, built in the Six Dynasties, was in what is now Nanjing. It was near the Black Gown Lane.
[2] Black Gown Lane, a residential area for the rich and powerful.
[3] Wang Dao and Xie An, two families of nobility of the Jin Dynasty, used to live here.

Liu Yuxi

刘禹锡

春词

新妆宜面下朱楼　　　　　新妝宜面下朱樓
深锁春光一院愁　　　　　深鎖春光一院愁
行到中庭数花朵　　　　　行到中庭數花朵
蜻蜓飞上玉搔头　　　　　蜻蜓飛上玉搔頭

A Spring Song

She comes downstairs with new
makeup that fits her face.
Spring scenes are shut out
from the doleful courtyard.
She walks to the mid-court and
starts counting flowers.
A dragonfly suddenly
alights on her jade hairpin.

劉禹錫　春詞

新○妝○
xīn zhuāng
new makeup

宜○面△
yí miàn
suitable for face

下△朱○樓●
xià zhū lóu
goes downstairs

深○鎖△
shēn suǒ
deeply locked

春○光○
chūn guāng
springime

一△院△愁●
yī yuàn chóu
courtyard is full of sorrow

行○到△
xíng dào
walking to

中○庭○
zhōng tíng
the mid-court

數△花○朵△
shǔ huā duǒ
to count flowers

蜻○蜓○
qīng tíng
a dragonfly

飛○上△
fēi shàng
flies and alights on

玉△搔○頭●
yù sāo tóu
jade hairpin

371

Li Yi

李益

夜上受降城闻笛

回乐峰前沙似雪	回樂峰前沙似雪
受降城外月如霜	受降城外月如霜
不知何处吹芦管	不知何處吹蘆管
一夜征人尽望乡	一夜征人盡望鄉

Hearing a Pipe at Night Over the Shouxiang Wall

Below the Huile Peak,
the sand looks like snow.
Outside the Accepting-Surrender City,
the moon is as bright as frost.
Where does the reed pipe's tune
come from?
For the whole night,
soldiers are all thinking of their home.

李益　夜上受降城聞笛

回○樂△峰○[1]
huí lè fēng
Huile Peak

受○降○城○[2]
shòu xiáng chéng
Accepting-Surrender City

不△知○
bù zhī
not knowing

一△夜△
yī yè
the whole night

前○
qián
front

外△
wài
outside

何○處△
hé chù
where

征○人○
zhēng rén
soldiers

沙○似△雪△
shā sì xuě
sand looks like snow

月△如○霜●
yuè rú shuāng
moon looks like frost

吹○蘆○管△
chuī lú guǎn
blow a reed pipe

盡△望△鄉●
jìn wàng xiāng
all long for home town

[1] Huile Peak is in present-day Lingwu County, Gansu Province.
[2] Shouxiang City (Accepting-Surrender City), located north of the Yellow River, was built in the Tang Dynasty for the purpose of defending against invading tribes,

373

Wang Changling　　　　王昌齡

长信怨

奉帚平明金殿开　　　奉帚平明金殿開
暂将团扇共徘徊　　　暫將團扇共徘徊
玉颜不及寒鸦色　　　玉顏不及寒鴉色
犹带昭阳日影来　　　猶帶昭陽日影來

Complaint in the Changxin Palace

Soon after the gate was opened at dawn,
she started to sweep the palace hall.
For a break, she moved around
with a round fan.
A pretty face could not even compete
with the hue on a winter crow,
who had bathed in the sunlight
from the Zhaoyang Court.

王昌齡　長信怨

奉△帚△ [1]	平○明○	金○殿△開●
fèng zhǒu	píng míng	jīn diàn kāi
sweeping with a bloom	at dawn	golden palace opened

暫△將○	團○扇△	共△徘○徊●
zhàn jiāng	tuán shàn	gōng pái huí
for a break	round fan	to move around

玉△顏○	不△及△	寒○鴉○色△
yù yán	bù jí	hán yā sè
jade-like face	not as good as	color of a crow

猶○帶△	昭○陽○ [2]	日△影△來●
yóu dài	zhāo yáng	rì jǐng lái
still can bring	Zhao Yang	sunlight with it

[1] After Concubine Ban had lost Emperor Cheng's favor, she became a court maid during the Han Dynasty.
[2] Zhao Yang (Bright Sun) was the name of the palace in which the newly favored concubine Zhao Feiyan lived.

Wang Changling　　　王昌齡

閨怨

闺中少妇不知愁
春日凝妆上翠楼
忽见陌头杨柳色
悔教夫婿觅封侯

閨中少婦不知愁
春日凝妝上翠樓
忽見陌頭楊柳色
悔教夫婿覓封侯

Sorrow of a Young Wife in Her Boudoir

A young wife shows no sign
of worry in her boudoir.
On a spring day, she dolls up
and climbs the emerald tower.
Suddenly she notices the color
of the roadside willows
and regrets letting her husband
away to seek official titles.

王昌齡　閨怨

閨○中○ guī zhōng in the boudoir	少△婦△ shào fù a young wife	不△知○愁● bù zhī chóu shows no sign of worry
春○日△ chūn rì on spring day	凝○妝○ níng zhuāng applies makeup	上△翠△樓● shàng cuǐ lóu goes up to emerald tower
忽○見△ hū jiàn seeing suddenly	陌△頭○ mò tóu the roadside	楊○柳△色△ yáng liú sè color of willows
悔△教○ huǐ jiāo regrets to let	夫○婿△ fū xù husband	覓△封○侯● mì fēng hóu seeking high position

Wang Changling   王昌齡

春宮曲

昨夜风开露井桃　　昨夜風開露井桃
未央前殿月轮高　　未央前殿月輪高
平阳歌舞新承宠　　平陽歌舞新承寵
帘外春寒赐锦袍　　簾外春寒賜錦袍

Song of Spring in the Palace

Last night, a wind set in bloom
the peach tree by the well.
Above the front palace hall,
the moon was bright and high.
For her song and dance, a new imperial
favor was granted to Pingyang:
a brocade robe to shield her
from spring chill outside.

王昌齡　春宮曲

昨△夜△	風○開○	露△井△桃●
zuó yè	fēng kāi	lù jǐng táo
last night	wind blew open	peach blossom by the well

未△央○[1]	前○殿△	月△輪○高●
wèi yāng	qián diàn	yuè lún gāo
Weiyang	front palace	the moon was high

平○陽○[2]	歌○舞△	新○承○寵△
píng yáng	gē wǔ	xīn chéng chǒng
Pingyang	song and dance	newly granted favor

簾○外△	春○寒○	賜△錦△袍●
lián wài	chūn hán	cì jǐng páo
outside the curtain	spring chill	bestow a brocade robe

[1] Weiyang, name of a palace built by Han Gao Zu, the founder of the Han Dynasty.

[2] Pingyan, refers to Princess Pingyan's singer-dancer, who became the queen of Emperor Wu (Han Wu Di,157—87 B.C.)

Wang Changling

王昌齡

出塞

秦时明月汉时关　　　　秦時明月漢時關
万里长征人未还　　　　萬里長征人未還
但使龙城飞将在　　　　但使龍城飛將在
不教胡马渡阴山　　　　不教胡馬渡陰山

Passing the Frontier

Still the same moon of Qin,
the same passes of Han.
Marching for three thousand miles,
the soldiers have not yet returned.
If only the Flying General
of Dragon City were there,
the Tartar horses could not
have crossed the Yin Mountain!

王昌齡　出塞

秦○時○	明○月△	漢△時○關●
qín shí	míng yuè	hàn shí guān
Qin's	bright moon	Han's passes

萬△里△	長○征○	人○未△還●
wàn lǐ	cháng zhēng	rén wèi huán
ten thousand *li*	long march	people not yet returned

但△使△	龍○城○[1]	飛○將△在△
dàn shǐ	lóng chéng	fēi jiàng zài
if only	Dragon City	Flying General still there

不△教○	胡○馬△	渡△陰○山●[2]
bù jiāo	hú mǎ	dù yīn shān
won't let	Tartar horses	cross Yin Mountain

[1] Dragon City, in what is now Mongolia, was the frontier where General Li Guang (Flying General) stationed and defended against the Xiongnu tribesmen.
[2] Yin Mountain, in what is now Inner Mongolia.

Wang Han

王翰

凉州词

葡萄美酒夜光杯
欲饮琵琶马上催
醉卧沙场君莫笑
古来征战几人回

葡萄美酒夜光杯
欲飲琵琶馬上催
醉臥沙場君莫笑
古來征戰幾人回

Song of Liangzhou

Good grape wine glistens in
a cup that glows in the night.
Before we can drink
the pi-pa summons us to mount.
Don't laugh, my friend, should I
lie drunk on the battleground.
Since ancient times, how many soilders
have ever returned to town?

王翰　涼州詞

葡○萄○
pú táo
grape

美△酒△
měi jiǔ
good wine

夜△光○杯●[1]
yè guāng bēi
a cup that grows in the night

欲△飲△
yù yǐn
about to drink

琵○琶○[2]
pí pá
pi-pa

馬△上△催●
mǎ shàng cuī
urges to mount the horse

醉△臥△
zuì wò
lying drunk

沙○場○
shā cháng
battleground

君○莫△笑△
jūn mò xiào
don't you laugh

古△來○
gǔ lái
since ancient time

征○戰△
zhēng zhàn
on an expedition

幾△人○回●
jǐ rén huí
how many have returned

---

[1] A cup made of jade that glows in the night.
[2] A Chinese musical instrument that resembles a four-stringed guitar.

Wang Wei 王维

渭城曲

渭城朝雨邑轻尘　　渭城朝雨浥輕塵
客舍青青柳色新　　客舍青青柳色新
劝君更尽一杯酒　　勸君更盡一杯酒
西出阳关无故人　　西出陽關無故人

Song of Wei City

A morning rain has moistened
the light dust in Wei City.
Outside the tavern, the willows
look fresh and green.
I urge you to empty
one more cup of wine:
West of Yang Pass,
no old friends will be in sight.

王維　渭城曲

渭△城○[1]
wèi chéng
Wei City

朝○雨△
zhāo yǔ
a morning rain

浥△輕○塵●
yì qīng chén
moistens light dust

客△舍△
kè shè
tavern

青○青○
qīng qīng
fresh green

柳△色△新●
liǔ sè xīn
willows look new

勸△君○
quàn jūn
I advise you

更△盡△
gèng jìn
to empty further

一△杯○酒△
yī bēi jiǔ
one cup of wine

西○出△
xī chū
west of

陽○關○[2]
yáng guān
Yang Pass

無○故△人●
wú gù rén
no more old friends

---

[1] Wei City, in what is now the city of Xianyang, Shanxi Province.
[2] Yang Pass, the name of an ancient pass, in Dunhuang, Gansu Province.

385

Wang Zhihuan   王之涣

出塞

黄河远上白云间	黃河遠上白雲間
一片孤城万仞山	一片孤城萬仞山
羌笛何须怨杨柳	羌笛何須怨楊柳
春风不度玉门关	春風不度玉門關

Passing the Frontier

The Yellow River flows
all the way to the white clouds.
A lone town lies beneath mountains
of many thousand feet high.
Why must you blow the sad
"Willow" tune with a Tartar pipe?
Spring wind will not reach
the Jade-Gate Pass.

王之渙　出塞

黃○河○	遠△上△	白△雲○間●
huáng hé	yuǎn shàng	bái yún jiān
Yellow River	rises all the way	among clouds

一△片△	孤○城○	萬△仞△山●[1]
yī piàn	gū chéng	wàn rèn shān
one	lone city	mountains of ten-*ren* high

羌○笛△	何○須○	怨△楊○柳△[2]
qiāng dí	hé xū	yuàn yáng liǔ
Tartar pipe	no need to	blow sad Willow tune

春○風○	不△度△	玉△門○關●[3]
chūn fēng	bù dào	jù mén guān
spring wind	can't reach	Jade-Gate Pass

[1] *Ren* is a measure of length equivalent to about eight feet.
[2] "Willow Tree" was the name of an ancient song.
[3] Outside Jade-Gate Pass was what is now Xinjiang Province.

Wei Zhuang   韦庄

金陵图

江雨霏霏江草齐	江雨霏霏江草齊
六朝如梦鸟空啼	六朝如夢鳥空啼
无情最是台城柳	無情最是臺城柳
依旧烟笼十里堤	依舊煙籠十里堤

A View of Jinling

Rain falling thick and fast
uniformly on the riverside grass.
Birds crying blankly;
the Six Dynasties had vanished
like a dream.
The most heartless has to be
the willows of the Terrace City,
for they as ever shroud
the three-mile dyke in misty green.

韋莊　金陵圖

江○雨△	霏○霏○	江○草△齊●
jiāng yǔ	fēi fēi	jiāng cǎo qí
river rain	falling thick and fast	uniform riverside grass

六△朝○[1]	如○夢△	鳥△空○啼●
liù cháo	rú mèng	niǎo kōng tí
Six Dynasties	like a dream	birds cry blankly

無○情○	最△是△	臺○城○柳△[2]
wú qíng	zuì shì	tái chéng liú
heartless	has to be	willows of Terrace City

依○舊△	煙○籠○	十△里△堤●
yī jiù	yān lóng	shí lǐ dī
same as old	mist covers	a ten-*li* dyke

[1] The Six Dynasties (222—589) all made Nanjing their capital.
[2] Terrace City, also called Yuan (garden) City, was situated by the Lake Xuanwu, in Nanjing.

Wen Tingyun 温庭筠

瑶瑟怨

冰簟银床梦不成
碧天如水夜云轻
雁声远过潇湘去
十二楼中月自明

冰簟銀床夢不成
碧天如水夜雲輕
雁聲遠過瀟湘去
十二樓中月自明

Complaint of a Jade Lute

A dream cannot be made
on the cold mat of a silver bed.
The sky is as bluish as water;
the night clouds are thin.
Wild geese honk as they pass
far beyond the Xiao and Xiang.
The moon shines for no others
amid the twelve-story tower.

溫庭筠　瑤瑟怨

冰○簟△ bīng diàn ice-cold mat	銀○床○ yín chuáng silver bed	夢△不△成● mèng bù chéng dream can't be made
碧△天○ bì tiān emerald sky	如○水△ rú shuǐ like water	夜△雲○輕● yè yún qīng night clouds are light
雁△聲○ yàn shēng sound of wild geese	遠△過△ yuǎn guò passes into distance	瀟○湘○去△[1] xiāo xiāng qù through Xiao and Xiang
十△二△樓○[2] shí èr lóu twelve-story tower	中○ zhōng amid	月△自△明● yuè zì míng moon shines for itself

[1] Xiao and Xiang are names of rivers in Hunan Province.
[2] The twelve-story tower, an immortal place, is used here to refer to a beautiful mansion.

Wumingshi
(Anonymous)

无名氏

杂诗

近寒食雨草萋萋
著麦苗风柳影堤
等是有家归未得
杜鹃休向耳边啼

近寒食雨草萋萋
著麥苗風柳影堤
等是有家歸未得
杜鵑休向耳邊啼

Cold Food Day

As the Cold Food Day draws near,
grass appears lush in the rain.
Wind blows the young wheat;
willows shimmer on the dyke.
Like others, I cannot
go back home at this time.
O cuckoo, why don't you
stop crying in my ears.

無名氏　雜詩

近△寒○食△[1]	雨△	草△萋○萋●
jìn hán shí	yǔ	cǎo qī qī
near Cold Food Day	rain falls	grass looks luxuriant
著△麥△苗○	風○	柳△影△堤●
zhù mài miáo	fēng	liǔ yǐng tī
young wheat	wind blows	willows reflect on dyke
等△是△	有△家○	歸○未△得△
děng shì	yǒu jiā	guī wèi dé
I also	have a home	yet can't return to
杜△鵑○[2]	休○向△	耳△邊○啼●
dù juān	xiū xiàng	ěr biān tí
cuckoo	stop crying	at the side of my ears

[1] Cold Food Festival was an ancient Chinese custom during which food was supposed to be eaten cold.

[2] When a cuckoo cries, it sounds like "bu ru gui qu" (why not go home) in Chinese.

Zhang Bi　　　　　　张泌

寄人

别梦依依到谢家　　别夢依依到謝家
小廊回合曲阑斜　　小廊回合曲闌斜
多情只有春庭月　　多情只有春庭月
犹为离人照落花　　猶為離人照落花

To Someone

I dreamt of coming to your house
after we reluctantly parted.
I passed the circular veranda
with bent railings.
Only the moon was full of affection
on the spring courtyard.
It still shone on the fallen petals
for someone who was about to part.

張泌　寄人

別△夢△	依○依○	到△謝△家●[1]
bié mèng	yī yī	dào xiè jiā
in a dream after parting	reluctant to separate	arrived Xie's house

小△廊○	回○合△	曲△闌○斜●
xiǎo liáng	huí hé	qǔ lán xié
little veranda	circular	bent railings

多○情○	只△有△	春○庭○月△
duō qíng	zhǐ yǒu	chūn tíng yuè
full of tenderness	there is only	moon of spring courtyard

猶○為△	離○人○	照△落△花●
yóu wèi	lí rén	zhào luò huā
still for	the one to leave	shines on fallen flowers

[1] Xie, a famous family name in the Eastern Jin Dynasty, is used here to represent family in general.

395

Zhang Hu 张祜

赠内人

禁门宫树月痕过　　禁門宮樹月痕過
媚眼惟看宿鹭窠　　媚眼惟看宿鷺窠
斜拔玉钗灯影畔　　斜拔玉釵燈影畔
踢开红焰救飞蛾　　踢開紅燄救飛蛾

To a Court Lady

A moonbeam had just glided over the
trees inside the palace.
Her loving eyes focused only
on the egret perching in its nest.
She obliquely drew a jade pin
from her hair near the lamp,
and saved the fluttering moth
by brushing aside the red flame.

張祜　贈內人

禁△門○ jìn mén forbidden door	宮○樹△ gōng shù palace tree	月△痕○過● yuè hén guō moonbeam passed through
媚△眼△ mèi yǎn loving eyes	惟○看○ wéi kān see only	宿△鷺△窠● sù lù kē egret perching in its nest
斜○拔△ xié bá pull up obliquely	玉△釵○ yù chāi a jade hairpin	燈○影△畔△ dēng yǐng pàn by the shadow of a lamp
踢△開○ tī kāi kick out of the way	紅○燄△ hóng yàn red flame	救△飛○蛾● jiù fēi é to save the fluttering moth

397

Zhang Hu 张祜

集灵台 (一)

日光斜照集灵台
红树花迎晓露开
昨夜上皇新授籙
太真含笑入帘来

日光斜照集靈臺
紅樹花迎曉露開
昨夜上皇新授籙
太真含笑入簾來

Jiling Terrace (1)

Slanting sunlight shines
upon Jiling Terrace.
Red trees are blooming;
morning dew is thawing.
Last night the emperor bestowed
a title to a new Taoist.
Taizhen, with a smile on her face,
came from behind the curtain.

張祐　集靈台 (一)

日△光○　　　斜○照△　　　集△靈○臺●[1]
rì guāng　　xié zhào　　jí líng tái
sunlight　　shines obliquely on　　Jiling Terrace

紅○樹△　　　花○迎○　　　曉△露△開●
hóng shù　　huā yíng　　xiǎo lù kāi
red trees　　flowers greet　　morning dew is thawing

昨△夜△　　　上△皇○[2]　　新○授△籙△[3]
zuó yè　　　shàng huáng　　xīn shòu lù
last night　　the supreme emperor　　granted new Taoist title

太△真○[4]　　含○笑△　　　入△簾○來●
tài zhēn　　hán xiào　　rù lián lái
Taizhen　　with a smile　　entered from behind the curtain

[1] Jiling Terrace (Spirit Collecting Terrace), inside Hua Qing Palace, was used to worship spirits in the Tang Dynasty.
[2] Refers to Emperor Xuanzhong.
[3] Emperor Xuangzhong, who saw Yang Yuhuan, his son's concubine, and fell in love with her. He authorized her to first become a Taoist and later a court lady before she was bestowed the title of imperial concubine.
[4] Taizhen was the title given to Yang Yuhuan by the emperor when she became the Taoist.

399

Zhang Hu

张祜

集灵台 (二)

號国夫人承主恩
平明骑马入宫门
却嫌脂粉污颜色
淡扫峨眉朝至尊

號國夫人承主恩
平明騎馬入宮門
卻嫌脂粉污顏色
淡掃峨眉朝至尊

Jiling Terrace (2)

The lady of the Guo State
is bestowed imperial grace.
She often rides a horse
through the palace gate.
Disdainful of cosmetics that could
mar her facial complexion,
she lightly touches her eyebrows
before paying respect to the emperor.

張祜　集靈台 (二)

號△國△
guó guó
Guo State

夫○人○[1]
fū rén
lady of

承○主△恩●
chéng zhǔ ēn
grace granted by the emperor

平○明○
píng míng
at dawn

騎○馬△
qí mǎ
riding a horse

入△宮○門●
rù kōng mén
enters the palace door

卻△嫌○
què xián
yet dislike

脂○粉△
zhī fěng
cosmetics

污○顏○色△
wū yán sè
mar facial complexion

淡△掃△
dàn sǎo
lightly touches up

峨○眉○
é méi
beautiful eyebrows

朝○至△尊●
cháo zhì zūn
be received audience by the emperor

[1] Lady of Guo (name of an ancient feudal state), a title bestowed to the elder sister of Yang Guifei, the famous concubine of Emperor Xuanzhong.

401

Zhang Hu

张祜

题金陵渡

金陵津渡小山楼　　金陵津渡小山樓
一宿行人自可愁　　一宿行人自可愁
潮落夜江斜月里　　潮落夜江斜月裡
两三星火是瓜州　　兩三星火是瓜州

Written on the Wall of a Ferry Building in Jinling

In a little storied house
on the hill near Jinling Ferry,
a traveler for the night
is apt to feel anxious.
In slanting moonlight
the river is at ebb tide.
Guazhou must be where
I see two or three sparking fires.

張祜　題金陵渡

金○陵○[1] jīn líng Jinling	津○渡△ jīn dù a ferry	小△山○樓● xiǎo shān lóu a little storied building on the hill
一△宿△ yī sù lodge for the night	行○人○ xīng rén a traveler	自△可△愁● zì kě chóu be inclined to feel sorrowful
潮○落△ cháo luò ebb tide	夜△江○ yè jiāng night river	斜○月△裡△ xié yuè lǐ in slanting moonlight
兩△三○ liǎng sān two or three	星○火△ xīng huǒ star-like fires	是△瓜○州●[2] shì guā zhōu is Guazhou

[1] Jinling is present-day Nanjing.
[2] Guazhou, name of a town in Yangzhou, Jiangsu Province.

403

Zhang Ji 张继

枫桥夜泊

月落乌啼霜满天　　　月落烏啼霜滿天
江枫渔火对愁眠　　　江楓漁火對愁眠
姑苏城外寒山寺　　　姑蘇城外寒山寺
夜半钟声到客船　　　夜半鐘聲到客船

Mooring by Maple Bridge* at Night

The moon goes down,
a crow caws,
and the frost fills the sky.
River maples
and fishing torches
keep me anxiously awake.
The clang of a midnight bell
from the Cold Mountain Temple
outside the city of Gusu
drifts to my boat.

張繼　楓橋夜泊

月△落△　　　烏○啼○　　　霜○滿△天●
yuè luò　　　wú tí　　　shuāng mǎn tiān
moon goes down　crow caws　frost fills the sky

江○楓○　　　漁○火△　　　對△愁○眠●
jiāng fēng　　yú huǒ　　　duì chóu mián
river maples　fishing torch　anxiety keeps (me)
　　　　　　　　　　　　　awake

姑○蘇○[1]　　城○外△　　　寒○山○寺△[2]
gū sū　　　chéng wài　　hán shān sì
Gusu　　　outside the city　Cold Mountain Temple

夜△半△　　　鐘○聲○　　　到△客△船●
yè bàn　　　zhōng shēng　dào kè chuán
midnight　　clang of bell　reaches my boat

* Maple Bridge is located several miles west of Suzhou.
[1] Gusu, in present-day Suzhou, Jiangsu Province,
[2] Cold Mountain Temple remains one of the tourist attractions in Suzhou.

Zhang Xu 张旭

桃花溪

隐隐飞桥隔野烟	隱隱飛橋隔野煙
石矶西畔问渔船	石磯西畔問漁船
桃花尽日随流水	桃花盡日隨流水
洞在清溪何处边	洞在清溪何處邊

Peach Blossom Stream

A veil of wild mist
hides the tall bridge.
By a rock on the west bank,
I ask a fisher boat:
"The peach petals keep floating
with the water the whole day.
On which side of the clear stream
can I find the cave?"

張旭　桃花溪

隱△隱△	飛○橋○	隔△野△煙●
yǐn yǐn	fēi qiáo	gé yě yān
obscure and hidden	tall bridge	veiled by wild mist

石△磯○	西○畔△	問△漁○船●
shí jī	xī pàn	wèn yú chuán
water-surrounded rocks	west side	ask a fishing boat

桃○花○	盡△日△	隨○流○水△
táo huā	jìn rì	su liú shuǐ
peach blossom	whole day	follow flowing water

洞△在△	清○溪○	何○處△邊●
dòng zài	qīng xī	hé chù biān
cave is	clear stream	which side

407

Zheng Tian　　　　　郑畋

马嵬坡

玄宗回马杨妃死　　　玄宗回馬楊妃死
云雨难忘日月新　　　雲雨難忘日月新
终是圣明天子事　　　終是聖明天子事
景阳宫井又何人　　　景陽宮井又何人

At Mawei Hill*

Emperor Xuanzong returned on a horse
after the death of Lady Yang.
How could he forget his love for her
each new day and month!
It was, after all, a wise decision
of the Son of Heaven.
Why would he want to be another hider
in the well of Jingyang Palace?

鄭畋　馬嵬坡

玄○宗○ xuán zōng Emperor Xuanzong	回○馬△ huí mǎ returned on a horse	楊○妃○死△ yáng fēi sǐ concubine Yang was dead
雲○雨△ yún yǔ love affairs	難○忘○ nán wáng hard to forget	日△月△新● rì yuè xīn new day and month
終○是△ zhōng shì at the end	聖△明○ shèng mínng capable and virtuous	天○子△事△ tiān zǐ shì what an emperor did
景△陽○宮○[1] jǐng yáng gōng Jing Yang Palace	井△ jǐng well	又△何○人● yòu hé rén would be another person

* During the An Lushan rebellion, Emperor Xuanzong fled from the capital on his way to Sichuan. At Mawei Hill in the year 756, he put his favorite concubine, Yang Guifei, to death in order to quiet down the dissension of his own generals.

[1] The last emperor of Chen hid himself in a well with two concubines before he was captured by the Sui soldiers in the Jingyang Palace.

Zhu Qingyu　　　　　朱庆余

宫词

寂寂花时闭院门　　　寂寂花時閉院門
美人相并立琼轩　　　美人相並立瓊軒
含情欲说宫中事　　　含情欲說宮中事
鹦鹉前头不敢言　　　鸚鵡前頭不敢言

A Palace Poem

Flowers are blooming;
the courtyard is closed and quiet.
Standing side by side at the
elegant veranda, the court ladies
want to share their private feelings
about things in the palace.
But in front of the parrot,
they refrain from talking.

朱慶餘　宮詞

寂△寂△ jì jì quiet and lonely	花○時○ huā shí flower season	閉△院△門● bì yuàn mén courtyard gate is closed
美△人○ měi rén court ladies	相○並△ xiāng bìng side by side	立△瓊○軒● lì qióng xuān standing at elegant veranda
含○情○ hán qíng inner feelings	欲△說△ yù shuō want to talk about	宮○中○事△ gōng zhōng shì palace affairs
鸚○鵡△ yīng wǔ parrot	前○頭○ qián tóu in front of	不△敢△言● bù gǎn yán dare not to say

Zhu Qingyu 朱庆余

近试上张水部

洞房昨夜停红烛	洞房昨夜停紅燭
待晓堂前拜舅姑	待曉堂前拜舅姑
妆罢低声问夫婿	妝罷低聲問夫婿
画眉深浅入时无	畫眉深淺入時無

For Zhang Ji* Before Examination

Red candles were burning non-stop
last night in the bridal chamber.
At dawn, she must go to kneel and kowtow
to her husband's parents.
Having done her makeup,
in a low voice she asks her husband:
"Have I painted my eyebrows
just about right for the current fashion?"

朱慶餘　近試上張水部

洞△房○
dòng fáng
bridal chamber

昨△夜△
zuó yè
last night

停○紅○燭△
tíng hóng zhú
red candle kept burning

待△曉△
dài xiǎo
wait until dawn

堂○前○
táng qián
front hall

拜△舅△姑●
bài jiù gū
bow to husband's
parents

妝○罷△
zhuāng bà
after makeup

低○聲○
dī shēng
in low voice

問△夫○婿△
wèn fū xù
asks her husband

畫△眉○
huà méi
blacken eyebrows

深○淺△
shēn qiǎn
deep or shallow

入△時○無●
rù shí wú
fashionable or not

* Zhang Ji was the chief examiner of the civil service examination, which the poet was scheduled to take. He wrote this poem in an attempt to ask the examiner indirectly whether his poem was up to par.

413

PART 6

About the Poets

About the Poets

Bai Juyi (白居易 772—846)

Bai Juyi is best known for his two long poems "Everlasting Regret" and "Song of a Pipa Player." A prolific writer, he wrote many satirical poems that reflect his criticism of those in power. His writing style is plain, direct, and easy-to-understand. With his straight-talk approach, Bai frequently offended his superiors and other officials in the government. He eventually gave up politics and turned to drinking and poetry writing.

Cui Tu (崔塗 Birth and Death Dates Unknown)

Little is known about Cui Tu's age and place of birth. The only thing that is certain is that he was born in Jiangnan, the area south of the Yangtze River. He wrote mainly poems that reflect a sense of loneliness and parting sorrows.

Dai Shulun (戴叔倫 732—789)

Dai Shulun was born in present-day Jiangsu Province. A friendly and honest person, Dai was well-liked by his friends and colleagues. He worked hard and served the people well. For his dedication and services, the Emperor Dezhong even sent him a poem to show his appreciation. Dai wrote poems from his heart. The themes of his poetry are usually about scenery and country life.

Du Fu (杜甫 712—770)

Du Fu and Li Bai were universally regarded as the two greatest poets in China. He was born in present-day Shanxi Province. For all his accomplishments as a poet, Du Fu failed to pass the *jinshi* and become a successful candidate of the national civil service examination. As a result, he did not have a successful political career. During the An Lushan Rebellion, Du Fu held a small appointment under Emperor Xuanzhong.

Du Mu (杜牧 803—852)

Du Mu was born in Chang'an (present-day Xian). He became a *jinshi* in 828. He was best known for writing beautiful *jueju* (seven-character truncated verses). His writing style can be described as charming, warm-hearted, and powerful. He held a number of official positions over the years, but was not given the top-level jobs, perhaps due in part to his tendency to criticize superiors.

Du Xunhe (杜荀鶴 846—907)

Du Xunhe was born poor and failed the civil examinations several times. He did, however, eventually pass the *jinshi* rank in 891. He wrote his poems in everyday language with a common theme of complaints over poverty. He was not well-known until he reached his later years.

Gao Shi (高適 701—765)

Gao Shi did not start writing poetry until he reached the age of fifty. He was better known for writing poems about the frontier life. People liked to read his poems because his lines often reflected true feelings. He was a friend of Du Fu and Li Bai.

Gu Kuang (顧況 725—814)

Gu Kuang was a pleasant and humorous person. He was good at landscape painting in addition to writing poems. In his later life, he retreated to a mountain residence and became interested in the practice of the Taoist alchemy, trying to make pills of immortality.

He Zhizhang (賀知章 659-744)

He Zhizhang lived a long life by the standard of his time. He was eighty-six years old when he died. He was well-known in his youth because of his elegant writings. He had a charming personality and an open-minded attitude. Most students today in China are familiar with his poem "Coming Home."

Huangfu Ran (皇甫冉 716—769)

Huangfu Ran began to write good essays when he was only ten years old. Zhang Jiuling, the prime minister, was impressed by the quality of his writings. To avoid the turmoil created by the war, he drifted to the rural areas. His poems reflect the sorrow of a poet wandering from place to place.

Jiaoran, the monk (皎然 Birth and Death Dates Unknown)

Before he became a monk, Jiaoran had a family name of Xie. He was believed to be a descendent of the famous poet Xie Lingyun. The date of his birth is unknown. His famous friends included the poets Wei Yinwu, Liu Yuxie, and Li Duan. He wrote poems mainly about landscapes and religious life.

Li Bai (李白 701—762)

Li Bai or Li Bo was recognized as one of the greatest poets in China. He moved from Shandong to modern Sichuan with his father at the age of five. He enjoyed traveling and drinking. Li Bai was known for his unique writing style: unconventional, romantic, powerful, and natural. He was awarded the title of Hanlin (a high literary degree) by Emperor Xuanzhong.

Li Duan (李端 Birth and Death Dates Unknown)

In his youth, Li Duan studied under Jiaoran, the monk. He liked to live a quiet life in the mountain and often interacted with monks. He was gifted in poetry writing and was able to write poems on the spot.

Li Pin (李頻 818—876)

Li Ping was well-known for his personal and professional integrity. It was said that he walked a long distance to ask Yao He, a famous poet of the time, to evaluate his poetry. Yao He not only liked his poems but also liked him as a person. Eventually Li Pin became his son-in-law. Li Pin's poems are filled with the spirit of patriotism.

Li Qi (李頎 Birth and Death Dates Unknown)

Li Qi was not motivated to achieve fame and wealth as many other people were. He was, however, quite interested in practicing Taoism. Many of his friends were Buddhist priests. He liked to write poems that depicted the frontier life.

Li Shangyin (李商隱 813—858)

Li Shangyin was one the greatest poets in the late Tang period. Some of his famous poems evoke strong feelings about romantic love. He liked to use allusions that are difficult to figure out. His verses are elegantly written with a very unique style.

Li Yi 李益 (748—829)

As a *jinshi*, Li Yi was not very successful in politics. He gave up a government job to pursue other interests after failing to get a promotion. He served in the military as an advisor and was therefore quite familiar with the frontier life. He wrote quite a few poems about life in the army.

Liu Changqing (劉長卿 714—790)

Liu Changqing was one of the most influential poets after the high Tang period. As a straightforward person, he often offended others. He was once wrongly convicted and spent time in the prison. He wrote quite a few poems that reflect his grievance over his treatment.

Liu Fangping (劉方平 Birth and Death Dates Unknown)

Liu Fangping was not only a good poet, but also an artist. His paintings, which depicted the beauty of natural landscapes, are considered among the very best of his time. Like his art work, he also wrote short poems that reflect his love for beauty and nature.

Liu Yuxi (劉禹錫 772—842)

Liu Yuxi, a political innovator and philosopher, suffered a long period of banishment after his supporter in a high position had lost power. He wrote a number of poems that reflect political life and the life of the common people. Bai Juyi had some nice words to say about his poetry. Liu Yuxi also wrote excellent essays.

Lu Lun (盧綸 748—800?)

Although he failed several times in the highest civil examination, Lu Lun was recognized as one of the ten most talented persons in his time. Emperor Wenzhong liked his poems so much that he, on hearing his death, ordered his officials to compile Lu's poems for his perusal.

Ma Dai (馬戴 Birth and Death Dates Unknown)

Ma Dai liked mountains and rivers so much that he would rather live a simple life than chase fame and power. His poems remind one of Tao Yuanming, the famous poet of the Eastern Jin Period.

Meng Haoran (孟浩然 689—740)

Meng Haoran did not pass the *jinshi* examination until he was almost forty. Among his friends were Li Bai, Wang Wei, and Wang Changlin. Most of his poems depict rural life, landscapes, and hermitage.

Qian Qi (錢起 722—780)

Qian Qi was one of the most famous poets in the Mid Tang period. His poems were elegantly written. Other poets, such as Wang Wei, were quite impressed with his unique style. His poems show some creative and thoughtful ideas.

Qin Taoyu (秦韜玉 Birth and Death Dates Unknown)

Qin Taoyu obtained a government position without passing the highest civil examination. He was known for his writing skill, especially in the seven-character regulated verse.

Shen Quanqi (沈佺期 Birth and Death Dates Unknown)

Shen Quanqi was known for his skill in writing five-character regulated verse. His poems were elegantly written and rarely deviated from the prescribed tonal pattern. At one time, he was banished to the remote area because he committed bribery. Some of his poems reflect the sorrow of a banished official.

Sikong Shu (司空曙 Birth and Death Dates Unknown)

Sikong Shu was a person of high moral integrity. He would rather live in poverty than to seek a good life through dishonest means. At one time, he became a wanderer and a friend of monks. He wrote elegant poems that lament human sufferings.

Wang Changling (王昌齡 698—757)

Wang Changling was a very talented poet. Some of his poems depicting frontier life are still very popular today. He also wrote some essays discussing the techniques and style of poetry. He was wrongly put to death by a government official who envied him.

Wang Han (王翰 Birth and Death Dates Unknown)

Wang Han was known for his unconventional and unbridled lifestyle. As a young man, he liked to drink and play with song girls. He wrote some of the best four-character truncated verses.

Wang Wei (王維 701—761)

Wang Wei was one of the most famous poets in the Tang period. A person with many talents, he was also good at painting, calligraphy, and musical composition. His wife died when he was still young, but he never married again. He became interested in Buddhism later in his life. His poems reflect his love for a quiet life and deep thinking.

Wang Zhihuan (王之渙 688—742)

A friend of Wang Changling, Wang Zhihuan was known for his chivalrous spirit when he was young. He failed repeatedly in the highest civil examination. As a result, he devoted himself to poetry writing. His poems about frontier life are smooth and magnificent. One of his four-character truncated verses is still widely recited.

Wei Yingwu (韋應物 Birth and Death Dates Unknown)

When he was young, Wei Yingwu served as an imperial guard to Emperor Xuanzhong. After the death of the emperor, Wei studied very hard but became less ambitious. His poems, which are simple and lucid, were influenced by the nature poet Tao Qian.

Wei Zhuang (韋莊 Birth and Death Dates Unknown)

Wei Zhuang lived at a time when the Tang Dynasty was on the decline. His father died when he was only a child. He encountered many hardships during his life. His poems reflect his unpleasant life experiences.

Wen Tingyun (溫庭筠 812—870)

Wen Tingyun was often compared to Li Shangyin in poetic style. He was better known for his *ci* poetry in the late Tang period.

Xu Hun (許渾 Birth and Death Dates Unknown)

Xu Hun passed the highest civil examination and became a *jinshi*. He often suffered from poor health because he studied very hard when he was young. He enjoyed the landscape of mountains. His poems reflect his personal experiences and retreat in the mountains.

Xue Feng (薛逢 Birth and Death Dates Unknown)

Xue Feng was a very gifted individual. He ranked third in the highest civil examination of his exam year. However, he was not very successful in public services as he quite often offended his superiors with his sarcastic writings. His poems were sometimes criticized for not being refined enough.

Yuan Zhen (元稹 779—831)

A close friend of Bai Juyi, Yuan Zhen was a person of unusual talent. He wrote good essays when he was only nine years old. He and Bai Juyi were the leaders of the "song poetry" movement. He argued that poetry should reflect real life. He was especially noted for writing touching love poems.

Zhang Bi (張泌 Birth and Death Dates Unknown)

Little is known about the life of Zhang Bi except that he was a government officer during the Southern Tang dynasty.

Zhang Hu (張祜 Birth and Death Dates Unknown)

Zhang Hu enjoyed traveling and sightseeing. Although he was very talented, he never got the kind of recognition that he deserved. He liked to write landscape poems and those that reflected life in the palace.

Zhang Ji (張籍 Birth and Death Dates Unknown)

Zhang Ji became famous after he met Han Yu (768-824), the literary giant of the Tang dynasty. He was better known for his interest in writing poetry for the music. Zhang Ji, along with Bai Juyi and Yuan Zhen, became masters of the literary style known as "the Yuan He Ti."

Zhang Ji (張繼 Birth and Death Dates Unknown)

Zhang Ji was not among one of the greatest poets at the time when he lived. He was and still is well-known because his short poem "Night Mooring at the Maple Bridge" has made the Cold Mountain Temple famous.

Zhang Xu (張旭 Birth and Death Dates Unknown）

Zhang Xu was recognized as one of the greatest calligraphers in the Tang Dynasty. Only six of his poems have been handed down.

Zheng Tian (鄭畋 823—882）

He passed the highest civil examination and became a *jinshi*. He was Emperor Xizong's prime minister. Only sixteen poems he wrote survived.

Zhu Qingyu (朱慶餘 Birth and Death Dates Unknown)

Zhu Qingyu liked to write five-character regulated verses. Although he was well-known at the time when he lived, the number of poems that have been handed down is rather limited.

Zu Yong (祖詠 Birth and Death Dates Unknown)

A native of Luoyang and a friend of Wang Wei, Zu Yong often faced financial difficulties. He was well-known for his short poems that depict the landscape. He is close to Wang Wei in poetic style.

References

Herdan, I. (tr.). The Three Hundred Tang Poems. Taiwan: The Far East Book Co., 2000.
Liang, S. C. (ed.). Far East Chinese-English Dictionary. New York: U.S. International Publishing Inc., 1996
Wu, J. (ed.). The Pinyin Chinese-English Dictionary. Beijing: The Commercial Press, 1979.
Weinberger, E. Nineteen Ways of Looking at Wang Wei: How a Chinese Poem is Translated. Kingston: Asphodel Press, 1987.
Xu, Y. Z., Loh, B.Y., and Wu, J. (tr.). 300 Tang Poems: A New Translation. Hong Kong: The Commercial Press, 1996.
Yip, W. Chinese Poetry: An Anthology of Major Modes and Genres. Durham: Duke University Press, 1997.

邱燮友【新译唐诗三百首】，台北市三民书局印行，一九九四年二月初版。

李淼、李星 【唐诗三百首译析】，吉林文史出版社，一九八六年四月第一版。

沙灵娜【唐诗三百首全译】，贵州人民出版社，一九八三年三月第一版。

郝敏、史铁良、邓绍基【唐诗三百首】，大连出版社， 一九九二年八月第一版。

庄惠文【唐诗赏析】，台南市文国书局，一九九七年十月第一版。

戴扬本 【唐才子传】，香港海啸出版事业有限公司，二零零五年九月出版。

王力【诗词格律十讲】，北京商务印书馆，二零零二年第一版。

余照春亭【增广诗韵集成】，台南市大孚书局有限公司，一九九九年十二月初版。

周渊龙【对韵合璧】湖南大学出版社，二零零二年十二月第一版。

萧涤非等著【唐诗鉴赏词典】，上海辞书出版社，一九八三年十二月第一版。